The Complete Guide to
Nonprofit Management

NONPROFIT LAW, FINANCE, AND MANAGEMENT SERIES

Charity, Advocacy, and the Law by Bruce R. Hopkins

The Complete Guide to Nonprofit Management by Smith, Bucklin & Associates

Developing Affordable Housing: A Practical Guide for Nonprofit Organizations by Bennett L. Hecht

Financial and Accounting Guide for Not-for-Profit Organizations, Fourth Edition by Malvern J. Gross, Jr., William Warshauer, Jr., and Richard F. Larkin

Fund-Raising: Evaluating and Managing the Fund Development Process by James M. Greenfield

Fund-Raising Fundamentals: A Guide to Annual Giving for Professionals and Volunteers by James M. Greenfield

Fund-Raising Regulation Letter by Bruce R. Hopkins

The Law of Fund-Raising by Bruce R. Hopkins

The Law of Tax-Exempt Organizations, Sixth Edition by Bruce R. Hopkins

A Legal Guide to Starting and Managing a Nonprofit Organization, Second Edition by Bruce R. Hopkins

Modern American Philanthropy: A Personal Account by John J. Schwartz

The Nonprofit Counsel by Bruce R. Hopkins

The Nonprofit Law Dictionary by Bruce R. Hopkins

Nonprofit Litigation: A Practical Guide with Forms and Checklists by Steve Bachmann

The Nonprofit Management Handbook: Operating Policies and Procedures by Tracy Daniel Connors

Nonprofit Organizations' Business Forms: Disk Edition by John Wiley & Sons, Inc.

Partnerships and Joint Ventures Involving Tax-Exempt Organizations by Michael I. Sanders

Planned Giving: Management, Marketing, and Law by Ronald R. Jordan and Katelyn L. Quynn

The Tax Law of Charitable Giving by Bruce R. Hopkins

Tax Planning and Compliance for Tax-Exempt Organizations: Forms, Checklists, Procedures, Second Edition by Jody Blazek

The United Way Scandal: An Insider's Account of What Went Wrong and Why by John S. Glaser

The Complete Guide to Nonprofit Management

Smith, Bucklin & Associates

**Edited by Robert H. Wilbur, Susan Kudla Finn, and
Carolyn M. Freeland**

*RW Fingue
Feb 1999
Toronto*

John Wiley & Sons, Inc.

New York • Chichester • Brisbane • Toronto • Singapore

Foreword

When Smith, Bucklin & Associates was founded after World War II, neither I nor any of my early associates envisioned how important nonprofit organizations would become to our society. While hospitals, museums, and universities were long part of our scene and Americans have always joined together to solve community problems, the strength and contributions of these and of our hundreds of thousands of charitable and service organizations are greater today than ever before. Nonprofit organizations have become the recognized "third sector" of our society, working cooperatively and intimately with both for-profit business and the federal, state, and local government sectors of our economy.

Nor did we understand at that time the growing professionalism and indeed, the professional respect which would follow for those who make their careers with nonprofit organizations. As these organizations acquire the recognition they deserve, the accomplishments of their leaders, whether volunteer or staff, have been recognized as well.

Smith, Bucklin & Associates has been fortunate to have been able to contribute to this evolution in the role of nonprofit organizations. Most of our clientele come from one segment of the overall nonprofit world—that of trade and professional associations. However, the majority of the 600 men and women who now work in our firm also participate as board members or volunteers of local civic and charitable organizations. From this work we know that the qualities we stress in working for our clients—commitment to their organizations and to the causes they pursue—and management that is both creative and efficient—are as essential to the full range of nonprofits as they are to trade and professional associations.

Management of the well-run nonprofit is not—or at least should not be—as different from the management of a successful for-profit organization of comparable size as is often assumed. While techniques of management drawn from for-profits need adaptation to the nonprofit world—the relationship between staff and leadership is the most obvious difference—the lessons of management are, we believe, adaptable. Our close relationship with the for-profit organizations that provide the board members and volunteer leadership of the organizations we serve has taught us this. From our forty years of working to adapt management skills to nonprofits and striving to work with our boards and members cooperatively and energetically, we hope we have developed lessons of use to others. If so, that will be the ultimate reward of the work of our own men and women.

William Erby Smith
Chairman
Smith, Bucklin & Associates

Preface

In the last twenty years, the nonprofit sector of the U.S. economy has grown rapidly in size and significance. More than 1,100,000 nonprofit organizations registered with the Internal Revenue Service in 1992. According to author and management consultant Peter Drucker, nonprofits are "America's largest employer," with 90 million paid employees and volunteers. Charities, the largest segment of the nonprofit world but not the whole, had total expenses of $327 billion in 1990—equivalent to approximately six percent of the nation's total economy.

What accounts for this rapid growth? One reason is the evolution of our economy from agriculture to manufacturing to services and information technology. Another is the precedent set by increased government funding for health, education, and social welfare programs during the past 25 years, which stimulated the formation and growth of many nonprofit organizations, especially in service areas. When Federal cutbacks occurred in the 1980s, local communities, corporations, and individual citizens, rather than seeing these service organizations disband, often stepped in to fill the void.

America's tradition of solving problems with the help of volunteers is not new. As early as 1835, the French writer Alexis De Tocqueville noted the American tendency to band together in voluntary association to take on community problems:

> Americans of all ages, all conditions, and all dispositions constantly form associations. They have not only commercial and manufacturing companies, in which all take part, but associations of a thousand other kinds, religious, moral, serious, futile, general or restricted, enormous or diminutive. The Americans make associations to give entertainment, to found seminaries, to build inns, to construct churches, to diffuse books, to send missionaries to the antipodes; in this manner they found hospitals, prisons, and schools. If it is proposed to inculcate some truth or to foster some feeling by the encouragement of a great example, they form

a society. Wherever at the head of some new undertaking you see the government in France, or a man of rank in England, in the United States you will be sure to find an association.

                                        Alexis De Tocqueville
                                        "Democracy in America"

More than 200 years later, volunteerism continues to spread, with nonprofit organizations providing the backbone of this vital force.

The word "nonprofit" is often misunderstood. Technically, it describes only an organization which does not distribute profit (either dividends or capital gains) to its owners; it has no owners in the sense of the private or for-profit sector. But the nonprofit world is immensely varied. It includes such large organizations as the Massachusetts General Hospital, Stanford University, and the American Red Cross as well as local community organizations ranging from churches and temples to soup kitchens and shelters. Sources of revenues vary as well. A recent study published by the Foundation Center estimated that 51 percent of the income of all nonprofit service organizations comes from fees and other charges for services, 31 percent from government, and 18 percent from charitable giving (this latter largely from individuals but also from corporations and foundations).

Despite the great variety of organizations, of purposes, and sources of funding, one common element stands out: these organizations have become critical to the quality of life in America. They serve us and they deserve our support.

Given the growing importance of nonprofit organizations in our society, it is surprising that relatively little has been written about the management issues facing their staff and leaders. While the measures of employment and compensation in the nonprofit sector inevitably are weighted by the larger organizations, it is the smaller, independent organizations which are more typical of the true nonprofit world. The majority of charitable organizations, excluding churches, have annual budgets of less than $500,000. The managers of these smaller, more typical, nonprofit organizations have largely been left to improvise and learn effective management skills on their own.

At long last, the art and science of managing nonprofits are receiving attention. Nonprofit managers are re-examining common assumptions and learning from misperceptions about their responsibilities and those of their elected leadership. Until recently, many believed that nonprofit organizations could not be "managed" in the same way as for-profit organizations. There was a bias against using the "bottom line" orientation of the corporate business world to manage nonprofit organizations. But nonprofit organizations today must operate as effectively and efficiently as for-profit organizations or go out of business. With escalating costs and diminishing resources, nonprofit executives are under the same pressures as for-profit organizations to justify every dollar spent. The days are past when a certain casualness of management might be excused because the work of the nonprofit was from the heart or because their staff were less well-paid than those of comparable for-profit organizations.

For the most part, nonprofit organizations still do not face the same financial exigencies as the typical corporation: extinction is not as likely if they fail to turn a profit (or, in nonprofit terms, provide a surplus of income over expenses) from services or activities. But nonprofits are not excused from balancing their budgets. Under the pressures of "right-sizing," this exemption from the laws of economics is being repealed. Even the most loyal donors and contributors to nonprofits are now far less willing to support fund-raising campaigns whose goals increase in direct proportion to the shortfalls from operations, or which lack a compelling explanation of how the funds will be spent. When revenues shrink in the face of rising needs or desires, the "bottom line" exerts its discipline. Members of our boards of directors expect us, quite rightly, to operate at the same level that they demand from the staff of their own organizations. Peter Drucker has noted the change, stating that nonprofits have entered the world of "accountability."

The Complete Guide to Nonprofit Management is intended to help nonprofit executives and their volunteer leaders take a new look at the management issues being confronted by nonprofits in an increasingly complex world of accountability. The contributors to this book work for a for-profit organization which manages over 180 nonprofit organizations. Most have business backgrounds, often with additional experience in education or government. With over 600 employees, we have been able to draw on diverse backgrounds and experience in working with these nonprofit organizations more effectively. As our nonprofit clients always have the option of going somewhere else, we live under a market discipline in many ways similar to that of the for-profit world. We believe our success, and much of what we have to share in this book, lies in our ability to adapt for-profit management strategies and techniques to the unique demands of the nonprofit world. In addition to client responsibilities, most of us also serve as volunteers, either on boards of directors or as participants in the work of charitable organizations. We've tried to bring both perspectives—paid manager and volunteer leader—to this book.

There are elements of art as well as science in managing nonprofit organizations. Relations between paid staff and boards of directors differ between nonprofits and typical for-profit organizations, and differ as well from one nonprofit to another. Management styles are perhaps more likely to be "interactive" in nonprofit organizations, based on teamwork and communication, but individual management styles and varying sizes of organizations make generalizations difficult. Nonetheless, limits of budgets mean that most nonprofit managers and staff wear several hats; CEOs must also perform much of the day-to-day work, not just facilitate.

Despite their diversity, most nonprofit organizations have common management concerns: clarifying their organization's mission, raising funds, marketing programs, managing staff and finances, deciding how to communicate with constituents, the public, and government. To help both the nonprofit executive and the board member who wants to know more about the tasks facing these organizations, we have structured this book in three sections:

   I. Building the Foundation
  II. Pursuing the Mission
 III. Managing the Organization

The first three chapters deal with basic management issues confronting almost all nonprofits: establishing (and re-evaluating) the organization's direction (or "mission"); maximizing board/staff effectiveness; and developing and implementing fund-raising strategies. These elements of nonprofit management should, we believe, be re-evaluated constantly. Without a practical sense of mission, organizations often flounder, unable to develop effective action plans. Without an understanding of board/staff relationships and of the way these may change in the evolution of an organization, much of the available talent and energy will be wasted. Without adequate funding and a realistic appraisal of how and where an organization can look for funds, the best of dreams remain unrealized.

The second section, pursuing the mission, turns to the design and execution of strategic and operational programs. As we have noted, most nonprofits get more than half of their revenues from services. Establishing a marketing orientation does not mean giving up the altruistic goals on which most nonprofits are founded; it does mean developing the awareness that charity requires an assessment of what revenues the organization can expect from its services. Subsequent chapters deal with specific programs—educational activities, meetings and conventions, public relations, advocacy—which are often essential to a nonprofit's success. Examples from our own or others' experience illustrate how these activities can effectively be planned and executed.

The third section focuses on issues of day-to-day management, emphasizing the tools essential to running a nonprofit organization: understanding basic nonprofit accounting principles, choosing the right information systems in an age of technology, managing staff and resources, meeting legal requirements, selecting and using consultants.

In addressing these management topics, we have outlined strategies that have been used successfully by professionals with responsibilities ranging from overall executive management to such critical details as finances, meetings, and public relations. We have also reviewed such ever-present issues as the relationships between staff and their boards of directors and the constantly changing face of information technology. We hope these discussions will be of value to the most seasoned nonprofit executive, as well as to those coming into new responsibilities. We also hope that our discussions will give nonprofit boards of directors a better understanding of the efforts and responsibilities of management in this vital part of our economy, as well as an appreciation of their own leadership role in working with both staff and volunteers.

Finally, we recognize that our observations and recommendations will not fit every organization's need. But we hope to provide a starting point for those looking for practical tools and techniques, drawn from experience and proven in practice, for meeting many of the day-to-day challenges of "accountability" in this growing world of nonprofits.

Robert H. Wilbur
Susan Kudla Finn
Carolyn M. Freeland

Smith, Bucklin & Associates, Inc.
June 25, 1994

Acknowledgements

We wish to take this opportunity to thank the dedicated officers, board members, committee chairs, and volunteers of the nonprofit organizations we serve. These men and women have been active participants in the programs and projects we describe; they have brought to these organizations their own knowledge and experience, providing us with ideas and inspiration; they have pressed us to think beyond what we have done in the past, searching always for new and more effective ways to work toward their organizations' goals.

To them this book is dedicated.

Many executives and staff of Smith, Bucklin & Associates have contributed to this book. Among those who offered insight and valuable information as they reviewed and edited our chapters are Duane Ekedahl, Roger Albert, Drew Albritten, Walter Coleman, Cele Fogarty, Sheila Hoffmeyer, William Kelley, and Diane Winterberg. Joseph Ho contributed research and suffered through redraft after redraft with professionalism and diplomacy.

Samuel Harahan and Patricia Skillman, Executive Director and Associate Executive Director of the Council for Court Excellence, Richard Ingram, President and CEO, Association of Governing Boards, Paul T. Schindler, President and CEO, African Wildlife Foundation, Steven F. Stanton of Arthur Andersen & Co., Holly G. Shelton of Crestar Bank, and Ray Platig reviewed key chapters, providing us with their valuable perspective.

Carter Keithley, Peter Trimmer, and William Greer, colleagues and valued friends, and Nora Greer, experienced writer and editor, worked with us on several chapters.

Bruce Hopkins, author of several books in the Wiley nonprofit series, reviewed and critiqued the chapter on legal responsibilities of nonprofit executives. We also thank him for introducing us to Marla Bobowick of John Wiley & Sons, Inc. and recommending that we undertake this ambitious assignment. Marla Bobowick brought tact, prodding, and a sharp editorial eye to her difficult job of working with a consortium of writers more concerned with their responsibilities to client associations than to the deadlines of editorial production.

And finally, we express again our admiration and appreciation to William E. Smith, founder of Smith, Bucklin & Associates, who has been a friend, mentor, and supporter to us throughout our careers. While building a company with over 600 employees, he has never lost sight of the fact that every one of us has an obligation not only to the nonprofit organizations we serve, but also to the communities in which we live and to our society as a whole.

Contributors

Robert Hunter Wilbur, Vice President for Government Relations at Smith, Bucklin & Associates has been executive director or director of government relations and public affairs for nonprofit organizations ranging from health care policy to telecommunications. Before joining Smith, Bucklin in 1972, he was a member of the public affairs department of Chrysler Corporation, special assistant to the United States Ambassador to the United Nations, and Director of Communications for the National Alliance of Business. He has a Ph.D. in Comparative Literature from Columbia University and also taught English at Northwestern University.

Susan Kudla Finn has been executive director of five nonprofits, including one foundation, ranging in budget sizes from $25,000 to $1 million, and has over 20 years of experience in client services, government relations, and fund-raising. Ms. Finn graduated from Georgetown University with an A.B. degree in American Government, received her M.A. in Legislative Affairs from George Washington University, and is a graduate of the Executive International Business Certificate Program at Georgetown University.

Carolyn M. Freeland has served for ten years as executive director or interim executive director for a range of nonprofit organizations with emphasis on health services and education and has served as a facilitator and strategic planning consultant for professional organizations, foundations, educational institutions, and government agencies. She currently heads Smith, Bucklin's organizational audit team. She also taught for ten years in higher education, having obtained her Ph.D. at Purdue University in communication theory and educational psychology.

Ute Duncan has been Director of Human Resources for Smith, Bucklin & Associates' Washington, D.C. office since 1986. Her prior experience in the field was at the Rochester Institute of Technology. A native of Norway, she received her B.A. degree in Economics from the State University of New York.

J. Michael Hall is a Government Relations Director at Smith, Bucklin & Associates, specializing in Congressional representation services. Prior to joining Smith, Bucklin, he served on the staff of the U.S. Senate Committee on Appropriations. His last assignment on the Committee was as Staff Director of the Subcommittee on Labor, Health and Human Services, Education and Related Agencies responsible for $240 billion of federal programs. Mr. Hall has both his B.S. in Economics and M.B.A. degrees from the University of Illinois.

Jennifer A. Lewis, the director of office services for the Washington, D.C., office of Smith, Bucklin, oversees the facilities management and centralized operational services Smith, Bucklin provides its clients. Ms. Lewis was Vice President of Administration for Copeland Krieger, an interior architecture and design firm, prior to joining Smith, Bucklin in 1992. She earned her undergraduate degree from Smith College.

Michael Payne serves as a vice-president for Smith, Bucklin and manages one of its largest professional associations. He also currently heads Smith, Bucklin's Washington, D.C. Convention and Trade Show Division. Prior to joining the company Mr. Payne spent ten years with the Federal government in various capacities, including Deputy to the Assistant Secretary for Congressional Affairs of the Department of Commerce. A graduate of the University of South Carolina, Mr. Payne has degrees in Journalism, Political Science, and History.

William J. Peyser is a Certified Public Accountant with over 10 years experience serving nonprofit organizations. He heads the accounting department of the Washington, D.C., office of Smith Bucklin & Associates. He is responsible for overseeing the finances of 50 nonprofits with annual budgets totaling over $20 million. Prior to joining the firm in 1989, Mr. Peyser practiced in the audit division of Arthur Andersen & Co. His undergraduate degree in political science is from Tufts University and he received his masters degree in accounting from Northeastern University.

Dennis E. Smeage has more than 21 years of professional experience in the health care field. Prior to joining Smith, Bucklin & Associates in 1988, he served eight years as executive director of the Arthritis Foundation's Washington State Chapter in Seattle. He also spent nine years with the American Heart Association in the San

Francisco area and Seattle as an executive in public relations and public education. He has an undergraduate degree in broadcast communications from Michigan State University.

Judith Walker Thomas heads the public relations department of the Washington, D.C., office of Smith, Bucklin & Associates. She is the Executive Director of a large national medical association while also helping other nonprofits design public relations and marketing programs to promote their organizations' goals. Prior to joining Smith, Bucklin in 1983, Thomas was Director of Marketing for a national education association. She holds a B.A. in English from St. Mary's College, Notre Dame, and an M.A. in Education from Trinity College.

Contents

Part 1: BUILDING THE FOUNDATION

Chapter 1   Establishing the Organization's Direction   **1**

Strategic Management and Strategic Planning   1
Why Strategic Plans Fail   4
Key Elements to Successful Strategic Planning   5
Implementing the Strategic Plan   25
Document the Process, the Outcomes, the "Strategic" Plan   26
Monitor the Implementation Plan   26
Checklist for Your Strategic Planning Effort   28

Chapter 2   Working Together: Maximizing Board and Staff
Effectiveness   **31**

Governing Boards: Caretakers of the Public Trust   31
Roles and Responsibilities of Governing Board Members   33
Committees   42
Roles and Responsibilities of the Chief Executive Staff Person   48
Checklist for Maximizing Board and Staff Effectiveness   58

Chapter 3   Raising Money to Achieve Your Goals   **61**

Identify Your Fund-Raising Needs   63
Fund-Raising Program Options   66
The Internal Action Plan   67
The External Action Plan   69
Fund-Raising Strategies   76
The Solicitation Package   79

Strategies for Small- and Medium-Sized Nonprofit
Organizations   85

Fund-Raising Checklist   88

Fund-Raising Resources   89

Suggested References   90

Part 2   PURSUING THE MISSION

Chapter 4   Creating a Marketing Orientation in the Nonprofit Organization   93

What is Marketing?   93

The Role of Marketing in the Nonprofit Organization   94

The Benefits of a Marketing Orientation   95

Identification of the Market and Its Needs   97

Examining the Environment   102

The Written Marketing Plan   104

Creating the Market Budget   113

Evaluation   115

Who Holds the Marketing Responsibilities in the
Organization?   117

Chapter 5   Providing Needed Educational Programs   119

Is Your Organization in the Education Business?   120

How Do You Determine the Need For Education?   121

How Do You Plan a Successful Program?   123

What is the Most Appropriate Medium to Use?   124

How do You Build Credibility Into Your Program?   128

Why Are Promotion and Easy Access So Important?   130

What Do You Need to Understand About Your Budget?   135

Why Is Program Evaluation Important?   137

Checklist for Effective Education Programs   139

Chapter 6   Mastering the Meeting Planner's Puzzle   143

Designing Your Meeting   144

Conference Activities   156

Postconference Activities   162
Wrap-up   162

Chapter 7   Using Public Relations Tools Effectively   167

What Is Public Relations?   168
Communications Tools   175
Communications Tactics   186
Forward-Looking Public Relations   198
Summary   199

Chapter 8   Getting Political Support for Your Cause   201

Establishing a Government Relations Program at the Local
Level   202
The Importance of a Government Relations Program   203
Participation in Your Government Relations Program   204
Starting a Government Relations Campaign   204
The Importance of Facts for a Government Relations
Campaign   206
Facts Are Not Enough for a Government Relations Campaign   206
A Letter-Writing Campaign is Important   207
Making the Campaign More Effective   209
Coalitions   210
Lobbying   210
Checklist for Creating a Government Relations Program   216

Part 3:   MANAGING THE ORGANIZATION

Chapter 9   Financial Management   219

What is the Accounting Process?   220
Getting Started: Opening a Bank Account   221
Staffing the Accounting Function   224
Accounting System   225
Chart of Accounts   227
Accrual and Cash Basis Accounting   228
Cash Receipts   229
Cash Disbursements   230

Accrual Entries and Other Journal Entries   231
Closing Procedures   232
Budgeting   233
Financial Statement Preparation   234
Review and Analysis   237
Does Your Organization Need an Audit?   242
Tax Returns   243
Policies and Procedures   244

**Chapter 10   Choosing and Nurturing An Information
                        System   247**

Selecting an Information System for Your Organization   247
Staffing Your Information System   252
Preparing For Change   253
Maintenance   255
Summary   257

Chapter 11   Your People and Their Environment   259

Human Resources   260
Start-up and Growth   261
Finding and Hiring Staff   263
On the Job   268
Down . . . and Eventually Out   269
Personnel Policies and Procedures   270
The Office Environment   272
Summary   276

Chapter 12   Knowing Important Legal Requirements   279

Forming and Operating a Nonprofit Organization   279
Avoiding Potential Legal Pitfalls   289
Special Circumstances Requiring the Help of Counsel   294
In Conclusion   296

Chapter 13   Selecting and Using Consultants   **297**

How to Select and Use Consultants   297
Working with Your Consultant   308
Assisting the Consultants   313
Final Reports   314
Checklists/Points for Review   314

CHAPTER ONE

Establishing the Organization's Direction

"If you don't know where you're going, any road will do." Identifying your mission will help you choose the right road and make your organization stronger. This chapter will show you how to formulate a mission statement and then develop goals and strategies to carry out that mission.

How recently have you reflected on the effectiveness of your nonprofit organization in meeting the current and future needs of the constituents or publics you serve? Too often, a crisis occurs before staff and elected leaders feel the need to reexamine the mission and goals of the organization. Rather than waiting for that crisis, leaders of nonprofit organizations must **think strategically**, continually analyzing emerging trends affecting their organizations.

At the very least, organization leaders—both executive staff and governing board members—should periodically analyze whether the original mission of the organization is still relevant to the needs and expectations of its members and constituents. There should be a well-defined and understood strategic plan which the organization's staff, as well as its board or other governing body, uses to guide program activities, allocate resources, and assess the organization's achievements. This process should be part of "strategic management"—a proactive, rather than a reactive, tool.

STRATEGIC MANAGEMENT AND STRATEGIC PLANNING

Strategic management first requires that the organization's leaders identify their collective vision or mission for the organization. It requires them to assess long-term opportunities and threats to that vision, mobilize assets to address those opportunities and threats, and carry out a successful implementation strategy. **Strategic planning** is the essential first step—planning that establishes the *direction* for the organization, that provides the navigator's chart to achieve the organization's **mission**. A good strategic plan will provide staff and leaders with the guidelines to:

- Establish the organization's program of activities;
- Allocate human and financial resources to accomplish those activities;
- Assess whether objectives are being met; and
- Evaluate programs, staff, and resources.

Strategic planning does not summarize the wish lists of all contributors; rather, it is realistic, based on what is going on in the real world, taking into account that changes will take place both inside and outside of the organization in the timeframe of the plan. Strategic planning requires that we not only look inward at what we might desire for our organization, but also—and perhaps more important—that we look outward to the external environment to understand those forces and trends which will affect our nonprofit's future and the accomplishment of its mission. As shown in Exhibit 1–1, strategic planning, as opposed to "traditional" planning, requires **strategic thinking**.

A strategic plan does not provide a detailed chronology of action; that is a function of an "operational" or "business" plan. Rather, a strategic plan broadly maps the activities the organization should pursue to maintain its desired character and identity. It is a tool to guide decision-making by the organization's leaders on issues which are fundamental to the organization.

A well-developed strategic plan provides the framework for responding to a changing environment. Among the questions the organization's leaders should ask during the planning process are:

- What is the essence of the organization? What makes it unique?
- What are the core values and beliefs of its constituents?

Exhibit 1–1   Strategic vs Traditional Planning

Traditional	Strategic
1. Emphasis on stability	Dynamic and change-oriented
2. Tradition-oriented	Mission-oriented
3. Blueprint for future decisions	Vision of future guides today's decisions
4. Reactive	Proactive
5. Inaction in face of ambiguity	Action-oriented, even in face of ambiguity
6. Internal focus	External focus
7. Relies on tried and tested	Emphasizes innovation and creativity
8. Lock-step process	Continuous, ongoing process
9. Facts and quantitative emphasized	Options and qualitative emphasized
10. Efficiency orientation	Effectiveness orientation

Schwartz, Michael A. with Timothy N. Burelle, *Guidelines for Strategic Planning for the Colleges of Pharmacy*. Alexandria, VA: American Association of Colleges of Pharmacy, 1990.

- What is its mission? Who is served and what do they get? Should the mission be amended?
- What does it do best, and how does that relate to what the world needs?
- What are its strengths? Its weaknesses?
- What are the keys to the success of the organization?
- Of those factors making a difference, what is changing in the environment and what is the competition doing?
- How can the organization really make a difference in the lives of its constituents and in society?
- What activities are worth undertaking and committing to over the next three years? Five years?
- What must be done to implement the strategy?

When completed, a strategic plan should not be a long, onerous document; it should be focused, containing a mission statement, principles, goals, and strategic objectives. Through its strategic plan, an organization says to the world: this is who we are and what we want to be, and here's how we plan to fulfill our mission.

Working from the strategic plan, nonprofit organizations can develop coherent, focused, realistic **operational plans**, describing the specific actions that must be taken to accomplish each objective identified in the strategic plan. With both strategic and operational plans developed and adopted by the leadership and staff, the executive is positioned to manage strategically. Without these critical tools, nonprofits often find themselves using their resources indiscriminately, limiting their opportunities for greater success.

WHY STRATEGIC PLANS FAIL

There are a number of ways to approach strategic planning. One educational association began with a board-appointed standing committee on long-range planning. The committee took considerable time surveying the membership, conducting environmental analyses, and using a variety of processes to gain consensus. After two years, a document was prepared setting forth great expectations for the organization—expectations which had neither the intellectual nor financial commitment of the organization's leadership.

Does this sound familiar? Many nonprofits use this approach as their first step. But only when a governing board is convinced of its own responsibility and limitations for matching planning with reality will the process move forward.

Perhaps you already have a strategic plan which was developed a number of years ago but was not actually used by the organization or referred to since it came off the press. Have you analyzed why? There are a number of reasons why strategic plans fail. Among the pitfalls you want to avoid are:

- All of the ideas and all of the wish lists of the contributors are included in the document. So many ideas are presented that the real focus is unclear.
- The "wish lists" fail to take into account what is actually occurring in the real world or to realize that the environment and the organization have changed since the organization was chartered.
- The strategic plan is not tested against current and anticipated resources (human and fiscal) of the organization.
- The executive, elected leaders, and/or staff lack commitment to the plan.

- No operational plan is developed for the strategic plan; thus, there is no carry-through on the plan.

- As leaders change, there are no mechanisms in place to gain commitment and continue the strategic plan; thus, again, there is no carry-through on the plan.

KEY ELEMENTS TO SUCCESSFUL STRATEGIC PLANNING

There are two maxims to remember as you move through the strategic planning process:

- A strategic plan is a statement of important, but flexible, guidelines, not rigid doctrine.

- The process of strategic planning—the development, implementation, and assessment of a plan—is not a single, one-shot event; rather, it is an ongoing, continuous process, which must adapt to environmental changes, both external and internal.

Lessons learned over the years can help shorten the developmental process for organizations beginning strategic planning, making it more efficient and satisfying for all those involved. Among them are those discussed in the next several sections.

Obtain Support and Commitment of Leadership to Pursue Strategic Planning

This may appear as a simple observation; however, it will be critical to have the agreement and commitment from the nonprofit's elected leaders to pursue strategic planning. In situations where there may be an overlap of board elections, be sure "new" board members agree with the proposed activity. An executive who believes he or she "knows best" and therefore begins the process without the approval and commitment of elected policy makers will be jousting with windmills. In some cases, the nonprofit's leaders will need to be convinced that strategic planning is necessary. There may be those who have been through a poorly conducted process and may find little value in spending time and resources on such a "spurious" activity. Others may toss the responsibility back to staff, saying, "You know what we want. Handle it."

Involve Leadership, Staff, and Other Major Constituents in the Strategic Planning Process

Elected policy makers cannot just give lip service to the idea of strategic planning, but should be at the center of the planning process whenever possible. Other leaders or outside experts can likewise be involved in the process, including founders and other stakeholders. It also would be wise to consider involving individuals who would be identified as "visionaries" or "futurists" as well as "distractors" or "outliers" of the organization. They will provide perspectives not readily apparent to those in the mainstream of the organization, challenging the status quo. In addition, gaining major constituents' involvement and commitment early in the process should help pave the way for easier implementation. Key staff will necessarily take responsibility for helping to implement the plan and, therefore, should be a part of the planning process.

Without the support and commitment of the organization's elected leaders, your strategic plan will die a slow death. Their involvement, along with committee chairs, past and future leaders, visionaries, and even outliers should facilitate the development of a good strategic plan. In addition, opportunities must be provided to allow other constituents to participate in the process, whether through a questionnaire in the organization's newsletter or through requests for review and comment on draft plans.

If recommendations for changes in the organization evolve from the strategic planning process, constituents must not only be aware of those changes, but understand why the organization is changing. Sufficient information should be provided to address how the changes will benefit them and allow them to manage the change. Those constituents who perceive they had an opportunity to provide input into the plan are more likely to embrace it.

Think "Strategically" — Go Beyond the Boundaries

The differences between traditional and strategic planning can be equated with the differences between traditional and strategic thinking. A person who thinks strategically is proactive, externally focused, allowing the vision of the future to guide decision-making. A person who thinks traditionally, on the other hand, is reactive, focused on the organization's internal activities only, and uses the past to determine future decisions. Thinking strategically allows one to push beyond the boundaries and think and act creatively. Strategic thinking helps an organization focus on shaping the future rather than on reviewing the past.

Throughout the strategic planning process it will be important for all participants to think strategically—to "stretch"—and be willing to go beyond the boundaries in their thinking and allow themselves to really "hear" and understand the trends and environmental changes that will affect their organization. The concerns and issues that drove our constituents ten years ago are not the same concerns and issues that drive them today.

Too often, organizational leaders can identify well the emerging trends, opportunities, and potential threats to their nonprofit, but are unwilling to change their mind-set about *their* organization, allowing it to crumble before their eyes, rather than to be willing to address impending changes.

Identify a Consultant/Facilitator for Assistance

If resources are available, an outside facilitator can be immensely helpful. We have all heard the adage, "You can not be a prophet in your own country." Well, neither can the chief executive officer—nor another staff member—manage the strategic planning process in its entirety. Many aspects of the process do not require the assistance of a facilitator; however, a qualified, unbiased facilitator from outside the organization can assist in a number of ways. Specifically, a facilitator can:

- Assist in developing the overall strategic planning process which will be used by the organization;
- Assist in the development and analysis of questionnaires designed to assess emerging trends and critical issues for the organization;
- Assist in the development of meeting agendas for working through the group's strategic planning process;
- Assist in identifying individuals both within and outside the organization who should participate in the process;
- Facilitate the group process in a retreat atmosphere that will allow elected leaders and key staff to focus on the issues rather than on the process;

- Balance competing participant perspectives and facilitate consensus-building;
- Prepare the summary report from the retreat, which should include the first draft of the organization's strategic plan;
- Provide ongoing counsel to the executive and elected leaders to ensure the strategic plan is completed, an operational plan is developed, and monitoring and evaluation mechanisms are established; and
- Provide heightened credibility to the strategic planning process.

If resources are not available to pay for an outside facilitator, nonprofits often solicit assistance from a governing board member whose for-profit organization may have used a facilitator or consultant for its own planning process. Sometimes, the consultant or facilitator may contribute his or her services in support of the nonprofit's mission.

You will want a facilitator who has or will gain the respect of the participants. Costs, as for all consulting activities, will vary depending on location and the amount of time you will require of your facilitator; however, in 1994 fees ranged from $85 per hour to $150 per hour. Time spent facilitating a strategic planning session generally was doubled, since additional time and energy are expended in preparing summaries after hours for the participants to review while they are together.

Management consultant Peter Drucker has developed an excellent guide and participant's workbook for the analytical phase of a nonprofit's strategic planning: *The Five Most Important Questions.* These materials, which should be indispensable for any nonprofit carrying out its own self-assessment, are available from the Drucker Foundation for Nonprofit Management in New York.

Conduct an Environmental Analysis

A critical step in the strategic planning process is to understand what is happening in the environment: externally to the organization, including trends, challengers, competitors, and other interested parties; and internally, with the organization's constituents, structure, technical and economic capabilities, and culture.

Through an environmental analysis, the organization's leaders can identify those **external trends/issues** which may have an impact on the organization. Generally, it is helpful to begin with categories of trends which can be analyzed, such as:

- Sociological/demographic
- Economic/financial
- Technological/scientific
- Political/legislative/regulatory
- Professional/educational

These categories are those used by a number of organizations. You should be able to adapt them to your nonprofit. For example, current economic trends affect all organizations; however, the impact on each nonprofit may be different depending on the nonprofit's mission and its usual source of funding. A social services nonprofit may depend heavily on state grants that have been cut because of state financial difficulties; another nonprofit may look to philanthropic foundations and be able to maintain or even increase their support.

An analysis of the **internal environment** means assessing the organization's strengths and weaknesses in all aspects of the organization:

- Communication and marketing capabilities;
- Constituents' satisfaction with the organization;
- Governance and staffing structures;
- Culture of the organization—as perceived both internally and externally;
- Financial and human resources; and
- Technological and scientific capabilities.

Often leadership and constituent questionnaires are used to assess both the external and internal environments. These questionnaires may also be sent to outside publics to obtain their perspectives on the organization. Other sources of information also may be available through other data collected by the organization as well as through meetings and current publications.

The need for an environmental analysis can not be overstated. Without a good, clear understanding of the trends both within and outside the organization, a "strategic" plan cannot be developed. The computer GIGO rule will prevail: garbage in, garbage out. An example of a questionnaire designed to develop information for an organizational assessment is provided in Exhibit 1-2. Tabulating and summarizing constituent responses can be a task of staff or the facilitator. In either case, summaries should be developed for use during the strategic planning retreat along with any other documents or materials that provide information regarding the trends and environmental conditions of the organization.

Plan and Conduct a Strategic Planning Session with Key Leaders and Staff

Generally, a meeting away from the office in a different environment eliminates distractions and brings a clear perspective to elected leaders as they map out the future for their organization. With an initial environmental analysis completed, most strategic plans can be developed in a two-day to two and one-half day leadership retreat. For very large organizations, several meetings over a period of a year may be required. Your facilitator, if involved, will work with you in developing the agenda for the retreat. This should allow for open discussion and active listening, testing of theories and practice, discussion by both advocates and detractors, free time to allow issues to "gel," and sufficient opportunity to build consensus.

The amount of time provided for the retreat may need to be modified based on the time elected leaders have free to spend away from home and their willingness to commit 100 percent of the time available to the task. Generally, however, it would be most preferable to allow two to two and one-half days. Some nonprofits find it most convenient to hold the session prior to another meeting—such as a board meeting—to reduce travel costs. The downside, of course, is the length of time the volunteer leaders are away from their jobs and families. Since strategic thinking and planning are arduous processes, requiring much concentration and creativity, the retreat should not be held *after* another meeting.

You will want to address a number of topics/issues during a strategic planning session or retreat. Each is critical to the outcomes of your strategic plan.

Exhibit 1–2 Sample Questionnaire

1. How would you define the mission of the _____ organization?
2. What are the current main goals of the organization?
3. Using the attached form, (a) identify those environmental trends/changes that are occurring, or will occur within the next two to five years, which will have an impact on your organization. Next, on the same form, identify the threats and/or opportunities created by these same environmental trends for your organization. You may wish to consider Economic, Technological, Educational/Training, Sociological, and Regulatory trends.
4. Using the same form, identify the organization's greatest assets or strengths in making an impact on those trends.
5. Again using the same form, identify the organization's greatest weaknesses in making an impact on those trends.
6. What do you perceive as the three (3) most critical issues for the organization at this time? Please prioritize. (1 = most critical)
7. With respect to the organization's internal capabilities, which issues do you consider most essential to the organization's ability to successfully implement its objectives?
8. What recommendations do you have to increase the organization's effectiveness? Please prioritize. (1 = most important)
9. What is your personal "vision" for the organization's future?
10. If one objective could be accomplished or one issue could be resolved for the organization, what would you want it to be?
11. In your opinion, what is the greatest obstacle to overcome to achieve this objective or resolve this issue?

Test the Outcomes of Your Environmental Analysis. During the retreat, the environmental trends and issues can be analyzed to determine whether they present **opportunities or threats** for the organization. Often, a trend or issue may present both opportunities for your organization and challenges to the status quo. The analysis continues by assessing the **strengths and weaknesses** of the organization in dealing with the threats and opportunities. The entire analysis is often called a *S.W.O.T. analysis*—Strengths, Weaknesses, Opportunities, and Threats. Again, this assessment can be conducted via mailed questionnaires; however, often this part of the process is conducted during a leadership retreat.

A SWOT analysis worksheet is provided to assist you in working through the process (see Exhibit 1-3). Identify one critical issue for your nonprofit; identify whether this issue provides opportunities,

Exhibit 1–3 Strategic Planning: Environmental S.W.O.T. Analysis Worksheet

Environmental Trends	Threat	Opportunity
Trends:		
Strengths/Assets:		
Weaknesses/Limitations:		

or threats, or both to your organization; and identify your organization's strengths and weaknesses in addressing the issue.

Determine Whether Immediate Action is Required.   It will be particularly important for the organization's leaders to identify specific opportunities or threats which may require immediate action or close observation in the immediate future. Using the chart below (Exhibit 1-4), identify those environmental issues and trends (external and internal) which may have a high impact on your organization and determine whether there is a low, medium, or high probability of occurrence within the next five years. Those which emerge as high priority—"high impact/high occurrence"—become the critical, "strategic" issues which will require the organization's immediate attention.

Exhibit 1–4   Environmental Issues Alert Matrix

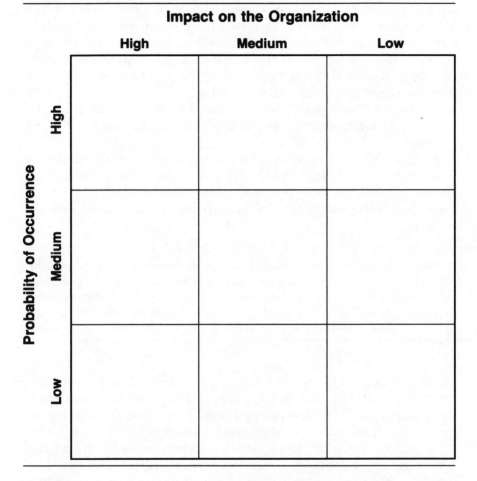

Nonprofit leaders who think and manage strategically can and should develop mechanisms to continuously (not just during the strategic planning process) monitor emerging trends, opportunities, and threats to the organization. The earlier such elements are detected, the more efficiently they can be addressed.

Identify the Leadership's Collective Vision for the Organization. Once the environmental analysis is completed, retreat participants can be asked to step back and identify their **visions** for the future of their organization. Often the pre-retreat questionnaire includes questions regarding the respondent's vision for the organization.

The group can discuss what consensus, if any, emerged and, again with a facilitator's assistance, identify the "collective vision" for the organization. "Visioning" requires letting go of preconceived notions about the organization and allows for creative and strategic thinking about what the future could be like for the organization. One facilitator used the tactic of asking the participants to describe the newspaper headlines which would appear about their nonprofit five years into the future. Visioning helps to describe the organization as the collective group would like to see it at a point in time in the future.

William Taylor, Executive Director for the American Society of Association Executives (ASAE), has noted that ASAE, through its visioning and strategic planning processes, is stretching to be more than it has been historically, working to reach out in new directions.

> "Before visioning, when asked about ASAE, I described it almost exclusively as a continuing education organization. That's how we perceived ourselves. But the vision and the [strategic] plan reach out in many ways—technology, partnerships, internationalism, diversity, and others. This represents a breadth that we have not aspired to previously."

Develop Scenarios for the Organization's Future. Some nonprofits find it helpful to develop both positive and negative **scenarios** about the organization's distant future (15–20 years into the future). In these situations, participants develop scenarios based on a future environment which has many positive opportunities for the organization and other scenarios which describe an organization based on threats. Some people have a difficult time thinking twenty years into the future, making this an excellent exercise for individuals in the organization who can be identified as the "futurists."

One health care nonprofit, the American Association of Blood Banks (AABB), developed a series of scenarios that focused on various views of the world of medicine and the effects of potential future technological developments on the role of blood banking, transfusion medicine, tissue banking, and transplantation medicine. Although members who were involved in the development of the scenarios did not agree on all issues, the scenarios did present possible alternative futures that the organization can be prepared to address proactively, rather than reactively.

Review the Organization's Mission Statement. Strategic plans can never be well developed until the organization is clear on its fundamental mission. Most often, a number of board members cycle on and off the board each year, leaving staff to provide the continuing direction for the organization. Unless the board of directors, the chief executive, and staff are all working with a *clear and concise mission statement* for the organization—one which they all understand, accept, and commit to—each of the parties, working under different perceptions of the *actual* mission of the organization, will try to lead the organization, each in a different direction.

All too frequently, however, it is not until the organization's leaders participate in the strategic planning process, identifying the trends and, consequently, the critical, "strategic" issues which are affecting, or will affect, the organization, that they become aware of the group's lack of unity in direction. It is at this point in the process that the group should begin examining the organization's current mission, principles, goals, and strategic objectives.

> **Mission Statement:** A succinct statement which sets forth the organization's purpose and philosophy. Although brief, the mission statement will specify the fundamental reason(s) for the organization's existence; establish the scope of the organization; and identify the organization's unique characteristics.

In some cases, the *actual* mission is clouded by all kinds of information included with the nonprofit's so-called mission statement. Often the mission is imbedded in a one- to two-page statement that includes the organization's goals, objectives, and program plans as well as the principles or "values" held by the constituents of the organization. Because the nonprofit's mission cannot be culled easily from the mass of information, no one remembers exactly what the mission actually is, allowing individuals on the board, staff, and committees to selectively retain that piece of information which agrees with their singular perception of the organization, rather than acknowledging its actual mission.

A good mission statement should be succinct, stating the nonprofit's purpose and philosophy, identifying the uniqueness of the organization. It should provide the overall direction, guiding the development of the organization's principles, its goals, and its strategic objectives—those targets for the organization's primary activities. Goals, strategic objectives, or program activities not relevant to the nonprofit's mission should not be pursued; they would be a distraction for the organization.

In 1960, the year the American Society for Psychoprophylaxis in Obstetrics, Inc./Lamaze (ASPO/Lamaze) was founded, the mission of the association was "to promote the psychoprophylaxis (natural childbirth) method of childbirth education." In 1986, the mission statement was revised to read: "to promote an optimal childbirth and early parenting experience for families through education, advocacy and reform." In 1990, the ASPO/Lamaze Board of Directors again examined the mission of the organization, this time in a climate of competing organizations and financial distress. While a difficult time for the Board, members worked to focus the organization for its future in identifying its unique characteristics, its scope, and its fundamental reason for existence—and again revised their mission statement: "To develop and promote standards for prenatal education, Lamaze childbirth education and early parenting education and family-centered maternity care through education, advocacy, and reform."

*This mission statement has held through subsequent years, with the organization addressing its actual mission, i.e., to **develop and promote standards** not only for childbirth education but also for early parenting education and for family-centered maternity care. The standards will be promoted through education, advocacy, and reform efforts, thus providing the organization's policy direction for both short- and long-term initiatives.*

Some nonprofits, particularly one-purpose membership organizations, may perform well for years without ever having developed a mission statement. Usually, in these cases, the mission is implicit in the by-laws or the collective minds of the members or governing board members. Making the mission statement explicit, however, ensures the nonprofit's long-term success. Take for example, the Sgt. Peppers Society.

Named after the U.S. Congressman Claude Pepper, an advocate for the aging, the Sgt. Peppers Society was a small volunteer organization formed by young singles who, rather than spend their free time meeting in bars, decided to spend their time together conducting fund-raising events to support the elderly. Armed with the motto, "Health, Housing, and Happiness," the leaders of the Sgt. Peppers Society identified the organization as a social and charitable group. They touted having planned and conducted four Monte Carlo nights, five Christmas dinners, five Senior Olympics, as well as facilitating eight marriages and four births over their brief, five-year history.

Through their fund-raising programs, they had provided over $55,000 for programs and services to support the elderly in the

Washington, D.C., area. At the same time, they recognized that many of the original founders were "burning out," with few new members willing to take on the many tasks developed over time by the founders. With concerns over the future direction of Sgt. Peppers, including conflicts among old and new members about the purpose of the organization and how monies were distributed to the elderly, the executive committee obtained the voluntary assistance of a consultant who helped plan and facilitate a day and a half retreat to begin development of a strategic plan for the Society.

Retreat participants assessed their organization's external and internal environments, identified the opportunities and threats to the organization, and prioritized the most critical issues the organization must address over the next several years. The process then led to specifying the organization's mission statement, principles, goals, and strategic objectives. It is not unusual for those involved in a strategic planning retreat to debate long and hard over the mission statement for their organization. Those at the retreat for the Sgt. Peppers Society were no different.

Among the concepts they wished the mission statement to convey were: the organization is charitable; members raise funds; they are interested in interacting with the elderly; they support and provide services for the unmet needs of the elderly; and they wish to enhance the quality of life for the elderly.

The first "final" draft of the mission statement was:

> "The Sgt. Peppers Society is a charitable organization which raises funds and provides support and direct services to improve the quality of life for the elderly."

Make Changes in the Mission Statement When Appropriate. Upon further reflection, the retreat participants agreed that the Society's mission was not to "raise funds," but rather to *raise funds in order to improve the quality of life for the elderly*. The revised mission statement is succinct and yet captures the intent of the leaders at the retreat:

SGT. PEPPERS SOCIETY IS A CHARITABLE, FUNDRAISING
ORGANIZATION DEDICATED TO IMPROVING THE QUALITY
OF LIFE FOR THE ELDERLY BY PROVIDING
SUPPORT AND DIRECT SERVICES.

Test yourself, your organization's elected leaders, and your key staff with the same question:

"How would you define the organization's mission?" Do responses come easily? Are they consistent with one another?

Test your mission statement as it is identified in your organizational documents and publications.

Does your Mission statement:

	Yes	No	Unsure
• Specify the fundamental reason(s) for your organization's existence?			
• Establish the scope of your organization?			
• Identify your organization's unique characteristics?			
• Provide a consistent message to all constituents?			
• Provide overall policy direction for the organization?			
• Direct your short-term as well as your long-range and strategic planning initiatives?			

Identify Your Organization's Principles. Every organization carries with it its own life—its own values and beliefs—whether it is for issues which must be addressed, standards to be developed, or support for others who are disadvantaged. These principles (values/beliefs) should both guide your organization's initiatives and help evaluate the success of those initiatives in fulfilling the nonprofit's mission.

Principles: Statements which identify the philosophical guidelines for all of the organization's activities.

Values and beliefs that recognize constituent needs and expectations can be captured as **principles** that define the philosophical guidelines for the organization's activities. For some organizations, principles may be imbedded in a longer mission statement or not stated at all. It is important to list the organization's statements of organizational principles separately so that they are clearly understood by constituents, board, and staff.

For ASPO/Lamaze, the following values and principles emerged as important in forming the organization's philosophy:

- Birth is a normal, healthy experience, belonging to the woman and her partner.
- Education for childbirth educators should be high quality and academically based.
- The association values childbirth educators and recognizes the need to support them in educating expectant parents.
- Child-bearing women/couples/families should be educated to make self-determined choices.
- All population segments should have access to high-quality childbirth education.

For the Sgt. Peppers Society, the following principles were established:

- Everyone has the right to a high quality of life, regardless of age.
- Members of Sgt. Peppers are committed to the organization's mission and goals.
- Sgt. Peppers members respect the wisdom of the elderly and appreciate the benefits they are deriving from the contributions made by the elderly.
- Contributions of all members as well as non-members are appreciated whether they are financial or time contributions.
- The Society supports individual member's personal goals in their involvement in the Society, whether they are for social, professional, or service reasons.
- All activities of the Society will be guided by the strategic plan.
- The primary responsibility of the Society's officers and directors is to identify the resources for the Society's activities and provide the leadership that will support the implementation of the Society's strategic plan.

It is important for the organization's leadership to embrace and commit themselves to the organization's strategic plan as it is developed to ensure it does not become a document that just sits on the shelf. With such a statement of principles included in the plan and in other organizational documents, it will be clear to all constituents, both inside and outside the organization, that the strategic plan will provide the direction for the organization's efforts and that the governing board has the responsibility to ensure its success.

Test your own organization's documents and promotional materials. Do they include philosophical statements which:

	Yes	No	Unsure
• Identify the principles held by your constituents?			
• Capture the essence of the organization's philosophy?			
• Recognize and are sensitive to your constituents' needs and expectations?			

Specify Targeted Goals for the Organization. While the mission statement identifies general policy directions of an organization, *goals*—or purposes—specify how these general policy directions will be carried out. For our discussion, we will use the term "goals" rather than "purposes" to translate a mission statement into major policy directives.

> **Goals**: A limited number of statements which translate the association's mission into *major policy directions.*

As noted previously, some organizations have included goals within their mission statement. Again, they should be separated from the mission statement so that they can be used as a tool to assess the success of the organization in fulfilling its mission. Goals will necessarily be broad statements, limited in number, and focused on the unique characteristics of the organization.

The Sgt. Peppers Society had two goals:

- To raise and distribute funds to support programs for the elderly.
- To maintain and improve the organization.

The goal statements for the American Association of Blood Banks (AABB) clarified the Association's mission statement, but also, even more importantly, set out measurable tasks against which progress could be gauged:

Mission: "To establish and promote the highest standards of care for patients and donors through leadership in all aspects of blood banking, transfusion medicine and tissue transplantation."

Goals: The AABB provides leadership in blood banking, tissue banking, transfusion medicine and tissue transplantation by:

- Educating members, other health-care providers, donors, patients, policy makers and the public;
- Providing a forum for professionals to exchange information and ideas;
- Improving the quality and efficacy of transfusion and transplantation practices by establishing and promulgating standards;
- Assisting our members in ensuring a safe and adequate supply of blood and transplantable tissue; and
- Assisting our members in effectively and efficiently implementing technological advances.

A regional nonprofit organization, the Fish Middleton Jazz Scholarship Fund, Inc. (FMJS), set its mission "to be a viable part of sustaining, nurturing and perpetuating American Jazz." This organization, which showcases jazz musicians through a number of music concerts, including an annual three-day music festival that provides the venue for awarding competitive scholarships, has identified two clear goals:

- To present quality music and educational events; and
- To promote and support emerging jazz artists to enter the international jazz arena.

Test your organization's *goals* by asking yourself the following questions.

Do the goals identified for your organization:

	Yes	No	Unsure
• Clarify your organization's mission statement?			
• Specify the overriding purposes of the organization?			
• Provide the foundation for developing targeted programmatic activities and operational plans?			
• Provide the basis for assessing the major priorities of the organization?			

Translate the Leadership's Visions into Strategic Objectives.
Evolving from an organization's mission, principles, and goals
should be the major accomplishments (strategic objectives) the organization seeks to achieve over a specified period of time (e.g.,
five years). Organizations use a number of terms to identify these
major accomplishments. Often, strategic objectives are confused
with the more general policy directives we've called goals. The difference is the level of specificity: the term *"strategic* objective" is
used to identify the major accomplishments the organization
hopes to achieve in a defined timeframe which address the critical,
"strategic" issues identified during the environmental analysis.
Importantly, strategic objectives may relate to one or more of the
organization's goals.

> **Strategic Objectives**: The major *accomplishments* that the organization
> seeks to achieve over a specified period of time (e.g., five years).

More specifically, strategic objectives should:

- Support the mission and goals of the organization;
- Provide clarification of the goals;
- Translate the critical, "strategic" issues identified for the organi-
  zation into *specific* policy directions;
- Provide the foundation for the development of detailed opera-
  tional or business plans for the organization; and
- Provide the basis for assessing the organization's accomplish-
  ments.

Of major importance, strategic objectives should not only respond to the needs of constituents, but also be realistic with respect
to the organization's environment, both externally and internally,
including the available human and financial resources required to
accomplish them.

The strategic objectives identified by the American Association of
Blood Banks (AABB) related to those issues that are critical to the
organization's future: quality, education, legislative and regulatory
issues, research, relationships with other organizations, and public
image. Within AABB's strategic plan, the strategic objectives appear
as follows:

I. Develop and promote quality management and improvement programs for blood centers, transfusion services and tissue banks to ensure the safest blood and tissue supply possible.

II. Increase professional educational opportunities for the membership and provide educational programs related to transfusion medicine and transplantation for the public and other related professionals (individuals and groups).

III. Establish a legal, regulatory and public policy environment conducive to the effective and efficient operation of our members in providing the highest level of health-care services.

IV. Actively promote the application of basic scientific discoveries to the continuous improvement and enhancement of blood transfusion and tissue transplantation practices.

V. Form a mutually beneficial working relationship with other organizations, including state and regional blood banking associations, to address areas of common concern and promote the AABB as the leader in its chosen fields.

VI. Develop acceptance and understanding of the AABB members' activities and their roles in the health-care profession, with the public sector and other professionals.

The Fish Middleton Jazz Scholarship Fund identified four strategic objectives:

I. Sponsor annual jazz concert events.
II. Facilitate in-school programs.
III. Conduct jazz workshops and seminars to enhance students' skills and understanding of jazz.
IV. Grant scholarships to emerging jazz artists.

A basic challenge to strategic thinking is the ability of the organization's leadership to create strategic unity among the leadership themselves, staff, and constituents. To build commitment to the strategic plan, everyone within the organization should be *aware* of what the organization is trying to accomplish, *accept* the organization's mission and goals and understand their implications, and *recognize* the actions that they and the leadership are taking toward the accomplishment of the stated mission, goals, and objectives.

Develop a Three- to Five-Year Plan Based on the Strategic Objectives. Typically, group consensus on all of the preceding retreat agenda items are captured on flip chart paper as they are developed and taped to the walls of your meeting room so everyone can review them as the discussion continues. The individual who facilitates the strategic planning session generally is the person who develops summaries as the meeting progresses and prepares a "first draft" of your strategic plan for all retreat participants to review. Comments returned to the facilitator are incorporated into the organization's "final draft" which can then be submitted to other constituents for their reactions.

To summarize, a strategic plan that focuses on the next three, four, or five years will not be a lengthy document; rather, your plan should consist of the following:

1. Introduction which may include:
   - The process the leadership pursued to develop the strategic plan;
   - A summary of the environmental issues, documenting those which were identified as "critical" issues; that is, high impact on the organization and high probability of occurrence; and
   - Identification of the organization's strengths and weaknesses in addressing those critical issues.
2. Organization's mission statement.
3. Statement of principles.
4. Statement of goals.
5. Strategic objectives.

Examine the Implications of the Strategic Plan on Your Organization's Current Programs and Structure. As the plan is developed, current programs and activities should be tested to determine their relevance to the **new** plan. Some programs or activities that have been part of the organization's past may not address the newly revised mission, goals, or strategic objectives, and, therefore, do not fit within the *new* strategic plan.

Similarly, the plan should be re-examined in light of the organization's current governance structure to determine whether the current structure will facilitate the organization's new directions. In many cases, each board member agrees to accept the oversight responsibility for one or more of the strategic objectives to monitor both staff and committees' success in achieving the objective.

Depending on the needs of the new strategic plan, it may be wise to review both the number of board members and their terms, again to facilitate the organization's refocused agenda. Roles and responsibilities for committees will undoubtedly change. In some cases, new committees or task forces will need to be appointed, whereas in other cases committees should be dissolved. Just as changes may be necessary within the governance structure, so too the internal organizational structure will need to be assessed, including staffing patterns, activities, and the utilization of human and fiscal resources.

Once the organization's governing board adopts the new strategic plan, and as modifications within the organization are implemented, a carefully planned communications program should be executed so that all constituents and stakeholders, including staff and outside publics, understand the changes and how they came about.

IMPLEMENTING THE STRATEGIC PLAN

An **operational plan** should accompany a strategic plan. Although time during the retreat may not be available to permit the development of an operational plan, the process for developing such a plan should be discussed at the retreat and assignments should be made. Generally, staff prepare the bulk of the operational plan, with guidance and final approval from the governing board.

As noted earlier, an operational plan describes the specific actions that must be taken to accomplish each objective identified in the strategic plan. It should include the responsible parties, timelines, resource allocations, and an evaluation plan that identifies specific, measurable outcomes to be achieved. The strategic plan, therefore, focuses on the *what*, while your operational plan will focus on the *how*. Without the accompanying operational plan, the strategic plan will languish on the bookshelf, perhaps serving as a reproach for what was not accomplished, but providing no real guide to action. Details within the operational plan should include:

- **Tactics**: Identify what should be done; that is, outline the specific tasks that need to be accomplished to achieve the strategic objective.

- **Timelines**: Include exact dates (month and year) when each tactic should be completed.

- **Responsible parties**: Identify those individuals (staff members, board members, committee chairs, or others) who will be held responsible for accomplishing the task.
- **Resource requirements**: Identify all resources required to accomplish the task, including funding for supplies, equipment, staff time, board travel, etc.
- **Anticipated results**: Specify the desired or anticipated results and what will be accomplished by the selected timeline.
- **Evaluation measures**: Outline how you will determine that the task has been completed or that success has been achieved.

Exhibit 1-5 diagrams the strategic and operational planning processes, beginning with the environmental analysis through to the determination of tactics and their implementation.

DOCUMENT THE PROCESS, THE OUTCOMES, THE "STRATEGIC" PLAN

The report of the process, the outcomes of discussion, and the "draft" strategic plan should be documented and shared with the nonprofit's constituents for review and feedback. This may take the form of a mailing to all board members or even to all constituents, based on the number of individuals involved and the resources available. In addition, committee chairs and members should have an opportunity to review the document to assist in identifying their roles (if any) in the new plan. It will be important, however, to involve the organization's constituents and other stakeholders, including outside publics, to ensure that leadership has correctly identified the critical issues for the organization as well as good strategies to impact them.

MONITOR THE IMPLEMENTATION PLAN

Now that the organization has a strategic plan and an accompanying implementation plan, it is incumbent upon the executive to monitor the plans and provide updates to the governing body on the organization's accomplishments in achieving the plan's strategic objectives. Mechanisms should be established, through a committee or staff assignment, to monitor and assess impending threats or opportunities and to recommend changes in the organization's course.

Exhibit 1–5 The Strategic and Operational Planning Processes

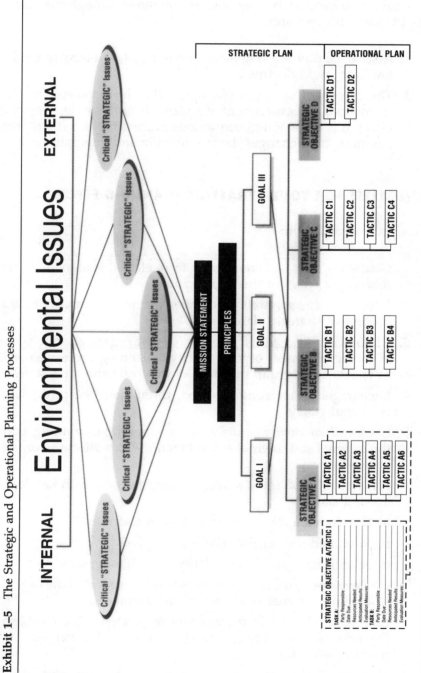

Again, two maxims to remember as you move through the strategic planning process are:

1. A strategic *plan* is a statement of important, but flexible guidelines, not rigid doctrine.
2. The *process* of strategic planning—the development, implementation, and assessment of a plan—is not a single, one-shot event; it is an ongoing, continuous process that must adapt to environmental changes, both externally and internally.

CHECKLIST FOR YOUR STRATEGIC PLANNING EFFORT

Has your organization:

1. *Obtained support and commitment* from elected leaders *to pursue strategic planning* for the organization?
2. *Involved leadership,* staff, and other major constituents in the process of strategic planning?
3. *Obtained assistance from a person outside* the organization to assist in the development of your strategic planning process as well as facilitate the group meetings of the leadership and staff?
4. Encouraged all persons involved, throughout the process, to *think strategically?*
5. *Conducted an environmental analysis,* carefully examining both the external and internal environments which affect the organization?
6. *Planned and conducted a strategic planning session* with key leaders and staff?
   a. Developed a clear, succinct mission statement?
   b. Identified the organization's principles?
   c. Established goals which clarify your mission statement?
   d. Developed strategic objectives which respond to the organization's internal and external environments?
7. *Established a process for implementing the strategic plan,* establishing priorities, identifying timelines, responsible parties, and resource allocations?
8. *Documented the process,* the outcomes, and the "strategic" plan?

9. *Continually monitored the implementation plan,* providing updates on the organization's accomplishments in achieving the plan's objectives?

The following chapters should help the nonprofit organization move from the essential first step—the strategic plan—to effective implementation: to turn from strategic planning to effective, strategic management.

CHAPTER TWO

Working Together: Maximizing Board and Staff Effectiveness

Governing boards and the executive staff share responsibility for their nonprofit's success. The successful nonprofit manager must understand the relationship between board and staff and be able to communicate effectively with elected leaders. This chapter will help both you and your elected leaders to understand the different—but equally important—roles of each group.

GOVERNING BOARDS: CARETAKERS OF THE PUBLIC TRUST

A nonprofit organization typically is born out of a group's desire to solve a problem, meet a need, or create new opportunities to help others. As the organization grows and gains strength with time and experience, it often evolves from a group of volunteers managing all aspects of its activities to one which depends primarily on staff to handle its day-to-day business.

Once the nonprofit moves into its formative years, most of its policies and procedures should be in place, with the governing board working closely with staff to fulfill the defined mission. Nonetheless, it is not unusual for difficulties to emerge as the nonprofit matures, perhaps with new constituents interested in moving the organization in a different direction from its founders. Often, it will not be until the nonprofit comes fully of age that a settling in again occurs.

31

As nonprofit organizations change, so do their governing boards. The relationships between committees, other volunteers, and staff differ from one period to the next. This chapter will help organizations identify troublesome areas before they become significant and overcome these transitional obstacles more quickly.

Types and Sizes of Boards

The size and nature of the board of directors is often determined by history, often without adequate thought. Many nonprofits are established with a 15- to 20-person board of directors that includes officers and directors who chair each of the organization's committees. A smaller board (e.g., 10–12 persons) can, however, provide direction for the organization, while other constituents chair committees and task forces.

Some nonprofits, because of their large size, their interest in involving as many constituents as possible, or simply tradition, have a small board (12–15 persons) but a larger "house of delegates"—individuals who represent regions or chapters and review policies recommended by the executive committee or board of directors. The size of a board will depend on many factors, including the laws of the state of incorporation (which generally dictate a minimum number of directors), the mission and philosophy of the organization, and its resources. However, any organization that has more than 30 board members should question its size. The board should be guided by several questions:

- What functions are required by the board?
- How many individuals, and in what roles, are needed to accomplish those functions?
- How many board committees are needed to accomplish the organization's goals?
- Are there sufficient individuals on the board to participate on board committees?

In most situations, the board will have an executive committee with the authority to act between meetings on behalf of the full board. Actions taken by an executive committee are reviewed, sometimes modified, and usually ratified by the entire board at its next meeting. With a large board, it is especially important to have strong, active committees to study issues in depth and make recommendations to the board. This streamlines the decision process by preventing the board from becoming enmeshed in details, unable to make decisions.

Most governing boards are elected: many by the constituents at large, some by the members of the governing board electing their own replacements. For some organizations, only the directors are elected by the constituents at large, and officers (president, vice president, treasurer, and secretary) are elected by the board. Decisions regarding policies and procedures for nominations and elections are organizationally unique. While one approach may sacrifice democracy, it may also provide greater efficiencies for the organization. Decisions regarding such policies should be driven by your nonprofit's mission and the constituents it serves.

ROLES AND RESPONSIBILITIES OF GOVERNING BOARD MEMBERS

Large nonprofits have sufficient staff to carry out all activities of the organization, with the board setting policy and the executive committee responsible for oversight and any policy decisions that must be made between board meetings. In most cases, however, much of the work of the organization is done by volunteers, through standing committees of the board or ad hoc committees and task forces. Regardless of the size or age of the nonprofit or the number of staff available to carry through the policies of the board, an individual accepting a position on a governing board has fiduciary, moral, and ethical responsibilities.

Ensure Mission is Carried Out

Nonprofit organizations are established to achieve a specific mission. Misunderstanding or misperceptions of the organization's mission—its reason for being—can cause havoc among board members, between board and committees, and between board and staff. Board members must understand the organization's mission and work together, with committee chairs and staff, to ensure the mission is fulfilled. Unless the organization's mission is clear, and all parties accept it and make a commitment to carrying it out, the organization will flounder: disparate goals will be pursued, conflict will arise among and between board members and staff, and the organization will cease to be effective. (See Chapter One, "Establishing the Organization's Direction.")

It is incumbent on the governing board to establish policies and priorities, approve the procedures to accomplish them, and monitor and assess the organization's success in achieving its mission. Once tasks are identified and responsible parties and time lines specified within an operational plan, nonprofit boards can better assess their organization's accomplishments between board meetings.

A board should periodically assess its own operations to ensure that both the board and the organization are working at optimum capacity and efficiency. Such an assessment can help ensure that the organization's mission remains in focus.

Meet Fiduciary Responsibilities

In addition to ensuring that the nonprofit's mission drives all the organization's programs, governing board members have a responsibility to assure that the organization remains financially sound. No board member wants to see the reserves of an organization depleted during his or her "watch." While the chief executive staff, the treasurer, and the finance committee have the chief responsibility for developing and tracking the budget, it is every board member's responsibility to understand the budget, the budgeting and investment procedures, and the organization's financial history in terms of reserves and restricted funds (if any).

Board members of one organization whose budget was well over $2 million were astonished to learn of imminent bankruptcy during a normal audit procedure. All had thought the organization was solvent, with plenty of reserves. When challenged, the executive staff member reported he was planning to "get a bank loan to carry the organization through a rough spot." Unfortunately, the problem was much deeper. Had responsible board members closely monitored the organization's fiscal status, drastic reorganization and downsizing would not have been necessary.

Contribute to the Organization's Bottom Line

Members of nonprofit governing boards are well aware of the need to give willingly of their time for meetings of the board—time that translates into financial contributions for many volunteers. In addition, board members bring their expertise, providing free counsel on a variety of issues.

As discussed in Chapter Three, fund-raising is critical for most nonprofits. This is true for established organizations seeking to expand or maintain existing programs as well as for small nonprofits whose success is measured by "getting to Friday." Board members will be expected not only to contribute their time and their expertise for program activities, but also to identify outside funding sources, and, in some cases, to provide direct financial support. In addition to direct financial contributions, a board member's organization may provide in-kind contributions for such activities as printing or mailing a conference brochure, stuffing envelopes, or providing assistance at a function's registration desk.

Members of nonprofit boards should be willing to dip into their own pockets to support the mission and goals of the organization for which they advocate. The amount is less important than the principle. It is much easier to solicit other individual and corporate support for a nonprofit's agenda when all governing board members of the organization have contributed as well.

Respect Other Board Members

Acceptance of an appointment on a nonprofit's governing board requires a commitment of time, energy, and expertise. Depending on the maturity of the nonprofit, its size, and its resource base, the commitment may be significant. It is incumbent on all board members, however, to respect other members by both attending and being prepared for meetings. If an assignment is accepted, it should be completed by the agreed-upon deadline.

While there may be unexpected circumstances that preclude attendance at a scheduled board meeting, any member of the governing board who fails to attend at least the majority of its meetings should assess his or her commitment to the organization and consider resigning from the board.

Respect for other board members also requires that members argue *positions*, not personalities. Decisions regarding the future of a nonprofit do not come easily and often there will be differing points of view. At these times, stepping into the other person's shoes and carefully listening to his or her perspective will be particularly critical to quality decision-making.

Maintain Professional and Ethical Standards

Members of a governing board are entrusted with the care and nurturing of their nonprofit organization. Board members must maintain high professional and ethical standards for the conduct of all activities within and outside the organization. Two areas of particular concern include confidentiality and conflict of interest.

Confidentiality.   The issue of confidentiality of board meetings and board decisions is often not addressed until a problem occurs. Although there may be disagreements within the board room, once board members leave the room they have the responsibility to maintain the confidentiality of the discussion and support the outcome, whether or not they agreed with it. When board members leave the board room and comment to other constituents that they did not agree with the outcome and that "so and so said . . . ," constituents lose confidence in the board's ability to lead. Airing dissension also creates distrust and additional conflict among board members and strains fragile interpersonal relationships.

Conflict of Interest.   Depending on the organization's mission and goals and the program activities it pursues, board members may have opportunities to benefit from board actions. Providing services for a fee, although not illegal, gives the appearance of self-interest. Contracts with board members for direct mail campaigns or other fund-raising services have been a cause of destructive publicity for several national nonprofits in recent years. When confronted with potential conflicts, board members should identify the conflict and remove themselves from the discussion and any vote on the matter. Some organizations have conflict of interest policies to prevent even an appearance of wrongful activity.

Respect and Support Staff

It is important for the board to support the executive staff leader. Whatever the title, the executive staff leader works at the pleasure of the governing board, implementing policies approved by board action. To ensure an effective, long-lasting relationship, the lines of communication between staff and board need to be clearly identified and maintained.

Lines of Communication.   Most nonprofits will clearly delineate the roles and responsibilities and reporting channels of the executive director. While the executive is accountable to the board as a whole, quite often the direct line of communication will be with the elected president or chairperson of the governing board. In some cases, the executive works just as closely with both the executive committee and the president. While all board members should feel free to contact the executive, the executive generally should confirm decisions with the president and/or executive committee, particularly if there are new policy or resource implications.

Staff, on the other hand, report to the executive, who has the authority to hire and terminate employees. In nonprofit organizations, whether small or large, board members should work with the executive in requesting staff time or support for activities.

The person hired to provide administrative leadership for a nonprofit organization is chosen to accomplish the tasks identified by the board at the time of hiring. Occasionally, a nonprofit outgrows its executive and chooses to hire someone new who can meet the new demands of the organization. Generally, however, with the support of the board, the executive grows along with the nonprofit. Boards need to recognize the talents of their executives and support them with opportunities for professional development. An executive director who has gained knowledge and responsibility through experience can be an organization's most valuable asset.

Generally, the president or chair of the governing board has the closest working relationship with the executive and should provide feedback on the executive's performance on a routine basis. A more formal review process, however, can also be developed so that all board members have an opportunity to provide their assessment of their organization's chief staff executive. The process developed should be agreeable to both parties.

Separation of Roles.   An area of particular concern for many executives is the distinction between the board's role as policy maker and the executive staff's role as administrator and implementer. Often, the line is quite fine: the executive will be expected to provide policy guidance for the board, not just take orders, and board members, as volunteers, may be called upon to handle some specific administrative tasks. It is important, however, for board members to refrain from managing the office activities. That is the purview of the nonprofit's executive. The board's responsibility is to identify priorities and establish the policy directives so that staff can manage the day-to-day activities of the organization.

As an organization grows, it is often difficult for board volunteers to wean themselves from the day-to-day activities, particularly those at which they have been successful. In working with such board members, the executive will need to be particularly sensitive and identify ways to involve them in the organization's activities. Relationships between board members and the executive staff will change as an organization grows and matures. Unless both the board and the executive are sensitive to changing needs, the process of maturation will be difficult.

After taking several courses in teaching students with learning disabilities, Mary Johnson found that she was able to help her own dyslexic son overcome, at least partially, his reading difficulties. Once he was in high school and no longer needed special tutoring, she founded a small nonprofit organization to make tutoring available to other dyslexic students.

Mary initiated a fund-raising campaign and raised sufficient funds to hire a full-time professional head tutor. Gradually the nonprofit acquired a staff of professionals, some working full-time and others part-time, and Mary was able to lease, at very low cost, an unused building that had formerly been an elementary school. Tuition income was now covering about half the organization's costs. A board of directors was formed, consisting largely of parents of former students who were willing to help the school in fund-raising and lobbying with the city government. Mary Johnson, still unpaid, became chairman of the board, while the director of tutoring became the full-time paid executive director of the organization, with responsibilities for hiring and supervising tutors, keeping books, managing space contracts, and other administrative activities. But when fund-raising fell off, Mary Johnson, frustrated, decided to resume more of a day-to-day management role. The professional educational staff, however, looked on Mary as an amateur, unable to guide them as educators. Conflicts grew, and the executive director, believing that she could no longer be effective as an administrator, resigned.

Mary Johnson had selected and recruited most members of the board of directors. Nonetheless, the board agreed that Mary, despite her role in creating the organization, was not the person to be the day-to-day administrator of the much larger, more professional organization which it had become, 15 years after its creation in her living room. Reluctantly, the board pressured her to resign as chairman. But, because the relationship between the just-resigned executive director and the past chairman was so strained, the board concluded that they could not rehire the director. They recruited another trained educational professional.

Although no written job description existed at the time the new executive director was hired, she had an agreement from the executive committee that she would develop one, with their input, as one of her first assignments. She met daily, at first, with other members of the professional staff, both in groups and one-on-one, to solidify their support and get their ideas on the future of the organization and involved both her faculty and the executive committee in decisions. She communicated frequently with the executive committee, telling them of decisions she was making in a way that allowed them to demur if they wished, but without expecting them to make decisions for her. This style evolved into her job description, giving the executive director the authority and autonomy necessary without displacing board responsibilities.

The new executive was also very careful to always show respect for Mary Johnson, who still had close friends on the board and among the parents of alumni. Although Mary boycotted the annual fund-raising dinner the first year, by the second year she had been won over and attended the banquet, receiving a standing ovation and an award for her creativity in founding the organization and guiding it through its formative years.

As in the case above, changes in staffing and board/staff relationships often are inevitable, particularly during the early growth and maturation years of an organization. Board members should be alert to situations when the board chair and the chief executive, perhaps for historical reasons, cannot work together effectively. Recognizing and addressing issues early can help to ensure personal conflicts do not interfere with the overall well-being of the organization.

Enhance the Public Image of the Organization

Members of governing boards of nonprofit organizations must assume an advocacy role on behalf of their nonprofit. Often board members are called upon to speak on behalf of the organization. The request may come internally from the president, through a board assignment, from staff, from another organization, or from the press. Board members should accept such invitations to speak for their organization only with full knowledge of the requester's expectations so as to be sure they can respond "on behalf of the organization." Any board member accepting such an invitation should notify the organization's chief elected officer or executive director (sometimes both) so that all parties may discuss how best to present the organization's policies.

Because such requests may come at any time, it is important for board members to know the official position of the governing board on all issues facing the organization. Many nonprofits have fact sheets or position papers clearly identifying the organization's point of view and the rationale for the position. Again, board members should review these carefully and obtain clarification on any points which they do not understand or do not agree with.

Whether in formal or informal situations, it also is important to acknowledge that even if a board member says "this is off the record" or "I am not speaking on behalf of the organization," those listening will not hear those words. Instead, they will assume the position the board member is advocating is the nonprofit's position. If a board member holds an opinion which is in conflict with the board's official position on an issue, the board member should either be willing to provide the "party line" or refrain from stating any position. If questions are expected, it would be advisable to refer the invitation to another board member. If a board member continues to have conflict with the board's official positions, he or she may wish to consider resigning from the board.

Recruit Other Volunteer Leaders

Of the responsibilities delegated to members of a nonprofit's governing board, one which is most crucial to the future of the organization is identifying and developing future leaders. Current board members are in the best position to know the kind of expertise needed on the board to replace those board members whose terms are ending. Is expertise needed in the financial area? Fundraising? Strategic planning? Research? Education or certification? Are there other considerations for the selection of board members, such as regional or racial representation? Careful thought should go into the qualifications and expertise required. Current board members can help identify individuals who meet the criteria and who would be willing to consider being nominated for a position on the board.

Most often, new leaders will be identified from having worked on a committee or task force. Equally important, therefore, is helping to identify new individuals for the organization's working committees.

One social service agency located in a major metropolitan area asked individual members of its board to personally recruit at least two other new volunteers for the organization. One board member who had served on and off the board for the past twenty years, and who felt she had called on nearly all her friends and acquaintances to actively support the agency during her tenure with the organization, decided to carry out her new assignment in a unique way.

She arranged to host an informal "get to know us" reception in her home to which she invited all other board members and their potential recruits.

The reception provided a non-threatening atmosphere in which the potential volunteers could chat with board members and other volunteers about the benefits of becoming involved in the agency's activities. Once everyone had gathered, the president gave a brief welcome and asked each board member to introduce and give a short biography of each of his/her potential volunteers. The president continued with a 5–10 minute overview of the agency and its mission. This was followed by two-minute reports by each of the agency's standing committee chairs highlighting the major programs and activities of the committees.

At the close of the reception, each potential volunteer was given a summary sheet of the information presented. Board members were asked to follow up by personally contacting their potential volunteers to obtain a commitment from each to serve on at least one committee and to participate in one program or fund-raising activity.

Within two months of the reception, 18 of the 20 potential volunteers who had attended the reception had become actively involved in the agency.

Assess your governing board members' understanding of and commitment to their roles and responsibilities by identifying the extent to which each of the roles and responsibilities indicated in Exhibit 2–1 is carried out.

Exhibit 2–1 Roles and Responsibilities of a Governing Board: An Assessment

	Always	Often	Sometimes	Never
All members of the governing board work to:				
1. Ensure the mission is carried out.				
2. Maintain fiduciary responsibility.				
3. Contribute to the organization's bottom line.				
4. Maintain ethical standards.				
a. Maintain board confidentiality.				
b. Recognize conflicts of interest.				
5. Respect and support staff.				
a. Maintain appropriate lines of communication.				
b. Understand and maintain separate roles.				
6. Respect other board members.				
7. Enhance the public image of the organization.				
8. Recruit other volunteers.				

Position Descriptions for Governing Board Members

In addition to the general roles and responsibilities of governing board members, officers will usually have specific tasks that are carried out on behalf of the board and the nonprofit organization. For many nonprofits, the chief elected officer carries the title of president, indicating this person is the primary spokesperson for the organization. For other organizations, the title of president is conferred on the chief executive staff person, again for the same reason. In this case, the chief elected leader generally is identified as the chairperson, or "chair," of the board.

Exhibit 2–2 provides sample position descriptions for these and other officer positions (vice president, secretary, and treasurer), along with a generic position description for a board director.

COMMITTEES

Any experienced nonprofit leader will tell you that committees can be the boon or bane of a nonprofit organization. The function of committees is to assist the board and staff with the work of the organization. When committees fulfill their charges, the organization's strategic plan can be realized, advancing the organization's mission. When committees fail, work does not get accomplished and expectations are shattered, frustrating board members, staff, and committee members.

For the most part, the governing board determines the types and sizes of committees that will assist in the conduct of the organization's business. In most cases, the chairperson and members of the committees are appointed by the president with nominations from and approval of the board. Terms of appointment vary, depending on the number of volunteers who are interested and willing to serve on the various committees; however, terms are usually designated for one or two years, with the opportunity for reappointment for a second and, sometimes, a third term.

Only standing committees, those which relate to the governance of the organization, should be included in a nonprofit's bylaws. For most organizations, these standing committees include the executive committee, the finance committee, and the nominations committee. These, as well as other important committees of the organization, may be "standing committees of the board"—those committees which are constituted exclusively of members of the board, precisely to keep the organization out of trouble.

Committees

Exhibit 2–2 Sample Position Descriptions—Elected Officers

PRESIDENT (or CHAIRPERSON): Chief elected officer of the organization

Primary Responsibilities:

Ensure that the organization abides by its bylaws and established policies.

Serve as chairperson of the board of directors and the executive committee.

Preside over all meetings of the board of directors and executive committee, and the annual business meeting of the organization.

Support the executive director.

Prepare agendas for all meetings of the board of directors in collaboration with the executive director.

Report to the membership.

Represent the organization to other organizations, the media, and the public at large.

Appoint committee chairpersons.

Additional Responsibilities:

Communicate regularly with the executive director.

Report periodically to the board of directors.

Train and otherwise prepare the president-elect for the responsibilities of the presidency.

Charge committees.

Serve as ex officio member of all committees, with the exception of elected committees.

Receive reports from all officers and committees.

Review communications, reports, and proposals of the staff.

VICE PRESIDENT: Assume the role and duties of the presidency if the president is no longer able to continue. (The role of the vice president is sometimes performed by the president-elect or immediate past president.)

Primary Responsibilities:

Perform the responsibilities of the president during absence or disability of the president.

Accede to the presidency in the event that a permanent vacancy in the presidency arises.

Serve as a voting member of the board of directors and executive committee.

Familiarize him- or herself with the responsibilities of the president, the activities and positions of the organization, and the functioning of the executive office.

Additional Responsibilities:

Assist the president as appropriate.

Exhibit 2–2   *(Continued)*

Represent the organization at the request of the president.

Serve on appointive committees.

SECRETARY: Custodian of records for the organization.

Primary Responsibilities:

Generally oversee the keeping of records of meetings, policies, activities, membership, and any other records required by law.

Oversee minutes of all meetings and teleconferences of the board of directors and executive committee, as well as the annual organizational business meeting.

Within thirty days after a meeting, provide the board of directors with minutes, including a list of motions made and the voting results. (Preparation of minutes may be delegated to staff, with the secretary responsible for approval.)

Review the policies of the organization and present to the board any policies which may need to be amended, rescinded, or reaffirmed.

Serve as a voting member of the board of directors and executive committee.

Additional Responsibilities:

Assist the president as appropriate.

Represent the organization at the request of the president.

Serve on appointive committees.

TREASURER: Monitors financial condition of the organization.

Primary Responsibilities:

Oversee, with the executive director, the fiscal affairs of the organization.

Present to the board of directors an annual budget for the organization, developed in concert with the executive director.

Monitor budgetary performance of the organization, recommending modifications as needed.

Review for approval all actions and policies with major financial implications.

Serve as a voting member of the board of directors and the executive committee.

Additional Responsibilities:

Serve as chairperson of the finance committee.

Assist the president as appropriate.

Serve on appointive committees.

Exhibit 2–2 *(Continued)*

DIRECTOR: Assists officers in overseeing health and direction of the organization

Responsibilities:

Attend board of directors meetings and participate in conference calls.

Attend any annual business meetings of the organization.

Participate actively in organizational strategic planning.

Vote on organizational policy and program issues.

Serve as a resource of knowledge and counsel to the executive office, committees, and other board members.

Assist in locating and developing funding sources for the organization.

Review and respond to all action and information requests from the executive office.

Serve as a liaison between the board of directors and committee chairs.

Represent the organization at the request of the president.

Other committees, which do not relate to governance issues but are ongoing committees of the organization—such as the annual conference program committee, awards committee, research committee, education committee, legislative committee—should not be listed in the bylaws, but may be referred to as "special" committees or committees of the organization. Keeping lists of committees out of the bylaws allows the board more flexibility to conduct its business. In addition, many nonprofit boards also will appoint ad hoc committees or task forces which are given a specific charge to be completed in a specified period of time. Ad hoc committees are often the most productive, specifically because the charge and time lines are clear.

Governance Committees

As noted above, standing committees provide guidance on the organization's governance issues.

Executive Committee. The role of an executive committee is to provide guidance for the nonprofit organization between meetings of the governing board. The roles and responsibilities of the executive committee should be explicit: only in emergency situations should the executive committee make policy decisions. The executive committee then reports its actions to the board at its next meeting, at which time the board ratifies, amends, or negates those actions taken. Executive committees can be a useful instrument of the board but should be careful not to usurp board responsibilities. Decisions reserved for the board should be included in the bylaws; for example, the board should be responsible for hiring the executive, encumbering funds, and approving the budget.

The executive committee is generally composed of the officers of the organization, with the executive director serving as an ex officio (non-voting) member. Some nonprofits include one or two additional members from the board to expand board input into the organization's policy decisions.

Finance Committee.   A nonprofit's finance committee should work closely with the executive in the critical role of financial oversight for the organization, advising the board on issues related to the budget and the financial affairs of the organization. The finance committee is usually chaired by the treasurer and includes other members of the executive committee, with the executive director serving ex officio.

Nominations Committee.   The critical role of the nominations committee is to identify the future leaders of the organization. To eliminate conflict among potential nominees or factions in the organization, policies should be in place to govern the procedures the nominations committee follows to select a slate of officers and directors.

As noted previously, the nominations committee often is elected by the nonprofit's constituents. There are organizations, however, in which the president appoints the nominating committee members—in most cases, from members of the governing board. Because of its critical function, the procedures for electing or appointing members of the nominations committee are included in the bylaws.

Exhibits 2–3 through 2–5 provide sample charters for these governance committees.

Other Committees

The number and assignments of other committees will vary depending on the size of the organization, its resources, and the number of volunteers willing to serve. Often, organizations will have a program planning committee to design and promote the annual meet-

Exhibit 2–3 Sample Charge for Executive Committee

Provide consultation and guidance to the executive director on matters related to the affairs of the organization between meetings of the board of directors.

Approve any extraordinary expenditure of funds, subject to board ratification.

Evaluate the performance of the executive director.

Perform other such duties as established by the board of directors.

Exhibit 2–4 Sample Charge for Finance Committee

Develop, with the guidance of the executive director, a budget for the organization based on forecasted income and expenses.

Recommend to the board of directors fiscal policies and procedures for the organization.

Review budget requests from all organization components.

Advise the board of directors regarding budget considerations and financial affairs of the organization.

Review all grants and contracts regarding their fiscal implications for the organization.

Review monthly financial statements of the organization.

Develop a long-range plan with strategies to ensure the fiscal viability and growth of the organization.

Exhibit 2–5 Sample Charge for Nominations Committee

Solicit nominations for elected positions from the membership at large.

Select, from the nominations submitted by the membership, a slate of nominees for each prospective vacancy in elected positions.

Verify and submit elections results to the board of directors.

ing of the organization. Other committees may include an audit committee, a fund development committee, an awards committee, a membership committee, a public relations or marketing committee, a government relations committee, an ethics committee, a research committee, and/or a certification committee. Again, depending on the needs of the nonprofit, these types of committees are generally ongoing, long-term committees, appointed on a yearly basis by the president, in consultation with the board of directors.

Ad Hoc Committees and Task Forces

Short-term, project-specific committees are generally termed ad hoc committees or task forces. These committees have a time-related, specific charge, and when the task has been accomplished, the ad hoc committee or task force is thanked for its work and disbanded. Examples of such ad hoc committees and task forces are: Ad Hoc Committee on Certification Test Development; Task Force on the First World Congress; Ad Hoc Committee on the 25th Anniversary Celebration.

Successful Committees

There are certain ingredients for successful committee outcomes. Examine each of your nonprofit's committees to determine if they meet all of the criteria listed in Exhibit 2–6.

ROLES AND RESPONSIBILITIES OF THE CHIEF EXECUTIVE STAFF PERSON

Titles—and therefore, responsibilities—of the chief executive staff person vary depending on the size, maturity, and philosophy of the nonprofit organization. Most organizations identify their chief executive as executive director: the individual who provides leadership and guidance to the governing board, administers and manages all aspects of the organization, and speaks on behalf of the organization as delegated by the elected president and governing board.

As noted earlier, some nonprofits want their chief executive staff person to be the *primary* spokesperson for the organization, with the title of president. Other titles may include chief executive officer, executive secretary, manager—each with position descriptions developed for the needs of the organization. (See Exhibit 2–7 for a sample position description for an executive director.) As nonprofits grow and mature, their governing boards usually become more willing to delegate spokesperson responsibilities to the chief executive staff person. Whatever the title, there are common roles and responsibilities that the chief staff person must fulfill to ensure the success of the nonprofit.

Exhibit 2–6   Criteria for Successful Committees

- Clearly defined task(s) to be accomplished.
- Established time lines.
- A committed chair who has the time to pursue the task and prepare concise reports on the committee's accomplishments for board review.
- Committee members who, likewise, are committed to the task and are willing to expend the time to accomplish the task.
- Time for the committee to meet face to face as needed (other meetings can be conducted by mail, fax, or conference call).
- Resources, based on a budget developed by the committee, adequate to accomplish the task(s).
- A board member, appointed as liaison to the committee, who will act as both advisor and advocate.

Understand the Organization — Inside and Out

A good chief executive will be familiar with all aspects of the non-profit he or she is managing. A new executive staff person will want to review all organizational materials: bylaws, policies and procedures manuals, past board meeting minutes, publications, historical documents, and promotional materials. The bylaws of an organization, depending on their specificity, can be an excellent source for determining the roles and responsibilities of the executive and the purview of the board. This should be supplemented with conversations with past officials and minutes of previous board meetings, with the focus on specific motions addressing board/staff relations.

The day-to-day reality of working with any particular governing board may differ from what is written in the bylaws or position descriptions. The personal interests and the personalities of board members are important factors in how the executive relates to the board and carries out their directives. Often, the executive will have to rely on intuition, interpersonal relations, and management skills in deciding how to proceed in a particular circumstance. The bylaws may not, for example, contain information regarding conflicts of interest between board members on a specific matter pending before the board. Clearly, if such an instance surfaces, the executive will want to ensure that board members are not embarrassed or placed in difficult situations.

Clear and concise bylaws, board directives, job descriptions, and other written documents are critically important in establishing the

Exhibit 2–7 Sample Position Description of Executive Director

---

EXECUTIVE DIRECTOR: Chief executive staff person of the organization.

Responsibilities:

Provide leadership and policy guidance for the organization.

Manage and direct all operations, programs, and activities of the organization.

Implement the policy decisions and directives of the board of directors.

Uphold and adhere to the policies and bylaws of the organization.

Report regularly to the board of directors and otherwise ensure that the board is fully informed of all organization activities.

Advise the board of directors in a timely fashion of any developments which may affect the organization's well-being.

Approve all financial disbursements and otherwise monitor all financial and accounting activities of the organization.

Prepare annual budgets with the assistance of the treasurer and finance committee.

Hire, supervise, and evaluate office staff.

Maintain organization records, files, documents, and archives.

Enter into contracts on behalf of the organization, with approval of the board of directors.

Regularly inform the membership at large of organization activities.

Represent the organization to other organizations, the media, and the public at large.

Prepare agenda books, bulletins, reports, testimony, daily correspondence, and other necessary materials and communications.

Maintain confidentiality of sensitive information.

---

executive's role and associated relationship with the board. Written directives, however, need to be supplemented with a more personal and thorough understanding of the board and the way individuals on the board wish to operate. Time should be spent with the chief elected officer as well as with other officers, board members, current staff, and former executives (if appropriate) to obtain a historical perspective on the organization as well as insights about the organization and its future. Particularly for a new executive, these discussions can be very helpful in providing supplemental information regarding organizational issues, board politics, and individual sensitivities.

Provide Policy Guidance and Leadership for the Board

For most nonprofits the role of the executive extends well beyond day-to-day activities. It is critical for the staff executive to monitor the organization's environment (both internally and externally) on an ongoing basis, identifying for the governing board those issues that will affect the organization. As noted in Chapter One, it is the responsibility of the executive to be able to discuss the implications of the strategic issues and provide recommendations for board action.

By thinking and managing "strategically," providing insights for board members who may have limited time to consider all of the issues' implications, the executive has the opportunity to help shape the policy directions for the organization.

Establish and Maintain Effective Communication Systems

A good working relationship between the nonprofit executive and the board of directors is critical to an organization's success. Nonprofit executives who do not communicate appropriately with their leadership or fail to read correctly the politics of their boards, create major, sometimes irreversible, problems.

Establishing good rapport and communication with the board is basic. This requires *respect* for members of the governing board: respect for their talents, their experience, and their perspectives. When respect between and among the executive and board members is mutual, honest and open communication will result. Without such respect, communication channels become strained, opening the door for mistrust and misperceptions.

Most often, nonprofit executives favor flexibility and independence to manage activities with little, if any, oversight by their governing boards. However, caution is warranted. With each degree of independence granted an equal degree of responsibility is assumed. If mistakes are made, the executive is held wholly responsible. Conversely, when success is achieved, the board will assume credit, and rightfully so. After all, the board established policy and granted the executive the authority to pursue board directives.

Through the executive's leadership, communication systems can be developed which are mutually satisfying to all involved. For some nonprofits, and depending on the current issues for the organization, contact is made with the chief elected leader several times a week. For other nonprofits, a telephone or conference call may be scheduled with the elected leader once a week or every two weeks.

In still other cases, no schedule is maintained for regular contact, and staff use fax and mail to provide updates or obtain decisions when necessary.

Some nonprofit organizations find monthly updates of the organization's activities to be extremely helpful in keeping board members informed. These updates also can include action items which require board members' immediate response. One organization, which depends heavily on its volunteer board for accomplishing many of its activities, issues a monthly board bulletin with updates of both staff and board member activities and accomplishments. An "action list" is included that identifies tasks to be accomplished, party responsible, and date due, and confirms when the task is completed.

Similar communications must be considered for the rest of the nonprofit's constituents. For some organizations, a quarterly newsletter is sufficient to provide constituents with information relevant to the organization. Others may mail a "Friday Letter" at the end of each week to communicate with constituents. Most often, a monthly newsletter provides constituents with updates on activities of the board, committees, other member activities, upcoming conferences or seminars, or information on legislative or regulatory issues. Unusual circumstances require more frequent communications.

When the YWCA of the USA planned a major restructuring of its national office, careful attention was paid to planning its communication strategies. According to Gwendolyn Calvert Baker, Executive Director for the YWCA of the USA at the time, "constant, honest communications were key to ensuring enthusiastic participation by staff and volunteers at the national and local level." Project Redesign, which has been credited with revitalizing the 135-year old organization, began with a clear announcement to all constituents. The executive director wrote a progress report memo to all participants at each stage of the project. An advisory committee of board members and trustees was established and held biweekly teleconferences with committee members, reducing anxiety throughout the organization. In addition, outside publics, including union officials, were notified and kept informed of the project's progress, producing a comfortable working relationship.

It is also very important to remember that board/staff relations are not static. An executive cannot assume that the way things are done one year is the way it will always work. Presidents and officers change, and board members rotate off the board in some cyclical pattern, establishing a new set of dynamics at the board table. To succeed, the executive must be able to adapt to these changes. Note how one executive handled two different situations in the case below.

A newly hired executive director was given no specific charge and very minimal direction from the board of directors. He met with some of the board members and solicited their areas of concern and interest to determine the organization's needs. At his first board meeting, he proposed a program focusing the resources of the organization on regulatory and legislative issues and provided specifics on how this would be achieved. The board endorsed the plan and strongly commended the executive director's proactive initiative.

About a year later, however, the same executive director was criticized for using his own judgment in another matter. The board learned that a program being managed by an outside consultant had developed in such a way that it now advocated a position not supported by the board of directors. Believing the position to be appropriate, the executive director had supported the consultant. He was unaware that the board did not support this position until his management of the issue was criticized. The executive director successfully resolved the issue by calling a meeting of interested board members, modifying the position according to their input, and assuring the board that the board would be party to any subsequent discussions on the issue.

Educate Board Regarding Board and Staff Roles and Responsibilities

As noted previously, newly elected board members may be long-standing and active constituents of the nonprofit organization. Their new positions as directors on a governing board, however, will demand more detailed information regarding the organization's policies and procedures. Indeed, to fulfill their roles as knowledgeable spokespersons for the organization, additional education is required.

Board Orientation. Many nonprofits schedule an orientation session for new board members and, sometimes, as a refresher for existing board members. Such orientations may be scheduled for two to four hours prior to a board meeting or for as long as one and a half to two days in a retreat atmosphere. Generally the executive conducts the orientation, along with the president and treasurer and perhaps other members of the executive committee. Note the list of

Exhibit 2–8   Topics for a New Board Orientation Session

- Mission and goals of the organization.
- Overview of the organization's history.
- Strategic plan; strategic planning process.
- Roles and responsibilities of the governing board.
- Roles and responsibilities of the executive and staff.
- Organizational structure and policies; reporting lines of communication.
- Resources available, including the financial structure and financial policies.
- Review of major activities; e.g. fund-raising events, annual meeting, or government relations activity.
- Headquarters office operating procedures.

topics generally included in a board orientation in Exhibit 2–8. The list is not all-inclusive. Executives should design an orientation approach which best suits the circumstances of their organizations and the various interest and sophistication levels of board members.

Some members of the board will have business experience and some will not. Some will have served on previous boards and some will be novices. The level of interest and expertise of board members, even if they all are from the same discipline, will not be uniform. Briefings and other communications (written and verbal) need to reflect the diversity of board members.

In addition to the more formal presentation, it is helpful for the executive to meet with new board members for an informal lunch or dinner. This not only creates a more personable atmosphere but also enables board members to ask questions they may not be comfortable asking in a larger gathering. To establish the framework for working together throughout the year, it is particularly important for the executive director to have such an informal meeting with the incoming president or chairperson.

Board and Staff Interactions.   Executives often find themselves in a quandary determining how much direct contact should be allowed between the board and staff. Decisions should be made based on the expertise or skill level of the staff and the size and complexity of the organization. If the staff is small, with two or three persons, the board members generally will deal directly with the executive. If it is a larger, more complex, and multi-dimensional organization, the executive will not have the in-depth knowledge of all topics to discuss them sufficiently with board members, and direct communication with the key staff person will be more appropriate.

Whatever the reason for the board and staff contact, however, the executive should ensure there is a specified reporting mechanism to learn about that contact. Even if it is on a short-term, day-to-day operational matter, the executive should be informed. Staff want to please and often will accept an assignment from a board member without considering the consequences in terms of time, resources, and uncompleted priority projects. No matter how small or inconsequential the matter may seem, the executive director should never be left "out of the loop."

Further, board members should respect the executive director's role as staff supervisor. While the executive reports to the board through the president or chairperson, staff report to the executive. All board requests for organization resources or staff time should be channeled through the executive director. It is the executive's responsibility to coordinate the activities of the staff, and this becomes impossible if the executive is not aware of all activities.

The board orientation provides a good opportunity for the executive to discuss board and staff interactions. If problems occur, the executive should address the issue directly with the responsible board member or solicit assistance from the chief elected leader.

Maintain Fiscal Control

Monitoring the financial condition of the organization is a responsibility that neither can nor should be delegated. Not only must the executive fully understand the income and expense statements with background information on the source of expenses, but he or she must also have a thorough knowledge of the overall financial health of the organization. Financial statements provided during the year and year-end external audits should be presented clearly and concisely.

Just as staff should keep the executive informed so that there are no surprises, so it is with the board. Board members should be apprised of impending problems with income or expenses. Most organizations have both a treasurer and a finance committee who take responsibility to work with the executive in developing budgets and long-range financial forecasts. Often, the treasurer chairs the finance committee. Whatever the situation, the executive should prepare both the treasurer and the finance committee so that they can become the spokespersons for the financial reports during board meetings.

Encourage and Support Involvement of Volunteer Board Members

With very few exceptions, individuals serving on a nonprofit board do so in a volunteer capacity. It is critically important to remember that volunteers are motivated to serve by different reasons. Some are active in an organization because they are strong advocates of the particular cause or mission of the nonprofit group. Some become involved for the networking or business opportunities. Others serve on the board because of the recognition they receive from the nonprofit for their high visibility and/or their ability to raise funds. Still others agree to serve on nonprofit boards because of the recognition they receive from peers at home or office.

Understanding a board member's motivations for serving will provide the executive with tools to support the board member and, likewise, to obtain support from the board member. For some nonprofits, the amount of volunteer time required is extensive, yet expectations of what time the volunteer will be able to contribute must be reasonable. Sensitivity to the board member's other demands, particularly if the member is an active public figure at the local or national level, will ensure expectations will not be violated.

Similarly, when working with volunteers, even those who appear to have unlimited time to serve, the executive must keep expectations in check, eliminating the possibility of volunteer "burnout." As noted earlier in this chapter, clear and concise committee and task force charges that are realistic in terms of time lines and resources required will support and encourage volunteer involvement.

Strategically Manage All Aspects of the Organization

A basic responsibility for an executive is to manage the nonprofit efficiently, effectively and, for best results, strategically. While each executive may have interests or strengths in some aspects of nonprofit management, it is necessary to become a "jack of all trades" to manage a nonprofit organization well. Skills will be required in all aspects of nonprofit organizational management. Mastering the areas identified in this book is a good first step.

A major resource for any organization, in addition to its financial income and its volunteers, is its staff. Just as volunteer management and development are important responsibilities of an executive, so too are the management and development of staff members, whether there is one additional staff person in the office or an additional 100+ persons. (See also Chapter 11, The Staff and Their Environment.)

Nonprofit executives who excuse or cover up for poor staff work often find themselves looking for another position.

One executive, because of his generosity and kind-heartedness, allowed several staff members to work part-time because of family commitments. Rather than hiring additional staff to take up the slack, he took on their responsibilities to save the organization money. Work of the organization did not get accomplished and the person responsible, the executive, was replaced.

Another executive for a local charity, whose personal expertise was in research and grant writing, retained an office manager who could not track finances adequately or provide her with the answers to questions board members raised regarding the organization's financial status. This executive likewise was replaced when end-of-the-year audits indicated a more negative picture for the organization than had been presented in previous executive reports.

Thus, it is critical for the executive to have good staff, but also to be knowledgeable about all aspects of the organization and to be prepared personally for any and all questions. Nonprofit cannot mean non-performing.

Maintain Flexibility

A critical lesson for nonprofit executives to bear in mind is that issues, responsibilities, and board relationships may not be the same next month as last, and almost certainly will not be the same next year as last year.

Elected board officers come and go. Issues arise and are either solved or, at the least, outlived and put behind. New opportunities or new board members lead to changes in the nonprofit's strategic and operational plans, sometimes even to changes in mission. These changes, along with changes in personality or in operational styles of the elected leaders, require the chief staff executive to respond, creatively and constructively. The nonprofit executive who expects to do everything the same way every year is in the wrong profession.

Change can be difficult. It also brings opportunities, both for the individual and the organization. The chapters that follow try to outline specific management techniques that some experienced nonprofit executives have used to enhance their effectiveness and that of their organizations.

Executives can assess their understanding of and commitment to their roles and responsibilities by identifying the extent to which each of the activities listed in Exhibit 2–9 is carried out.

Exhibit 2–9   Roles and Responsibilities of an Executive Staff Leader

	Always	*Often*	*Sometimes*	*Never*
The executive staff leader works to:				
1. Understand the organization—inside and out.				
2. Provide policy guidance and leadership for the board.				
3. Establish and maintain effective communication systems.				
4. Educate board regarding board and staff roles and responsibilities.				
5. Maintain fiscal control.				
6. Encourage and support involvement of volunteers.				
7. Strategically manage all aspects of the association.				

To maximize board and staff effectiveness, governing board members, committees, and staff will need to work together cooperatively, recognizing how each of their roles and responsibilities link with each of the others, and all with one goal in mind: achieving the nonprofit organization's mission. Use the checklist below to assess how well your organization is maximizing the effectiveness of its governance structure.

CHECKLIST FOR MAXIMIZING BOARD AND STAFF EFFECTIVENESS

Has your organization:

1. Developed policies for board size, composition, and nominations and elections processes based on its mission and the constituents it serves?
2. Established a policies and procedures manual?
3. Included the following in your policies and procedures manual?
   a. Roles and responsibilities of board members
   b. Position descriptions for officers

   c. Roles and responsibilities for executive staff

   d. Position description for executive staff

4. Developed a new board orientation program?

5. Established effective lines of communication between and among the executive, the governing board, and committee chairs?

6. Established a program for recruiting new volunteers?

7. Established a review process for the executive's performance?

8. Established effective communication systems for interactions between and among board, staff, committees, and constituents?

Does your organization:

9. Provide support for the executive's professional development?

10. Hold board members accountable for timely completion of assignments?

11. Hold committee members accountable for timely completion of assignments?

12. Hold staff accountable for timely completion of assignments?

13. Provide opportunities for informal interactions of board and staff?

14. Conduct a periodic assessment of board operations?

CHAPTER THREE

Raising Money to Achieve Your Goals

Fund-raising is both an art and a science. How do you ask for and get the funds needed to make your organization's vision a reality? This chapter provides the proper fund-raising tools and techniques, as well as guidance on when and how to use them.

Fund-raising. Financial development. Non-dues revenue. Whatever words are used to describe it, all nonprofit organizations are in the fund-raising business. Whether you establish a major capital campaign to raise funds for a building, organize a community barbecue to pay for a specific project, or raise money to "get to Friday," fund-raising is an essential element for any nonprofit organization's continued viability and success.

In this chapter we will discuss the basics of fund-raising for organizations with budgets averaging from $300,000 to $1 million. While some suggestions are drawn from the experience of the larger organizations and may not be appropriate for your organization, many are relevant for all nonprofits regardless of size.

According to *Giving USA: The Annual Report on Philanthropy for the Year 1992*, individuals, foundations, and corporations gave $124 billion to "those organizations to which contributions are tax deductible." Your organization can successfully capture some of the monies through thoughtful fund-raising activities. However, the close to 70 percent of charities with budgets under $1 million take in only 5 percent of this revenue. The key to success is having a clearly defined goal, along with a specific action plan that sets realistic objectives, outlines strategies to achieve them, and identifies the right people who can successfully contact prospective donors. Successful financial development will not only help raise funds, but will garner increased recognition and volunteer support for your organization.

This chapter will help you to:

- Identify your fund-raising needs.
- Take an inventory of your resources.
- Choose from among the best fund-raising approaches.
- Develop an action plan for positive results.

Tools for a successful fund-raising campaign presented in this chapter are:

- Sample Donor Prospect Record Card.
- Sample corporate recognition plan.
- Special event budget.
- Sample solicitation letter.
- Donor pledge form.
- Checklist of basic steps to implement a fund-raising plan.
- Resource list for additional information.

Even with these tools, it is important to remember that there is no one right way to conduct a fund-raising campaign. Having the best and most comprehensive letter or proposal often is not what makes the difference. Always more important are the personal relationships you have developed with people who trust you, and the work you do. Eighty-eight percent of all funds come from individuals. Your base of supporters is an important starting point for getting operating funds so that your organization can "get to Friday," as Sam Harahan, Executive Director of the Council for Court Excellence in Washington, D.C., correctly points out. You need to look beyond Friday, but you do have to meet payroll and pay rent, utilities, and equipment costs to keep your nonprofit in business.

While a professional-looking solicitation letter may get the attention of a new prospect, that perfect letter will never substitute for a personal relationship. The ideal relationship is for you as the fund-raiser to be able to pick up the telephone and call a friend who you think might be interested in the project, discuss the idea with him or her and, if there is interest, send a follow-up letter with answers to the questions raised in your conversation. Often, they will tell you what to include in your letter to increase your chances of getting funds. That is the ideal, toward which every fund-raiser strives.

It is important to recognize that doing all the right things may increase your chances for success but it does not guarantee it. In fact, most of your fund requests will not be granted. There is a finite amount of money given to charities each year and someone may simply have been standing in line longer. You must be prepared for coping with rejection even when you have the best idea and the most effective strategy to achieve your goals. You cannot take it personally and you must persevere. It may be that priorities of a funding agency, corporation, or foundation may change or that the emphasis has shifted to funding certain types of projects. A goal of this chapter is to increase your chances for success.

IDENTIFY YOUR FUND-RAISING NEEDS

Develop a Clearly Defined Goal

Funding-raising must have a purpose, an identifiable and quantifiable need. Ask yourself: Why are we raising money? Is it for a new project or a continuing program? Is it for an endowment? Are we raising money to offer something to the public, such as a new wing for a hospital or computers for schools?

When choosing a fund-raising project, be creative. Examine prior fund-raising efforts both within and outside your organization. Early on, make sure the fund-raising project meets a need and is marketable. What gives your idea merit and justifies a donor's commitment? If the plan is not well thought out, it may be difficult to reach your financial goals. You must also create a sense of enthusiasm about the idea and of belief that your project will make an impact. You will not be able to sell it to prospective donors if they do not see or feel your enthusiasm about it.

To ensure maximum support, a fund-raising goal should relate to the mission of your organization. If the idea is a board member's pet project and has little to do with the organization, precious resources are expended that could be used elsewhere. It may become difficult, if not impossible, to gain enough support from other important members in the organization who are either prospective donors or could help identify some. Care must be taken not to have an institution held hostage by one powerful board member with a personal agenda. It is also politically unwise to put the entire organization behind something that does not benefit the entire organization or fit in with the strategic plan. It is important to think strategically and identify projects that are consistent with your mission and goals. You will be wasting precious time and valuable resources if you lose sight of the "big picture" by only focussing on the fund-raising process. At risk is your organization's credibility and future fund-raising initiatives.

A risk in any fund-raising strategy is to accept money from a donor who has specific interests that do not fit the mission or goals of your organization. To accommodate this donor, time, money, and manpower may have to be expended pursuing a goal that is not part of your organization's mission. As a high-ranking university administrator observed, "It is difficult to say no to a good idea, but we have to commit resources to a greater good." Stay focused on a few priorities and stick with them.

Begin to outline clearly and succinctly the project's goals, objectives, and budget in writing. Only then can you actually go to other organizations and individuals that share, or have the potential to share, in your mission. Your donors will want to know if your idea is viable. They will also want to know what is in it for them in terms of exclusive benefits and recognition.

As you are forming your fund-raising concept, keep in mind that different goals will have different strategies. While fund-raising strategies will be discussed later, it's important that the financial as well as administrative implications of different strategies be considered during the early stages of formulating a program.

Set a Specific Monetary Goal

Carefully assess how much money needs to be raised to achieve your monetary goal. To do this, you may need to solicit estimates from construction companies, develop in-depth cost analyses, investigate employee pay scales, and estimate the costs of the fund-raising project itself, such as expenses surrounding staff, equipment, and rent.

Estimate all costs involved in fund-raising, both variable and fixed. Variable costs include postage, printing, telephone, supplies, brochures, graphic design, and staff time. Fixed costs include accounting, data processing/computers, and rent for office space. Other costs that should not be overlooked are those associated with research, education/networking, marketing/promotion, travel, and consultants' fees. Be sure that your fund-raising costs do not exceed a reasonable percentage of the cost of your project. Some funding organizations stipulate that administrative costs are not to exceed one-half the cost of the project. There is no hard and fast rule, and guidelines vary. Use common sense to dictate what is a reasonable administrative cost to generate revenue. You do need administrative support to execute your plan.

What is a good estimating ratio between money expended and money received? Jim Greenfield states in his book, *Fund-Raising Management: Evaluating and Managing the Fund Development Process*, that the national average in fund-raising costs is $0.20 to raise $1.00. Percentages of expenses against income will vary depending upon the event, but Greenfield suggests the following reasonable fund-raising administration cost guidelines:

Direct mail acquisition	$1.00 to $1.25 per dollar raised.
Direct mail renewal	$0.20 per dollar raised.
Benefit events	50 percent of gross proceeds.
Corporation/foundations	$0.20 per dollar raised.
Planned giving	$0.25 per dollar raised.
Capital campaign	$0.05 to $0.10 per dollar

Ask for what you need. If you limit your horizons, the possibility of a more comprehensive plan is stifled. That is not to say you should be unrealistic in your goals. It simply means that thinking small usually leads to a predictably modest result. Often, such thinking makes it difficult to excite potential donors about your project. If you ask a donor to give $500 to a worthy cause, chances are he or she won't say, "I'd like to give twice that amount."

Identify In-House Resources

Your organization may have resources to offer to the fund-raising effort that can lower the overall cost of the entire project. Internal resources for fund-raising may include staff, phones and phone service, mailing lists, office space, computer services, volunteers, and supplies. Your organization may publish a newsletter or regularly hold meetings, all of which are channels for gaining support for your fund-raising idea or contributions to the fund itself. Using your own resources also shows a prospective donor that you are taking a risk on the project. It is important, however, to consider whether these internal resources may be used without adversely affecting other functions in your organization. If a staff member, for instance, is taken off one project to coordinate the fund-raising plan, who will do his or her job?

Identify Outside Resources

As you develop the fund-raising strategy, draw upon useful information and data from various sources such as government reports, newsletters, computer databases, and industry associations. Use these resources to learn about your prospective donors, about their issues and concerns. This way, you can tailor your solicitation to the donor's perspective rather than your own.

For information about an industry's issues, contact the associations that represent the industry and/or individuals involved in that industry. Many companies, nonprofit organizations, and associations produce annual reports and/or promotional materials along with newsletters, magazines, and journals that may provide background information.

For example, for information about the electronic media (television, radio, and/or cable stations), you could contact Cahners Publishing in Chicago, which publishes *The Broadcast and Cable Yearbook.* Some organizations offer comprehensive lists of industry professionals and mailing labels, either free or for a fee.

In the end, the bottom line is to know what the existing resources are, decide which ones are useful, and then take stock to see what information you still need and where to find it.

FUND-RAISING PROGRAM OPTIONS

As you define your mission and research prospective donors, it's time to consider the types of fund-raising options you will choose. Sometimes the match will be obvious; other times not. Among the established fund-raising methods are the following.

Annual assessments and/or dues revenues - Revenues derived from membership dues or annual assessments can provide a financial base to support the administrative costs of many fund-raising initiatives, as well as the normal overhead expenses of managing an organization.

Income from programs or services or from such sources as advertising in publications, publication sales, or credit card service fees has become a major source of revenue for many nonprofit organizations. (See the following chapter on Marketing for the Nonprofit Organization, but also be aware of the potential that taxes may be due on unrelated business income.)

Annual campaigns - Funds to support the daily programs and services an organization provides. Campaigns can occur once a year, or even all year long, and use several methods of solicitation. Emphasis is usually placed on direct mail, telemarketing, or special events. This campaign can help build a solid foundation for your organization's fund-raising success as it finds new donors, recommits old ones, and identifies future prospects.

Capital campaigns - Usually launched by large institutions, such as universities and hospitals, for a variety of reasons, including building projects and restorations. A capital campaign has a goal that is large in relation to the organization and should have specific target dates.

Planned giving - Allows donors to make gifts to nonprofits, which will be realized in the future through the following vehicles:

- Wills and bequests - A gift bequested in a donor's will, often as a percent of the estate.
- Pooled income funds - A simple trust agreement transferring cash or securities to a charitable organization's pooled income fund, which is similar to a mutual fund.
- Life insurance/wealth replacement trusts - Allow an individual to make your nonprofit the beneficiary of his or her life insurance policy or, in the case of the wealth replacement trust, to use the annual income to purchase a life insurance policy in the beneficiary's name, thus transferring the value upon the donor's death.

Organizations that are successful in planned giving are usually well established. However, if you are a young organization just starting out, you might consider developing a list of donors over 55 years of age so you can build a base of potential planned giving donors. A good place to start with these types of giving is with your board of directors. (For a comprehensive overview on planned giving, consult Jim Greenfield's *Fund-raising Management: Evaluating and Managing the Development Process* and Bruce Hopkins' *The Law of Fund-raising*.)

Endowment funds - Usually set up to perpetuate the educational, scientific, and/or charitable goals of the organization. Generally, only the interest of an endowment fund is used and some organizations specify that the funds are not tapped until the dollar goal of the entire project is reached.

THE INTERNAL ACTION PLAN

Developing an internal action plan is crucial if your fund-raising project is to succeed.

Consider establishing a steering or advisory committee to oversee implementation of the action plan so that someone always has the "big picture" in focus. The number of participants/volunteers and the use of existing internal resources will depend upon the scope of the project.

Establish an Organizational Structure

Whether your organization is small or large, you need a plan and people assigned to the specific areas of responsibility, as explained below.

Executive committee and board of directors/trustees - Establishes priorities and goals and approves the action plan.

Outreach/marketing committee - Coordinates efforts to promote the project and find prospective donors.

Fund-raising committee - Implements the priorities and contacts donors.

Volunteer coordinator - Coordinates volunteer efforts. Plays a crucial role in maximizing efforts to achieve your fund-raising goals and avoid duplication of efforts.

Information processing - Staff assigned to keep the database and other records up to date and accurate.

Accounting - Staff must be available to constantly provide the latest, most accurate account of monies collected. If you do not have an accountant on staff, be sure to have one affiliated with your organization to serve as the accounting advisor.

Donation processing - Staff to process donations and promptly acknowledge each donation. (A sample donor prospect form is Exhibit 3–1.)

Understand Your Responsibilities

No one should raise funds for your organization without the knowledge and approval of the leadership, which may include, but not be limited to, your executive committee, board of directors, and chief executive.

Be sure to consider any disclosures that might be required by law when fund-raising. (See Bruce Hopkins' book *The Law of Fund-raising* for an in-depth discussion of disclosures.)

The importance of accurate accounting, record keeping, donation processing, and follow-up cannot be overstated. Regardless of the scope of your project, you must be certain you have enough staff

Exhibit 3–1 Donor Prospect Record Card

DONOR PROSPECT RECORD CARD

Name:

Title:

Address: City/State/Zip:

Phone: Fax:

Employer's name: Employer's address:

Spouse name: Spouse occupation:

Children's names: Children's ages:

Children's schools:

Programs of Special Interest: Giving History: (Yr./Amt.)

Community Affiliations: Religious Affiliation:

Education:

General Comments:

Other Significant Information:

The above items represent necessary components for a donor's record card. A database with this information should be set up accordingly.

---

and phones to take and process donations and/or follow through on the administrative activities.

Often an organization agonizes over whether it should hire a development officer. If your nonprofit has a budget under $300,000, you most likely cannot afford to hire one. Use trained volunteers. If your budget is between $300,000 to $500,000, you can probably afford to designate a part-time fund-raising specialist on staff or on contract. Charitable organizations with budgets over $1 million usually have a staff person with designated responsibilities to coordinate fund development.

THE EXTERNAL ACTION PLAN

Cast your net far and wide when identifying the companies and/or persons outside your organization that might be interested in contributing to your project and organization. Your list of potential donors might include:

- Corporations.
- Foundations.
- Federal and state agencies.
- Trade/professional organizations.
- Individuals.

Research will yield benefits, since targeted lists promise a greater return than nontargeted ones. Investigate the general interests of potential donors, as well as funding history and appropriate contact persons. A donor with a track record of giving to similar projects is more likely to contribute to yours. The more closely a donor relates to your organization's image, resources, and objectives, the more likely a donation will be made.

When properly designed and executed, donor surveys yield a wealth of vital information that may result in superior fund-raising. In conducting a survey consider the donor source, sample size, response rate, questionnaire design, execution, and analysis.

As you begin to put your list of potential donors together, you need to begin considering what type of strategy you will use: corporate proposals, mass mailings of solicitation letters, telethons, auctions, grant applications. And so, begin to discern which approach is best for which potential donors. Carefully assess the scope of your fund-raising pool. If you feel that the general public will donate money to your case, ask yourself: Do we have the resources to reach a sufficient number? Or, in other words, can you afford to do a mass mailing or a telethon? The bigger the campaign, the more financial and human resources you will need. Caution is advised since campaigns directed to the general public can be labor-intensive and may be quite costly.

Soliciting Businesses

Many corporations have foundations that focus on supporting activities that will benefit the communities they serve or advance a specific corporate goal. For example, a newspaper company might have set funds aside to support literacy programs. Corporations do not, however, usually support projects with a religious goal or objective.

While many successful corporations have budgets for philanthropic efforts, finding the right corporation to fund your project is not always easy. The best place to start may be your own backyard. First identify the major companies in your local community, for most corporations feel a responsibility to the community in which they are located. Check with your board members for contacts in those corporations. After you have developed your local corporate list, search for corporations outside your immediate environment that share your area of interest. Throughout the process, do not limit yourself to large corporations. Small companies may also have monies available to donate to your cause. Be sensitive to fiscal policies of corporations; most fund-raising is done in the fall of the year when corporate monies are allocated for the following year.

With the list complete, create a computerized notebook of potential donors, through which you can track all donations. This database should be comprehensive and contain records of all past donations with pertinent comments. This database, then, will serve as an accurate resource for future projects.

When soliciting corporations be sure you can answer the question: What is the benefit of a donation for this company? Be prepared with specific information on how your project is unique, essential, or urgent. Do your research. Know each corporation's products, market, interests, issues, and concerns. At the same time, be flexible to ideas they might offer. Exhibit 3–2 is an example of a corporate recognition plan used by one nonprofit.

Most corporations will request a written proposal, particularly those with foundations. Be sure you know their criteria for awarding grants and include all materials they will need to consider your proposal. Standard attachments include a copy of your tax-exempt status, a list of your board of directors, a project summary, budget, and cover letter.

Soliciting Foundations

Not every company will have a foundation for special projects. There are, however, literally hundreds of public and private foundations in our country today, established either by corporations or wealthy individuals. Foundation grant writing is probably one of the most competitive areas of fund-raising today. It can be a very demanding process, requiring detailed answers to a series of questions. Submitting an incomplete application may immediately disqualify it from consideration. And to be successful, a proposal must be well-written, clear in its purpose, and include specific information about every aspect of the project. It's interesting to note that grant writing for the private sector tends to be less tedious than for

Exhibit 3–2   Corporate Recognition Plan

CORPORATE RECOGNITION

Corporations and foundations like to feel they will be getting some company visibility and recognition for their generous donation. Be prepared with a "Corporate Giving Plan," which outlines various benefits and levels for corporate donors. The following is a sample corporate giving plan for a national awards event sponsored by a nonprofit organization:

CORPORATE SPONSOR - $15,000 to $25,000

- Press release announcing contribution and support
- Recognition plaque
- Head table representation at annual benefit
- Table for ten at annual benefit dinner
- Listing in the printed program
- Special recognition at the annual benefit with plaque presentation
- Discount for all corporation's attendees to annual benefit
- Corporate name on scholarship program
- Article in national newsletter on contribution
- Complimentary ads in annual publications
- Full page ad in printed benefit dinner program

CORPORATE BENEFACTOR - $10,000

- Press release announcing contribution and support
- Recognition plaque
- Head table representation at annual benefit
- Table for ten at annual benefit dinner
- Listing in the printed program
- Special recognition at the annual benefit with plaque presentation
- Discount for all corporation's attendees to annual benefit
- Full page ad in printed benefit dinner program

CORPORATE PATRON - $5,000

- Recognition plaque
- Prominent listing in annual meeting brochure
- Head table representation at annual benefit dinner
- Table for ten at annual benefit dinner
- Half-page ad in printed benefit dinner program

CORPORATE DONOR - $2,500

- Framed certificate
- Prominent listing in annual meeting brochure

Exhibit 3–2   *(Continued)*

CORPORATE CONTRIBUTOR - $2,000

- Invitation to be a head table guest at organization's annual benefit dinner
- Table for ten at annual benefit dinner
- Framed certificate
- Listing in annual report
- Listing in organization's national newsletter

government agencies. Two references to foundation giving are *The National Directory of Corporate Giving* and *The Foundation Directory and Supplement*. These are available at the *Foundation Center* and at most libraries.

Researching foundations requires the same care as researching corporations. Personal contacts of a board member or supporter can be extremely valuable. While many worthwhile projects inevitably go unfunded, foundation grants have been an important source of start-up funds for new organizations or for creative projects of established ones. Foundations are far less likely to finance operational budgets or cover the deficits of existing programs.

City Lights, a nonprofit organization created to provide alternative schooling and intensive counseling for alienated teenagers in Washington, D.C., many of whom would otherwise be in juvenile detention, initially had difficulty in obtaining funding from city government sources, who thought the concept unlikely to succeed. The organization was able, through persistence, to obtain a 3-l challenge grant from the Agnes Meyer Foundation. Other foundations followed and the program was launched. Subsequently, after City Lights demonstrated abilities to help teenagers who had repeatedly been expelled from other schools and seemed headed for a lifetime of failure, the city school system provided the funds to continue its programs.

Soliciting Government Agencies

Government grantsmanship is a skill. Government grants are tax-based dollars and may be in great demand, and, therefore, difficult to obtain. In addition, the preparation of grant applications may be extensive and require careful attention to details. Grant record keeping and staff administration may be extremely time-consuming; therefore, before you submit a grant you should research all of the direct and indirect costs of receiving a grant. Lead time could be a year or more with Federal grants. If you or someone on your staff does not have any expertise in this area, a consultant skilled in this field could save you a great deal of time and money.

Funding and access to useful databases and a variety of in-kind professional services for international programs and projects are also available through the Federal government. U.S. nonprofits can benefit directly from assistance provided by Federal agencies to organizations interested in expanding their work into other countries. The majority of these programs are underutilized because American nonprofits do not know what programs exist or how to find them. For more information, consult William Delphos' book, *Inside Washington: Government Resources for International Business*.

Sister Cities International is an organization whose purpose is to "twin" cities in the United States with cities abroad for cultural, municipal, and educational exchange. In addition to receiving donations and funding from their membership, Sister Cities has also received government grants from The United States Aid for International Development (USAID) and the United States Information Agency (USIA).

"Operation Smile," based in Norfolk, Virginia, which organizes teams of volunteers to travel to foreign countries and help children with facial deformities, also receives Federal grant monies from USAID. Volunteers include plastic surgeons, anesthesiologists, speech pathologists, nurses, dentists, physical therapists, and people who simply wish to help children in need.

If your nonprofit deals in trade issues, you may receive free initial legal consultations regarding international trade. This service is provided by attorneys from the International Law Council as part of a cooperative effort between the Small Business Administration (SBA) and the Federal Bar Association. Local SBA offices can provide details on this program. Some nonprofits help facilitate international trade of agricultural and other products, such as organizing promotion of U.S. products in foreign markets. The Foreign Agricultural Service reimburses part of export promotion expenditures for qualifying organizations.

Soliciting Trade and Professional Organizations

Typically, trade and professional organizations support projects that specifically relate to their business or that of the members they represent. Careful research is needed to develop proposals that clearly meet the organization's needs.

Through a partnership with the University of California at Davis and the University of Illinois, the Pet Food Institute (PFI) funded dog and cat nutrition research which resulted in a revised nutritional standard for pet food diets. A second goal of the Institute is to break down barriers to pet ownership for senior citizens at the state and national level. This led the Institute to support research by several nonprofit organizations on the contribution of pets to their owners' health, both physical and psychological, including a study on pets living with senior citizens in apartments in California.

The Financial Stationers Association, whose members are check printers, raised funds from its corporate members to support an educational video being distributed by local banks as one of the components in an educational module to teach students about responsible money management, including how to open checking accounts and use them properly. This supports FSA's mission to promote the paper-based payment system as a method for paying bills.

Soliciting Individuals

Soliciting individuals may take a variety of forms, with the most popular being an annual giving campaign. This type of campaign is usually undertaken in the fall of the year and will be most successful if targeted to people who have some affiliation with your organization or institution and who have a track record of participation and/ or financial support.

While a national fund-raising campaign can cost millions, it could yield substantial returns, particularly if its mission is reacting to a social cause or crisis. Telethons, mass mailings, informercials, telemarketing, print advertising rallies, and radio and TV public service announcements are common ways to reach the general public, and are particularly effective with large organizations. While difficult to carry out, national campaigns can be tremendously effective for the right cause, as shown by Mothers Against Drunk Driving (MADD).

As with other potential donors, members of the general public will need to share your vision before they write you a check. Educate them. In many cases, this may mean an emotional appeal for community action/service, humanitarian aid, or patriotism to solve the problem. Assistance from a local advertising, marketing, or public relations firm, if available, will increase your chance of success.

FUND-RAISING STRATEGIES

An organization's fund-raising efforts may take on one or all of the types listed here. There are advantages and disadvantages to each of them. A telemarketing campaign, for instance, is best conducted as part of a larger fund-raising campaign, rather than as a stand-alone effort, although the latter is an option. Direct mail may offer a more cost-effective approach to general donor renewal than telemarketing. Many groups use telemarketing for contacting donors who fail to respond to repeated mail solicitations. The more personal approach of a phone call may also be successful when trying to upgrade donors. Carefully choose which strategy or combination of strategies will be most beneficial to your efforts.

One way to choose an approach is to identify your prospective donors and then consider their specific needs, goals, and funding policies. What strategies will motivate the prospective donor? A personal visit? A letter explaining your goals? An opportunity to share in recognition of a community leader? Be careful not to overextend yourself. You do not want expenses to outdistance receipts. If necessary, develop cost estimates of your various strategy options before settling on one or two.

Personal Solicitations

One fund-raising expert, Barry Nickelsburg, has succinctly noted, "People give to people, not organizations."

Person-to-person contact is probably the most effective fund-raising tool. Colleague-to-colleague or friend-to-friend contacts greatly increase your chances of success. If someone you respect takes the time to enlist your support for a particular project, you are much more inclined to donate to that cause. Not only that, but you most likely will give more money face-to-face or voice-to-voice than if you were solicited by mail. At the very least, make follow-up calls to prospective donors who received your letter or proposal.

Direct Mail

Requests for individual donations from a larger group of donors are most likely to be through direct mail. If they are targeted letters to people who know and support your organization, direct mail letters may be the most effective tool to generate money. They are already designated as interested parties by their prior donations or by referrals from friends or colleagues. Start with the list of your former and current supporters and add referrals from friends, colleagues, or other organizations. Targeted mailings usually yield under $500 per person; often the donation requested is in the range of $10 to $250.

Keep in mind direct mail postage costs. You will need to determine whether the mailings will be sent first class or the less expensive bulk rate or third class mail available to nonprofits. Third class mail, however, may take substantially longer to reach a prospective donor, so mailings that require a timely response should be sent first class. The use of bar codes and nine-digit zip codes can expedite your mailing. (Domestic mail manuals may be obtained by writing the Superintendent of Documents, Government Printing Office, Washington, D.C. 20402-9371.)

Your fund-raising letter must be designed to quickly capture the attention of the prospective donor, considering the deluge of unsolicited mail delivered nowadays. Spend time on designing an enticing envelope and letter. If possible, enlist help—perhaps a volunteer(s)—from a local public relations or design firm for effective, eye-catching designs. It may make the difference between success and failure. Bear in mind that direct mail to lists that are not well chosen or targeted can often cost more than they bring in contributions.

Telemarketing

For many potential donors, the telemarketing call may be the only personal contact they have with your organization. This is an opportunity to answer any questions the prospective donor might have. When planning a telemarketing campaign, be sure to create an effective script for your callers that provides accurate information and anticipates questions. Your telemarketers may be staff members or volunteers, or you may hire a telemarketing firm. A side benefit of a telemarketing campaign can be market research, because the telemarketers may learn the extent of support for your program.

According to the American Red Cross' *Manual for Financial Development*, a telemarketing campaign is best conducted as part of a larger fund-raising campaign, rather than as a stand-alone effort. Many groups use telemarketing for renewing donors who fail to respond to repeated mail solicitation. The more personal approach of a phone call is also successful when trying to upgrade donors. Many colleges and universities have student volunteers for annual fund-raising drives that help raise a substantial amount of money for their institution.

Special Events

Special events are as varied as the organizations that plan them. One common event is an awards program where individuals are honored for their outstanding contributions to a cause or to the organization. Other widely used fund-raising events include balls, marathons, telethons, and silent auctions. On a small scale, churches and schools have bazaars, "white elephant" sales, bake sales, car washes, and holiday gift-wrap programs.

For big events well-known, high-profile personalities are often invited and help attract media attention to the cause. Sponsorships of the event may be solicited and corporate tables sold to raise substantial funds. Markups on individual event tickets are often twice the actual cost of the meal.

A civic group in San Francisco, Chinese-Americans for Affirmative Action, featured Professor Lani Guinier as keynote speaker at its annual fund-raising dinner in April 1994, the year her nomination to be Director of the Division of Civil Rights at the Department of Justice was withdrawn in controversy over some of her positions. Her appearance drew a sell-out crowd and reaffirmed the organization's awareness of and participation in national affirmative action issues.

Whatever the special event, it should appeal to a wide range of people and be well planned, publicized, executed, and evaluated. An enthusiastic group of volunteers may be able to find fresh, new approaches for annual events, locate new and nontraditional sponsors, and ensure that your fund-raising concept has not been overexposed. Of course, an excellent secondary benefit of special events is heightened community awareness of your organization. Events may turn out to be the public relations needed to attract new supporters.

Planning a special event should start with answers to the following questions:

- Why have an event? Or, can the goal be reached without the event?
- What kind of event will it be? A theme can help focus the event.
- Who will chair the event? Consider a prominent community personality.
- Who will be invited? Target your market.

- Where will the event be held?
- When will the event be held? Check community calendars, as well as your own schedule.
- Who will staff the event?

Establish a budget with costs versus projected income (see Exhibit 3–3 for an example of the budget for one organization's awards program) as well as a time line of critical dates and a list of who is responsible for mailing invitations, telephone follow-up, and pre-event publicity.

General Follow-Up Strategies

Follow up your initial contact to confirm that prospective donors have received information about your fund-raiser. This is a good time to ask for donations. When donations come in, promptly follow up with thank you notes from your organization's leader, preferably within 48 hours. For substantial contributions, a personal call should be made immediately upon receipt of the check or letter of commitment from a donor. Plan a personal visit to the donor if the donation is over a certain established amount; one organization calls for personal visits to any donor sending in $2,500 or more.

You may need to train your solicitors, particularly those who are conducting personal visits to donors. If your solicitor is afraid or too shy to ask for money or does not wholeheartedly believe in the project, he or she will not be successful. When visiting prospective donors, dress professionally and present materials in an organized and serious manner, yet be cordial. Respect the potential donor's time. Light conversation showing an understanding of the individual's accomplishments is a good ice-breaker, but it must be genuine, not forced. Usually, prospective donors will signal when they want to move from pleasantries to business.

THE SOLICITATION PACKAGE

Information given to prospective donors about your fund-raising campaign needs to be well thought out and attractive and reflect the image of your nonprofit as a professional organization. Be creative with the solicitation package, but be sure that you develop a clear and concise message for prospective donors.

Exhibit 3–3   National Awards Program Budget

NATIONAL AWARDS PROGRAM BUDGET

INCOME

Registration	$15,000.00
Non-member Registration	4,000.00
Awards Plaque Sales	2,000.00
Program Advertising	20,000.00
Corporate Table Sales	48,000.00
Corporate Sponsorships	45,000.00
Corporate Benefactor	130,000.00
Total Income:	$264,000.00

EXPENSE

Accounting	$2,000.00
Judging	6,000.00
Awards Video Production	20,000.00
Awards Video Dubs	2,500.00
Audiovisual/Hotel	6,000.00
Advertising Commissions	1,000.00
Food Function/Hotel	16,000.00
Postage/Shipping	9,000.00
Public Relations Services	15,000.00
Meeting Planning Consultant	7,500.00
PR Promotion	8,000.00
Awards Plaques	2,000.00
Printing/Duplicating	8,000.00
Office Supplies	1,000.00
Administrative Support	25,000.00
Telephone	1,500.00
Travel	2,500.00
Total Expenses:	$133,000.00
Income over Expense:	$131,000.00

The purpose of the solicitation package is to:

- Provide a clean and concise statement about your fund-raising goals.
- Explain why your project is needed.
- Identify the specific benefits that the donor will receive, from public relations and publicity to meeting potential clients.
- Communicate your commitment and sincerity for the project.

- Demonstrate the legitimacy and effectiveness of your organization.
- Evoke sympathy and support for your cause.
- Offer options for support or participation.
- Contain materials on your organization demonstrating the value of the program and/or project.

Basically, these materials should answer three major questions: Why are you raising money? Why should a donor support the project? How much does it cost? While addressing all of these concerns, try to keep the package simple and brief.

Basic Elements of a Solicitation Package

Solicitation letter - The direct appeal letter should be produced on your organization's stationery and contain a personalized salutation, persuasive wording, brief description of need, and requests of gift amount. When writing the proposal letter consider the following:

- Keep the letter to one page.
- Use clear and concise language.
- Use letterhead with the organization's main phone number.
- Address letters to the appropriate person. Never write to "Dear Sir or Madam." Refer to any prior visits and/or telephone conversations.
- Capture the reader's attention in the first sentence. State project objectives in the first paragraph.
- Outline only the highlights of your request. Details may be covered in the proposal itself or discussed at a future meeting.
- Show how your program/project addresses the prospective donor's expressed interests.

Exhibit 3–4 is a sample solicitation letter a nonprofit wrote to a potential sponsor.

Prospectus - A one- or two-page summary of the project. It should be produced on your organization's letterhead and should be concise. The prospectus should answer: who, what, when, where, why, and how much. It should capture for the prospective donor

Exhibit 3–4   Sample Solicitation Letter

ABC Corporation
Anywhere USA

Dear

I enjoyed talking with you by telephone recently about XYZ's Foundation
project. As a follow-up to our conversation, it is my pleasure to write you
and request your support of our program. This extraordinary opportunity
offers you exclusive sponsorship of a nationally acclaimed program that
benefits (description).

As a sponsor, you would gain national visibility and advance your marketing
goals. Showing your support of this most worthwhile project advances your
corporation's expressed interests. This program also has much media
involvement, offering high exposure for all supporters. (Be specific about
how it does this.)

I am enclosing a proposal that outlines our media schedule, promotional
materials, time lines, budget, and sponsorship benefits.

I would like to have the opportunity to meet you personally to discuss XYZ's
Foundation program. I will be contacting your office next week for an
appointment.

Thank you for your interest in the XYZ Foundation.

Sincerely,

_____

Director
XYZ Foundation

Enclosure

---

the essence of your proposal. The prospectus may only be a short
summary; the proposal will contain a more detailed explanation.
   Proposal - A comprehensive proposal should contain the following:

- Title page.
- Table of contents.
- Project description.
- Sponsor visibility.

- Statement of need.
- Organization capability, philosophy, history.
- Budget, i.e. income/expenses.
- IRS letter of tax-exempt status.
- Other relevant documents.

Support materials - Annual reports, brochures, press clippings, and any other materials that help sell the project and demonstrate its legitimacy.

Donor response card or pledge form - A card or reply form may be appropriate, especially when soliciting small amounts from individuals. This may produce higher results because of the convenience to the donor. The card may or may not be stamped. (See Exhibit 3–5.)

Donor Categories

Allow prospective donors the opportunity to choose from several categories of donations. A common list is benefactor, sponsor, donor, friend, with pledges ranging from $25,000 for a benefactor down to $25 for a friend. You also have the option of giving exclusive sponsorship rights to an event or project, with a price tag that should be considerably high. If yours is an annual campaign, donors should have the option of renewing their gift. You might also give donors the option of making a substantially larger pledge over a longer period of time.

Donor Benefits

Prospective donors want to make a contribution to the betterment of their community in exchange for appropriate recognition by their peers and the public.

The Museum Trustees Association found that its prospective donors wanted to support projects that were unique and offered exclusivity. Some prospective donors wanted no public recognition at all. Instead, they appreciated invitations to exclusive previews, private luncheons with artists, and opportunities to "rub elbows" with other donors. At gala events they could be seated next to celebrities or people they might admire and would not otherwise get to know. That is enough of a "thank you" for some donors. In other cases, special rooms in galleries are named after major benefactors. Corporations that sponsor art exhibits might stipulate that their names appear on all press releases and printed materials about the exhibit.

Exhibit 3–5   Sample Donor Pledge Form
_____

(ORGANIZATION LETTERHEAD)

PLEASE COMPLETE THIS FORM AND MAIL WITH YOUR CONTRIBUTION IN ENCLOSED ENVELOPE.

Name _____

Title _____

Affiliation _____

Address _____

Home Phone/Fax _____

Amount Enclosed/Charged: $_____

DONORS WHO MAKE CONTRIBUTIONS IN THE FOLLOWING AMOUNTS ARE RECOGNIZED BY INCLUSION IN THE SPECIAL GIVING GROUPS BELOW:

President's Club	$1,000.00 - and over
Benefactor	$500.00 - 999.99
Patron	$100.00 - 499.99
Contributor	$50.00 - 99.99
Friend	$25.00 - 49.99

Please charge my contribution to my credit card: (circle one)

VISA   MasterCard   American Express

Name on card: _____ Exp. Date: _____

Credit Card Number _____
(Use digits please)

Please recognize my gift as follows:

_____ Please publish my name and appropriate special group and/or fund information in our organization's newsletter and other appropriate publications during the year.

_____ Please do not include my name in any published materials. I wish my contribution to be anonymous.

The Foundation of (organization) is a nonprofit 501(c)(3) foundation. Contributions are tax-deductible to the fullest extent allowed by law.
_____

Not everyone wants public recognition when they make a donation; respect for a donor's wishes of anonymity must also be honored. It will, obviously, depend on the donor, but a fund-raiser must be sensitive to special requests and be as accommodating as possible. Most of all, let donors know that they are appreciated. This helps pave the way for long-term relationships.

STRATEGIES FOR SMALL- AND MEDIUM-SIZED NONPROFIT ORGANIZATIONS

What if you are not mounting a capital campaign, building a new wing on a hospital, or working for a museum seeking funding for a major exhibit?

If you are a small- or medium-sized nonprofit organization with fund-raising goals of $1,000 to $100,000, the questions are the same, but the process may be different. You may want to target your donor list by first looking within your organization for financial support from members, honorary trustees, board members, allied groups who serve your members, and those who have a track record of supporting your organization's activities through event sponsorships and advertising.

If you invest time at the beginning of the process in carefully identifying your prospect list, you will save a great deal of time and money in the long run. A three-pronged approach is desirable. First, always look for the one donor who can afford to pay for the entire project. Write, call, and visit him/her first and offer an exclusive sponsorship of your event or idea. Second, as a back-up plan, prepare a second detailed donor list. Develop a range of categories for medium-to-larger donations. Offer your carefully selected potential donors in this price range several options. A list of suggestions is offered in Exhibit 3–5. Third, go to your "small" donation list last. This could be your most expensive option, yielding only modest results. Exhibit 3–6 is a sample fund-raising campaign worksheet.

If your organization is comprised of individual rather than corporate members, solicitation takes a different approach. Do not get trapped into soliciting designated funds for specific projects; you need unrestricted funds as well. One 2,500-member organization with a foundation sent a year-end letter to all members asking for their annual donations to support the educational efforts of its foundation. The monies were not restricted or earmarked for specific programs; rather the letter was soliciting general support. While most individual contributions were modest, the total raised was sufficient to continue several important educational programs.

An important resource for nonprofits of any size is the National Society for Fund-Raising Executives (see list of resources at the end of this chapter). The Society can provide your organization with a vast supply of information on fund-raising tools and strategies, as well as provide an excellent opportunity for networking with peers.

Exhibit 3–6 Fund-raising Campaign Worksheet

Project Plan Worksheets

Segment: _____

Priority _____ Implementation date: _____

1. Project Description:
2. Prospect identification method:
      Number of prospects:
      Estimated potential: $
      Goals: $
      Competitive situation:
      Identified project needs/benefits:
      Problems:
      Opportunities:
3. Information needs
      Methods:
      Cost to obtain: $
4. Solicitation package
      Methods:
      Costs: $
5. Strategies
6. Summary
      Plan costs: $
      Income Est: $
      Profit: $
7. Time Line
      Activities to be Accomplished   Responsible Party   Start Date   Due Date

CASE STUDY—GEORGETOWN UNIVERSITY'S COLLEGE OF ARTS AND SCIENCES FUND-RAISING EFFORTS

Establishing the Fund-Raising Goal: One of the first steps Robert Brooks Lawton, S.J., took as the new Dean of Georgetown University's College of Arts and Sciences was to identify where funding was needed in the college. After discussions with students and faculty, Dean Lawton set as priorities the sciences and fine arts. After further review of curriculum and other needs, Dean Lawton established an advisory council of business and professional leaders with interests in the university, thus bringing these groups into active participation in the process.

Lawton acknowledges that his plan was designed to capture and channel enthusiasm, benefit from the perspective of people outside the school, and enlarge the funding base to do the projects the advisory board was enthusiastic about. Once a board of directors and an advisory council invest in ideas, he maintained, they can lead the project to fruition. Lawton also hired a development officer.

Dean Lawton observes that a broader peer-to-peer network develops during the process. In Georgetown University's case, advisory board members chaired subcommittees and worked alongside specialists in the sciences and fine arts. All advisory board members and committee specialists, including university scientists and professors, worked together from the very beginning to identify projects that needed funding, according to Dean Lawton. This "created mechanisms for buying into" an idea.

A Plan to Achieve the Goal: Dean Lawton cautions that, "If you have too many priorities, you have no priorities." He adds, "I have a few priorities and I try to stick with them, stay in focus and keep moving forward to achieve them. No one, of course, may do this alone. A vision articulated by a leader is critical, but other people must commit themselves to the vision if anything is to be accomplished. I have brought 'new blood' into the process, people who have not been tapped by Georgetown in the past."

Where Are the Donors: Dean Lawton spends one third of his time fund-raising for the college and observes that "10% of the people give 80% of the money." His advice: "Events are not productive unless they are part of a strategy to ask for money or build a relationship." When he is contacting donors, he relies on donor research coupled with good advice concerning whether he should contact in person, by telephone, or by letter. He also relies on his development officer's advice and recommendations to determine how his time may be used to yield the maximum financial benefit for the college.

The university's alumni office is one of Lawton's main resources for identifying potential donors. Fund-raising consultants have been hired in the past to research estimates on the giving potential of a certain "market" of alumni. The advisory council also serve as "consultants." Dr. Lawton is also planning to develop a Parents Board and a Young Alumni Council.

How Much Will the Donor Contribute? Dean Lawton cautions that there are three risks in fund-raising: asking too early, asking for too little (and risk insulting the prospective donor), and not asking at all. He attributes much of his success to his advisory council. "People fund ideas that they are excited about," says Dean Lawton. People are interested in supporting "big ideas" to solve national problems or significant issues. They are not interested in donating to pay off loans or clear a deficit. They want to be around exciting, interesting people who have ideas and strategies on how to solve big problems.

FUND-RAISING CHECKLIST

The checklist below can help you become a successful fund-raiser.

1. **Clearly identify your project.** Project goals should be compelling, specific, attractive, and people-oriented, and should convey importance and sense of timeliness.

2. **Develop a list of prospects**. The proposal must be of value to the prospective donors. Develop criteria and specific reasons why.

3. **Prepare a professional written summary of your idea**. It must convey a seriousness of purpose and be attractively presented and it must also be easy to read. Keep it short and simple.

4. **Carefully review potential funding sources.** Find out when budgets are approved for the following year. There is no sense applying for monies that have already been given that year. Get your request in early in the budget cycle, when there is still money available for a project like yours.

5. **Prepare contact lists for personal visits or telephone calls.** Remember: People give to people. Identify your human resources. Do your research on the appropriate "matches" for calls and visits. It may be best to work in pairs on visits. Invite a board member along, if he or she knows the prospective donor personally.

6. **Identify an enthusiastic team to work on follow-up.** Attention to details is important. If you said that you will get back to the prospective donor by Monday with the additional information, do it. No delays, no excuses. Deliver on your promise to follow up and your chances of success increase 100 percent. If you do not, it either means that you do not care or that your systems are sloppy, and no one wants to give money to people who are not responsible and responsive.

7. **Send personal letters of thanks immediately after your visit.**

8. **When the donation arrives, send a thank you promptly.**

9. **Be prepared.** When meeting with your prospective donor, present an image of success, both in dress and in written materials. Be sure you will be able to answer the donor's questions.

10. **If you do not believe in the project, do not try to raise funds.** Your hesitancy may not be masked for long. Only raise funds for those projects in which you truly believe.

FUND-RAISING RESOURCES

- American Association Fund-Raising Counsel Trust for Philanthropy, 25 West 43rd Street, New York, NY 10036. Annual survey: "State Laws Regulating Charitable Solicitations."
- American Society of Association Executives, 1575 I Street, N.W., Washington, D.C. 20005; phone: 202-626-2723.
- Association for Healthcare Philanthropy (AHP), 313 Park Avenue, Suite 400, Falls Church, VA 22046; phone: 703-532-6243.
- The Chronicle of Philanthropy, 1255 23rd Street, NW, Suite 775, Washington, DC 20037; phone: 202-466-1032.
- Domestic and International Mail Manuals may be obtained by writing to: Superintendent of Documents, Government Printing Office, Washington, D.C. 20402-9371.
- The Federal Assistance Program Retrieval System (operated by the Office of Management and Budget), General Service Administration, 300 7th Street, S.W., Room 101, Washington, D.C. 20407.
- Foundation Center, 79 Fifth Avenue, New York, NY 10003-3076; phone: 800-424-9836; and 1001 Connecticut Avenue, N.W., Suite 938, Washington, D.C. 20036; phone: 202-331-1401.
- The Grantsmanship Center, P.O. Box 17220, Los Angeles, CA 90017; phone: 213-482-9860.
- INDEPENDENT SECTOR, 1828 L Street, NW, Suite 1200, Washington, D.C. 20036; phone: 202-223-8100.
- National Catholic Development Council (NCDC), 86 Front Street, Hempstead, NY 11550-3667; phone: 516-481-6000.
- National Center for Nonprofit Boards, 2000 L Street, NW, Suite 510, Washington, D.C. 20036; phone: 202-452-6262.
- National Society for Fund Raising Executives, 1101 King Street, Suite 700, Alexandria, VA 22314; phone: 703-684-0410.

- Society for Nonprofit Organizations, 6314 Odana Road, Suite 1, Madison, WI 53719; phone: 608-274-9777.
- The Taft Group, 12300 Twinbrook Parkway, Suite 520, Rockville, MD 20852; phone: 301-816-0210.

SUGGESTED REFERENCES

Blazek, Jody. 1990. *Tax and Financial Planning for Tax-Exempt Organizations: Forms, Checklists, Procedures.* New York: John Wiley & Sons.

Brakeley, George A., Jr. 1980. *Tested Ways to Successful Fund Raising.* New York: AMACOM.

Broce, Thomas E. 1986. *Fund Raising: A Guide to Raising Money from Private Sources,* 2d Ed. Norman: University of Oklahoma Press.

Connors, Tracy Daniel. 1993. *The Nonprofit Management Handbook: Operating Policies and Procedures.* New York: John Wiley & Sons.

Delphos, William A. 1992. *Inside Washington: Government Resources for International Business.* Washington, D.C.: Venture Publishing, N.A.

Fink, Norman S., and Howard C. Metzler, 1982. *The Costs and Benefits of Deferred Giving.* New York: Columbia University Press.

Glaser, John S. 1993. *The United Way Scandal: An Insider's Account of What Went Wrong and Why.* New York: John Wiley & Sons.

Greenfield, James M. 1991. *Fund Raising: Evaluating and Managing the Fund Development Process.* New York: John Wiley & Sons.

Gross, Malvern J., Jr., William Warshauer, Jr., and Richard F. Larkin. 1991. *Financial and Accounting Guide for Not-for-Profit Organizations, Fourth Edition.* New York: John Wiley & Sons.

Hodgkinson, Virginia A., Murray S. Wietzman, Stephen M. Noga, and Heather A. Gorski. 1993. *A Portrait of the Independent Sector: The Activities and Finances of Charitable Organizations.* Washington, D.C.: Independent Sector.

Hopkins, Bruce R. 1992. *Charity, Advocacy, and the Law.* New York: John Wiley & Sons.

————. 1991. *The Law of Fund-Raising.* New York: John Wiley & Sons.

————. 1982. *The Law of Tax-Exempt Organizations.* New York: John Wiley & Sons.

————. 1989. *Starting and Managing a Nonprofit Organization: A Legal Guide.* New York: John Wiley & Sons.

Kaplan, Ann E. 1993. *Giving USA: The Annual Report on Philanthropy for the Year 1992.* New York: AAFRC Trust for Philanthropy.

Salamon, Lester M. 1992. *America's Nonprofit Sector: A Primer.* New York: The Foundation Center.

Seymour, Harold J. 1966. *Designs for Fund Raising: Principles, Patterns, Techniques.* New York: McGraw-Hill.

Strong, Christine. "Using Strategic Planning in Fund-Raising." *The Journal,* January 1993, page 30.

CHAPTER FOUR

Creating a Marketing Orientation in the Nonprofit Organization

Have you identified *all* of your potential markets? Do you know what they want and how to provide it? This chapter includes strategies on identifying all of your constituencies, assessing their interests and needs, and planning and promulgating programs that meet those needs.

WHAT IS MARKETING?

Marketing is often confused with selling. For years, nonprofits did not engage in marketing, because they equated the term with the "hard sell," something that was viewed as unprofessional and inappropriate. In reality, though, while the outcomes may appear the same, marketing and selling are quite different.

Selling is offering something in exchange for money, i.e. "I have **something** that I want you to buy." The emphasis is on the seller and the object being offered. A statement expressing a marketing orientation might say, "**You** have a **need** that I understand, and I am offering a product or service to meet that need." The central difference is one of perspective, and with a marketing orientation the emphasis is clearly on the consumer.

Note: The terms consumer, market, and audience are used throughout this chapter. The "consumer" will vary depending on the type of nonprofit organization; it may be a client, member, donor, visitor, patient, parishioner, etc. All are assumed in the general terms of consumer, market, etc.

In *Marketing for Non-Profit Organizations,* Philip Kotler defines marketing as "the analysis, planning, implementation, and control of carefully formulated programs designed to bring about voluntary exchanges of values with target markets for the purpose of achieving organizational objectives." While that's a comprehensive definition, one that is probably more useful for non-academics and non-profit executives is that marketing is "a management process directed at satisfying customer needs and wants through an exchange process."

A community hospital found that its surrounding neighborhood was changing, with more young families moving in. As a result, the hospital improved its maternity wing, began offering tours to expectant parents, and established training classes in delivery and parenting of infants and young children.

The hospital recognized that a secure and pleasant place to deliver a baby and information on how to deal with the stresses of pregnancy and caring for infants were important needs of its potential consumers (patients), and thus it developed both a tangible product and services to meet that need. An exchange takes place as young parents take advantage of the new services the hospital provides.

THE ROLE OF MARKETING IN THE NONPROFIT ORGANIZATION

In the "old days," marketing had no role in a nonprofit organization. Nonprofits were content to set lofty goals, create a program of products or services that the board or staff liked, and wait for the consumer to participate. But, like for-profit organizations, nonprofits were eventually forced to re-examine this orientation and develop programs that were market- or consumer-driven.

In the for-profit sector, the change began to occur in the mid 1950s, when companies first began seriously studying consumer needs. Nonprofits generally lag behind for-profits in business trends, and marketing did not become a serious issue for the nonprofits until the mid-70s. Consumers of nonprofit services had begun to make their dissatisfactions known. Churches were losing members; colleges were having difficulties attracting quality students; cultural organizations were finding it difficult to interest donors and volunteers; and many professional societies and trade associations were experiencing declines in membership. These serious problems, along with a tightening of economic conditions, forced nonprofit organizations to change the way they related to their markets.

The first steps were small ones, and it took about ten years for marketing to assume its role as an orientation that pervades entire organizations and drives the daily work environment. Some organizations still aren't there.

THE BENEFITS OF A MARKETING ORIENTATION

A marketing orientation enables a nonprofit organization to achieve its objectives more effectively and will produce four major benefits.

1. **Greater consumer satisfaction.** Effective marketing is "user-oriented," and it stresses the importance of measuring and satisfying audience needs. Thus, the products or services developed are far more likely to provide a high degree of satisfaction.

   A social service agency wanted to offer a program for recently widowed women. Before beginning, the agency surveyed the community and held a focus group. From these activities, the agency learned that while there was interest in the program, the widows in its community were less likely to need traditional information on managing finances, returning to the work force, etc., because many were seasoned money managers who had worked out of the home for some time. What they did need was a place where they could express their grief and learn to cope with widowhood in a society where immediate families often live at great distances and fewer people are available to provide strong emotional support.

   Armed with this information, the agency changed the focus of the planned program and the time at which the programs would be held (from afternoons to evenings). The program was ultimately very well-received by its clients.

2. **Increased consumer participation.** It naturally follows that products developed to meet known consumer needs will be sought after, thus benefiting the organization as well as the audience—the classic "win-win" situation. If the agency in the previous example had not learned that most of its potential clients were in the workforce, it might have planned a very good program that was held in the afternoon, reducing client partici-

pation significantly. Instead, the marketing focus helped to ensure participation.

3. **Better attraction of market resources.** To serve their audiences and accomplish their objectives, nonprofits must not only *provide* resources, they must also *attract* resources such as volunteers, employees, donors, public support, etc. Marketing provides a framework for doing so.

   An example from the for-profit world probably illustrates this best. If you wanted to start a business, and you had a product, you might need a bank loan to get started. If you approached the bank, but had no plan showing that there was a need for your new product or that you had an efficient strategy for producing, delivering, and promoting your product, you would certainly not get your money.

   It is the same in the nonprofit world. Your resources might not be money from a bank—they might be donors or volunteers. But you will not attract these resources if you cannot show them that a need exists, and that you can meet that need through a well-designed and communicated program that will effectively serve your target audience.

4. **Greater efficiency.** To market means to exert total control and coordination of program development and delivery. Outside of a marketing framework, decisions regarding programs are made arbitrarily, and the results may be ineffective or unnecessarily costly or both. Nonprofits frequently operate on tight budgets, so it is imperative that they achieve maximum cost efficiencies. A well-integrated marketing plan is a giant step toward that goal.

A Pervasive Orientation

It is important to reiterate that marketing is a pervasive consumer orientation, one that holds that the very purpose of the organization is to determine the needs and wants of its markets and to satisfy them through the creation and delivery of appropriate and effective programs.

Do you serve the disabled or indigent in a nonprofit program? They should be treated like the wealthiest legal clients or the most socially prominent diners in a four-star restaurant. Clients do not exist to fit the needs or culture of an organization. A marketing perspective dictates exactly the opposite—that the organization exists to fit the needs of the client. Indeed, without the client need, there would be no organization.

A marketing orientation will transform a "top-down" or board-driven organization to one that is highly responsive and adaptive. Peter Drucker has said, "Marketing is so basic that it cannot be considered a separate management function. . . . It is the whole business seen from the point of view of its final result, that is, from the consumer's point of view."

IDENTIFICATION OF THE MARKET AND ITS NEEDS

Market and needs identification can be one of the most time-consuming yet fascinating aspects of marketing. Exactly who are your consumers or potential consumers and what do they need and want? This research is most important, because the more you know about your consumers, the better decisions you will make on how to serve them.

Useful information may already be in your files and is also available from public opinion polls, surveys, related organizations, government statistics, local or regional chambers of commerce, etc. The Census Bureau and the Bureau of Labor Statistics can often provide data, and colleges and universities, especially those that concentrate in your area of interest, are also good sources of information.

Targeting the Market

A common mistake made by inexperienced marketers is to assume that they have only one market. Someone who runs a small museum, for example, may think that current visitors are the only market. That is not likely to be true, but even if were, within the "current visitor market" lie several different markets, e.g., young people, older adults, minorities, those who visit frequently rather than rarely, those visiting for education, etc. All represent special interests, and their needs and wants are likely to be different.

Breaking down a large potential market into special interest groups is called *market segmentation*, or targeting the market, and that is how marketing is done today. Remember when radio stations just played some middle-of-the-road music and news on the hour? No more. That approach was designed to offer something to every potential listener with no thought to special interest. Today, we have stations dedicated to rap, all news, all talk, religion, classic rock, etc. These programs are designed to appeal to a very particular group within a wide potential listening audience, and the kind of programming, the advertising, and the time slot are strongly related to the listening habits and the demographics of that special group.

Consider other audiences in addition to the ones you currently serve. What about those who haven't joined, visited, participated, volunteered, or contributed yet? Those who previously participated in some way, but are no longer involved? Those who are involved in an associated way, perhaps as suppliers? All of these groups are potential markets.

In addition to the consumers of services, a nonprofit organization will have other very different audiences to be served. For example, you might have a board of directors or trustees that must be kept involved and committed to the organization's mission. Or you might rely on the goodwill of the greater community, or need to attract a significant amount of government support. While quite different from one another, these markets must all be researched and well-served by your program.

In addition, you probably have individual donors and volunteers, and to attract their continued support, you must identify and meet their needs. In fact, in today's climate, with diminished government resources and both men and women working long hours in the workplace, the attraction of individual donors and volunteers is one of the greatest challenges faced by nonprofits. To be successful, you must identify potential donors and volunteers, determine their needs, and position your program to meet those needs.

You Know Who They Are—What Can You Do About It?

Once you've identified potential markets, two important questions emerge.

Is the market accessible, *i.e., is there a way to identify the actual members of the market and reach them with information about products and services?*

You may be able to purchase a mailing list that includes the kind of people you need to contact. This is especially true if you're trying to attract donors or volunteers. Check your local library for the Standard Rate and Data Service (SRDS) book of mailing lists, which gives descriptions and prices of thousands of lists available for rent.

Also, other organizations may be willing to exchange or share lists of clients with you. If you can't identify individual prospects by name, you might be able to predict the kind of publications they would read and reach the market through those outlets. For example, an agency planning to serve the African-American community might advertise in a newspaper oriented to this audience.

Currently one nonprofit health service agency is working to put together a national roster of people suffering from a rare bone disease. New treatment services are available for this small population, but currently there is no way to identify who they are.

Is the segment large enough to warrant the development of products/services to meet its needs?

It may be that the market is too small to support such development; however, unlike for-profits that are usually driven only by bottom-line considerations, nonprofits may choose to go forward anyway, if they determine that the service is mandated by their mission.

One nonprofit executive noted that such a program can become an excellent example for the organization's fund-raising department to use for solicitations. A good fund-raiser can highlight the program and emphasize how the organization has stood by its mission—even at great cost—and that "only with the support of its givers is it able to survive." Frequently, more money can be raised in this manner than is lost in running the program!

A cautionary note must be added, however. "Nonprofit" is a legal identification, not a state of being. You must have a positive balance sheet to stay in business and continue to aid the people that the organization was established to serve. A well-researched marketing plan enables managers to undertake an unprofitable but important program with a high degree of certainty that other activities will generate the funds to subsidize it.

Assessing Consumer Needs

Once you have identified your consumers, exploit all opportunities to learn everything you can about them. If you have an existing (fairly recent) survey of your donors or clients, get it out and study it. If it doesn't yield useful information, or if a recent survey doesn't exist, consider spending some funds for a well-designed and well-executed survey. Exhibit 4–1 illustrates the kind of information you'll want to have on your markets. This is an investment in future success. In addition to surveys, focus groups made up of current or potential consumers and run by a skilled facilitator are an excellent way to gain information. Evaluation forms are also a source of feedback. And, if a consumer severs ties with your organization, do an "exit interview" to find out why. It might yield valuable information—better yet, it might bring back a lapsed donor or client.

Exhibit 4–1   Checklist of Market Information

- Age.
- Sex.
- Race.
- Habitat (e.g., urban, rural).
- Socioeconomic level.
- Religion.
- Occupation.
- Family size.
- Education.
- Hobbies.
- Publications read.
- Level of knowledge about your organization.
- Expectations regarding your organization.
- Other organizations in which they participate.
- Products/services used.
- Level of satisfaction.

If funds are available, consider hiring a market research firm. These professionals know how to design surveys and elicit the kind of information you need. In addition, their work may yield more honest and reliable information than that which is returned to the organization's address.

Don't be tempted to forego market research on the assumption that you know what the market wants and needs—even if you consider yourself an expert or a member of the organization's market. Organization leaders and staff are sometimes out of touch and may be quite different from other members of the market in terms of commitment, age, wealth, career progression, etc. In addition, board or staff often have strong proprietary interests in particular programs, and thus they cannot be objective. It is not uncommon for a board to fashion a program with great enthusiasm, only to have it met with total lack of interest from the potential consumers or donors.

Comprehensive research is the only solid basis for future marketing successes. The following example illustrates what can happen when market needs are ignored or misunderstood.

A major national organization, concerned that too many people die while awaiting a liver, kidney, or other organ transplant, is trying to alleviate the critical shortage of donated organs. Some nonprofit organ procurement organizations have proposed that donors or their families be financially compensated (i.e., paid) for organ donations as a means of encouraging these donations. However, recent market research has revealed that the three main reasons why people do not become organ donors are: (1) Religious beliefs; (2) Lack of trust in doctors and hospitals; and (3) Belief that organs are not or would not be fairly allocated. Concerns with lack of compensation are not evident. Thus, if everything else remains unchanged, it seems unlikely that this market (potential organ donors) will be moved to donate based on a new program of compensation. The market research should cause the procurement organizations to abandon this idea and seek other programs to better serve both donor and recipient audiences.

In addition, society views organ donation as a singularly humanitarian and philanthropic act—perhaps second only to giving up one's life for someone. To offer payment for such an act might be interpreted as cheapening its value, and thus procurement agencies run the risk of losing the community's good will and thus alienating another important market. Good market research would confirm or deny that speculation as well.

Research does take time; but if you don't ascertain the needs of your market, you will proceed blindly with no assurance that the course you chose was the correct one.

Diligent research will uncover a variety of needs from your market segments. Some will be for specific products or services such as job training, shelter, medical treatment, educational or cultural programs, etc. But other, less tangible needs will also arise, such as the need for flexible access to services, group identity, information, recognition, fraternity, or prestige. You should consider both tangible and intangible needs when developing or evaluating products or services.

A final note on identifying market needs: Once is not enough! Our environment is fast-paced and ever-changing. That means your market and its needs are changing, too, so do needs assessments on a regular basis.

Sometimes a board-driven organization has an "epiphany," where it comes to understand what it means to be market-oriented.

The board of a national health agency introduced a journal as part of the member benefits for its professional membership though no assessment had shown that those members wanted such a publication. The board felt that the journal "would be good for the organization." Dues were increased to include a required subscription to the new journal.

The reaction to this new "benefit" was lukewarm, and over the next few years many of the clinical members expressed dissatisfaction with the journal. At a long-range planning meeting, the issue of the journal was raised; and the board, somewhat wiser, decided to initiate another journal, this one positioned to meet the needs of the clinical members. *Discussion ensued about whether members should be allowed to choose either journal as part of their membership, or still be required to take the original journal and pay an additional fee for the new one. Finally, one board member said, "We can't allow members to choose, because it's possible that too few people will want our original journal, and we won't have the base to keep publishing."*

After a moment someone said, "But if very few of our members choose the other journal, why would we want to continue to offer it? Isn't satisfying the member what we're trying to do?"

The room was silent, as several individuals grappled with and then acknowledged the truth of that simple statement.

EXAMINING THE ENVIRONMENT

Once target markets and their needs have been identified, you must look further to internal and external environments that may affect your ability to deliver a program that meets those needs. This is called an environmental scan. Such a scan will be extremely useful in considering your future service offerings.

The External Environment

The assessment process might uncover a need for which you believe you can develop an excellent program, but a scan of the *external* environment reveals a barrier to market entry.

A local birth control clinic was alarmed by the rapidly increasing rate of sexually transmitted diseases (STD's) among the community's adolescents and began working with the local high school to fashion a program of education to combat the problem. The program included the free distribution of condoms at the school. The two organizations had the necessary resources and the established delivery channels to put forth an excellent program, but before beginning they found that the community was not willing to acknowledge the problem and was uncomfortable with the notion of teen sexuality. This was a barrier to market entry in the external environment. The program could not go forward unless community attitudes changed.

Lack of consensus in the community is a common barrier to market entry from the external environment. There are many others, including government regulations, strong competing organizations, unusually high start-up costs, and unfavorable political forces.

External forces include anything outside of your organization that can affect your market or your ability to enter the market or deliver a product or service. Such forces can generate good or bad outcomes, and sometimes a good outcome can be bad for an organization's market or mission or vice versa.

The National Foundation for Infantile Paralysis, better known as the March of Dimes, worked in the 40s and 50s to fund polio research and assist those stricken by this dread disease. A vaccine was discovered in 1955, and quite suddenly polio, and the March of Dimes' raison d'etre, disappeared. This development in the external environment forced the organization to either rethink its mission or cease to exist. The board recognized that the organization's strength was the existing fundraising structure, so its response was to redefine its mission to raising funds for birth defects, thus serving a new but related market.

When looking at external environments, also focus on the ramifications of the current forces, which can affect every aspect of the marketing process.

For example, how might emerging communications technology affect the way in which your activities are conducted? Perhaps soon your organization will no longer communicate with members or donors through a newsletter, but rather through electronic mail or CD ROM. The product (information) will remain the same, but the delivery of the product will be different.

A scan of the external environment will not only tell you about the factors affecting your market today, but also give you information about how you can plan for the needs of your market tomorrow.

The Internal Environment

Like external environments, internal environments have a significant impact on your ability to develop programs to meet consumer needs; however, internal environments can sometimes be changed, while external forces cannot.

Internal environments include the size and wealth of the organization; the availability and expertise of staff to direct projects; existing equipment; the commitment and orientation of the board of directors and donors; and the current program, the mission, bylaws, and policies that dictate how the organization is to be run.

For example, market research identifies several needs for which the organization could create successful programs, but your internal scan reveals that the current staff is not large enough to develop and manage all those products. Your board must decide if it should change the internal environment by expanding the existing staff, use outside consultants for project management, attract volunteers to provide the necessary labor, or set priorities regarding the market needs it will serve.

A local clinic wants to immunize a poor population not covered by Medicaid, and research clearly identifies this as a serious need. However, the clinic does not have enough staff or volunteers to administer the vaccines, nor does it have the financial resources to purchase all the vaccine necessary to cover the population identified. These are limiting internal environments. However, with persistence they can be changed. The clinic director contacted the local medical society, which offered to provide the volunteers necessary to administer the vaccine, and, through a board contact, also reached an executive in the pharmaceutical company who agreed to provide the vaccine at cost. Now the small clinic had the internal resources it needed, and it went ahead with the program.

It is possible that an assessment will identify a need that the organization can serve, but a scan of the internal environment indicates that serving that need is not appropriate to the organization's mission as it is currently defined. The governing board may then decide to expand the organization's mission, i.e., change the internal environment (remember the March of Dimes) or not to service the need.

THE WRITTEN MARKETING PLAN

A marketing plan for a nonprofit organization is really just a blueprint for action that follows from your market research and needs assessments. Exhibit 4–2 illustrates the basic elements usually found in a marketing plan.

Exhibit 4–2   Marketing Plan Checklist

The Marketing Plan

1. Identification of your target audience (markets) and a description of their need(s).
2. Discussion of problems and opportunities.
3. Listing of measurable objectives and strategies.
4. Budgets.
5. Methods of evaluations.

Information on market needs, along with the knowledge acquired from environmental scans, will be used to develop the beginning of the plan. Generally, you will review that data in an opening section that could be called a "Situation Analysis." Here you will describe your various "publics," and discuss the results of your market research; your organization's strengths, weaknesses, and marketing objectives; and the overall plan of action. The presentation should make it easy for anyone to pick up the plan and understand your markets, your objectives, the needs you plan to serve, and the reasons the organization can and should meet those particular needs.

Developing Objectives and Strategies

Objectives and strategies form the heart of a marketing plan and make use of all the items in the *marketing mix* (see Exhibit 4–3). While "The Four P's" might seem a bit too corporate for the nonprofit world, with a little delineation you'll see that they do apply.

For nonprofits, let's convert the word *Product* to *Program*. Your product is actually the program of services (or in some cases tangible goods) that you offer to your clients. Programs (e.g., job training) or products (e.g., low-cost housing) are what you produce in response to a need. They are what you deliver and promote.

Price may not seem relevant if you provide services at no charge, but in every case, for proper financial management you must know the price to your organization for the services that you provide. There's another "price" component for nonprofits to consider. What is the "price" that donors or volunteers pay to support your organization? It may be actual money expended on the organization or the loss of other opportunities because of time devoted to your organization.

Place and *promotion* remain the same for nonprofits. Like corporate managers, you also need to think about the geographical area

Exhibit 4–3   The Marketing Mix: The Four P's

PRODUCT	The good or service developed in response to perceived market need.
PRICE	Price at which good or service will be offered.
PLACE	Area to be covered by good/service, e.g., local, national, etc.; the method of delivery.
PROMOTION	Methods used to communicate to the market the availability and benefits of a product or service.

that your services will cover, the methods through which you'll deliver services, and the means by which you'll let your various audiences know of the value and availability of your program.

Your marketing plan may actually include two different objectives. The first is a **marketing objective,** which addresses the way in which an organization intends to interact with its market. The appropriate marketing objective will be determined by the environmental scan.

For example, a group that finds itself with several successful programs would probably not choose to concentrate resources on new program development, but rather on promoting the current programs to its existing market to achieve *market penetration*. On the other hand, a group whose current markets are growing smaller would be interested in *diversification*, i.e., introducing new programs to new markets. Exhibit 4–4 illustrates the possible interactions between programs and markets.

A small midwestern museum had an excellent children's program offering "museum school," special tours, field trips, and other hands-on activities. However, the number of children in the locale surrounding the museum was decreasing as families grew older and were replaced by singles and childless couples. Since one of its markets (children) was declining, the museum was interested in diversifying or offering new programs to new markets. As part of this plan, it developed a "Singles Night" when the museum stayed open late, waived admissions, and offered wine and cheese to singles visiting the museum. This became one of the museum's most popular programs and was the start of other programs to be offered to this new market (singles).

The above example illustrates a wise marketing decision. Because the children's market is declining, it doesn't make sense to move

Exhibit 4-4   Interaction Between Programs and Markets

	Present Programs	New Programs
Present Markets	Market Penetration	Program Development
New Markets	Market Development	Diversification

toward *program development* for children or to try to achieve greater *market penetration*. *Diversification* was the smart move, followed by *program development* (more programs for the current singles market). *Market development*, perhaps by offering the same kind of special museum night for seniors, might be the next step.

The overall marketing objectives should be explained in the situation analysis, before moving into the specifics of the marketing plan.

The second kind of objectives might be called the **plan objectives.** These refer to the objectives you hope to achieve as a result of the marketing effort. Such objectives should be clear and measurable, listed in order of priority, and followed by detailed strategies. Specific objectives will provide a method for assessing the success or failure of the marketing plan once it is implemented.

Let's suppose that you're creating a marketing plan for a church (yes, even God needs marketing at times!) with a declining congregation. You might develop the following objective: "to meet middle-aged adults' (particular market segment) needs for fraternity and flexible access to organized religion by offering several church activities at a variety of times and places (your program of services), by the end of the calendar year attracting 15% more middle-aged adults than we are currently serving."

An organization will usually identify several objectives, and each is formulated the same way. For example, the church just mentioned would have another objective for attracting teenagers, still another to meet the needs of seniors, and so on.

Once the objectives are articulated, strategies must be formulated that detail the exact means to reach the objectives. Other components of the marketing mix such as *place* (the location and channels of program delivery) and *promotion* (the way in which you will communicate with your market regarding your program) will be explained in your market strategies.

Returning to our church example, the strategies supporting the marketing objective for adults might be as follows:

1. To offer a worship service with sermon and readings geared to
   working adults every Wednesday night, to be followed by coffee and dessert in the social hall. These will be highlighted in
   the church bulletin and listed in the "worship section" of the
   local paper. Eighty people should be attending by the end of
   the year.
2. To introduce a regular column in the church bulletin geared to
   the problems of working adults.
3. To develop a church bowling team for adult couples during the
   winter months and recruit through the church bulletin and
   community newspapers. Twelve couples should participate
   the first year.
4. To facilitate the organization of adult groups to work in other
   existing social programs at given times. For example, Monday
   will become St. Stephan's night at the community clothes
   closet. By the end of the year over 100 people should be participating in these groups. Announcement of this activity will be
   made regularly from the pulpit.

Promotion and price are integral parts of marketing strategies.
While many nonprofits offer services at no charge, not all do; managers may have to determine a price for various services, as well as
their cost to the organization. The price will be determined by a
combination of factors, including the cost of developing and delivering the program, the ability of the market to pay for the program,
costs of similar programs, and the niche that the organization has
created for its products in general.

Market niche is determined by the image of the organization and
the kind of product it is known to offer, and it is an important factor
in creating the marketing mix. For example, does the organization
have an image as upscale, always delivering high-end products or
programs that are expensive but well done, or is it known as an
organization whose products are not fancy but reliable and inexpensive. Market niche affects the market's acceptance of a product and
the price it is willing to pay, and it is difficult to market a product
outside an established niche.

*A voluntary health organization in a large Eastern city was known as a
very upscale organization, attracting big-ticket donors and many socially
prominent volunteers. For years the organization held a glitzy grand ball
with roving celebrities, breathtaking decorations, and irresistible displays of
food. The ball was the highlight of the winter social season and raised*

thousands of dollars for the organization. However, as the economy weakened, and the well-to-do became concerned about perceptions of "conspicuous consumption," ball organizers decided that the event should be significantly toned down.

*The result was a disaster. Attendance **and** donations were dismal. The market associated the organization with a very upscale, high-end product. It was not willing (or ready) to accept a "plain brown wrapper" social event, because that was not the niche that the organization belonged in.*

In retrospect, the organizers realized that rather than attempting to move to another marketing niche by substituting a toned-down version of an existing product (the ball), they should have created an entirely different product or service.

A change in image and marketing niche for nonprofits is possible, but it requires time and careful planning. The following example has a more positive outcome.

A small Midwestern university attracted its student population in large part because of its popular and nationally known football team. The academic program was acceptable, but the school was known for football, not scholarship. A new president was installed, and he was determined to turn the school into a strong academic center, thereby changing its image and its market niche. The president coined the term "academic excellence" as the rallying cry and the communications point to all the school's various markets, including students, faculty, administration, alumni, trustees, and donors and slowly went about making changes in the program. He upgraded the faculty, built a new award-winning library, increased the academic offerings, tightened the entrance requirements, and generally raised the academic standards. Over a period of years, the school started attracting a more scholarly faculty and more highly qualified students (two important markets for the university). Today the university has successfully completed the change in market niche and is regarded as an outstanding academic center (it still has a fine football team!).

One of the reasons this transformation was successful was that it took place over time. Many small steps were taken, and the school's markets were able to slowly change the way in which they regarded the university. Had the president tried to present the school to its various markets in this new niche within a year or two, and raised the tuition accordingly—even if he had had the program and faculty to back it up—it is unlikely that he would have been successful.

Note: In the for-profit world, companies can sometimes get around this problem by establishing a new brand with which they are not identified. That's how Honda brought to market the Acura Legend—many people don't realize that this expensive luxury sedan is made by Honda, the company best known for delivering a quality, low-maintenance, moderately-priced product. But this option is generally not available to the nonprofits.

Let's return to the issue of price and how it might operate in our previous museum example. One of the museum's objectives is to attract young single people, and one strategy is to have a "Singles Night." The museum staff must make several pricing decisions: Should the admission fee be lowered, waived, or left as is for that evening? Should wine and cheese be free or offered for purchase? Should the event be at cost or at a profit?

First, the total cost of the service must be determined; that includes all direct and indirect costs. Next the staff must decide if the museum budget can support whole or partial costs or if the program must pay for itself. If it is decided that the event must raise X number of dollars, the attendance must be estimated, which will then determine the per person price.

Finally, the staff must look at the potential consumers of the service. Are they upscale yuppies who can afford the necessary price and more, or working class singles for whom anything but the smallest price would be restrictive? If the staff determines that the audience cannot afford the necessary price, and the museum cannot cover the event, either an outside sponsor must be found or the event must be scaled down, e.g., offered less frequently or without refreshments.

However, market niche plays a role here, too. If the museum has an upscale image (e.g., a museum of contemporary art), and the intended audience is well-to-do, they are unlikely to participate in a pared-down event, such as a brief hour of viewing with pretzels and soft drinks.

If this market is important to the museum, a market that may eventually be not only consumers of services but also volunteers and donors, then it is even more important that staff devise a way to offer a program in keeping with the museum's image.

Promotion—The Final "P." None of the components of the marketing mix operates independently. They are related almost by definition. The type of program will affect the channels (place) through which it is delivered; the price will influence the quality and image of the program, and so on.

The final "P" to be considered is *promotion,* and promotional strategies are influenced by all of the other "Ps," as well as by the "readiness stage" of the consumer.

There are four main kinds of promotion: *Advertising, Direct Mail, Personal Selling,* and *Publicity.* They may be used alone or in concert, and an effective marketer will establish a blend that tells the consumer that the right program is available at the right price and the right time.

"Readiness stage" refers to the progression of consumer behavior that most experts believe occurs before purchase. The stages are: awareness, comprehension, conviction, and purchase.

The consumer first becomes aware of the organization or program (perhaps only by name recognition); then he or she understands the offering; then the prospect becomes convinced of the value of the offering; and finally he or she becomes a consumer of the product or service. The marketer tries to ascertain the readiness stage of the target market and match it to an appropriate message and medium.

For consumers in the early awareness stage, the message will have to be one of introduction, to acquaint them with the organization or the program. **Advertising**, which is paid promotion, might be a good way to do this, especially using a moderately priced vehicle that reaches a large percentage of the target market. If yours is a new organization, or you are offering a new service to a new market, advertising is an effective way to make potential consumers aware of your new program.

Recently, hospitals have begun to develop highly targeted programs for conditions like obesity, substance abuse, and eating disorders. Because it is difficult to identify exactly who suffers from these problems, hospitals frequently use radio and television advertising to make the programs known to the general public, many of whom might be potential consumers (or know of some).

Direct mail can be targeted to a very specific group and provides an opportunity for you to explain at length the merits of an organization or product. It can be particularly effective at moving potential consumers from comprehension to conviction or conviction to purchase. Many highly specific mailing list are available for rent, and users can purchase by area of the country, state, even by zip code.

This is the time-honored method for reaching potential donors, because the cost per contact is low, and a mailing can simulate a personal letter and even include photographs, if they provide an strong emotional appeal.

St. Jude's Children's Hospital in Memphis makes masterful use of direct mail. Each month those who have made a pledge receive a letter that usually includes a story about a young patient and his or her family. Sometimes the letters are signed by parents of a current or former patient; every letter includes at least one picture. Some letters tell of triumphs and some of losses, but each has a heart-rending story that moves the donor to give over and over again.

Personal or direct sales is most often used during the advanced stages of consumer readiness and is frequently the method employed to "close the sale" (particularly if an expensive donation or complicated purchase is involved).

For example, fund-raisers seeking very large corporate or individual contributions for a capital campaign for a hospital or college may lay the groundwork with advertising and personal letters, but the actual request will almost always be made through a personal visit.

Publicity, i.e., unpaid stimulation of demand, may be sought throughout the consumer readiness stages. If, for example, your organization began a shelter for battered women, you might try to interest the local reporters who covers women's issues in the program. You might send a press release describing the program or invite reporters to visit the shelter. Any resulting coverage would be publicity—a highly sought-after commodity—partly because publicity is assumed to be more honest than advertising.

Because members of a target market will not move simultaneously through the readiness stages, an effective marketer use a variety of promotions simultaneously.

A small crisis hotline in Kansas found that use of its services by people in severe psychological distress was declining, but at the same time the agency became aware of a growing need for "latchkey children" to have a similar service. Thus, the hotline was extended to these children to call whenever they felt frightened, unsure, confused, or just lonely.

This is a new service to a new market; let's explore what promotional strategies might be used.

Advertising. Because this is the introduction of a new service to a new audience, advertising is a very desirable means of promotion. The agency might place small space ads in community newspapers, PTA newsletters, and/or church bulletins. Flyers might be posted in places where children and their parents are likely to gather, such as an ice rink, swimming pool, or daycare center

Direct Mail. While a list of latchkey children is not going to be available, the agency could rent a list of parents of young children. A letter could be written that announces the phone number and describes the service. In addition, the letter can do "double duty" by asking for a donation to help maintain the service. Letters could also be written to principals, elementary school teachers, ministers, pediatricians, and any other identifiable group that is known to work with children.

Personal Selling. Members from the agency might make themselves available to speak about the new hotline at PTA meetings, church meetings, scout gatherings, women's clubs, etc. Again, the staff can "sell" the service, not only to potential consumers, but to potential supporters as well.

Publicity. A press release describing the new service must certainly be written and sent to local news outlets and to any other locally read publication that might include a column on what's new in the community. In addition, staff might collaborate with related groups and approach television or newspaper reporters about a story on children home alone in the community. A description of the hotline could be a part of that larger story.

Obviously, many of these strategies cost money, and the agency is unlikely to have the finances or the staff to handle all of them at once. A plan with a budget can be developed that sets priorities and develops a systematic program of promotion. As the various promotions are used, they will be evaluated for effectiveness, and as the hotline program matures, strategies will probably be adjusted.

Volumes have been written on promotional strategies, and more information on this topic can be found in the chapters covering fund-raising (Chapter 3) and public relations (Chapter 7).

CREATING THE MARKETING BUDGET

The marketing budget is not just a series of columns with numbers. It should be an integral part of the plan that flows from the goals and objectives. The budget is actually a quantitative expression of the narrative statements in the plan.

In reality, marketing budgets take many different forms, ranging from budgets that merely attempt to capture the direct costs of promotional activities, to very sophisticated budgets based on sales response optimization, i.e., the theory that increased sales revenue is a function of increased marketing expenditure (often used in planning for major donor solicitations).

The greater the expertise of the person managing the marketing function, the greater the likelihood that the marketing budget will be comprehensive, technical, and based on known sales formulas.

Many nonprofit organizations, however, do not make regular "sales," and the majority do not employ marketing MBAs. But even someone not formally schooled in cost/benefit analysis or surplus maximization can develop a marketing budget that will work for the organization as long as the manager keeps in mind that the budget is essentially a projected profit and loss statement based on stated goals and objectives.

The budget should include a detailed list of the assumptions on which the numbers are based (e.g., how many meals will be served, how many FTEs are required, how many brochures will be mailed at what rate) and cover both revenue and expense.

Nonprofits are often the recipients of donated services or in-kind contributions. Monetary values should be assigned to these contributions, and they should be shown as revenue in the budget. Expenses usually include the direct costs of production, distribution, promotion, and personnel, and more sophisticated budgets will also include indirect costs covering a portion of the organization's overhead. Not all organizations allocate indirect costs, but for realistic future analyses of what the programs really cost the organization, indirect costs should be assigned. Your organization may already have a formula for doing this. If not, you might apportion indirect costs based on resource usage.

Some common mistakes made in the development of the marketing budget are (1) not allowing sufficient funds for market research, evaluations, or effective promotional strategies; (2) underestimating the costs involved in developing new programs; and (3) overestimating the level of contributions.

Revenue projections should be based on real numbers and past experience. It's unrealistic to project a 30% increase in donations if increases have never been over 7% for the last three years (this does occur, usually under outside pressure to balance the budget, save a pet project, etc.), unless a new variable is operating that will account for such a large increase. If that is the case, it should be documented in the budget narrative. (For example, a moving television story about people suffering from a particular disease may produce large increases in donations to organizations working to eradicate that disease or aid its victims.)

A well-planned marketing budget emphasizes organizational objectives and relates them to the inputs and expenditures necessary for their achievement. The result will be grouping by program area. This process facilitates making "tradeoffs" that may be necesary to reach objectives. If one program performs much better than anticipated, while another is underperforming, it becomes easy to move additional promotional dollars to the latter program.

EVALUATION

Evaluation is the final step in the marketing process, and no marketing plan is complete without this activity. It is interesting to note that the marketing process began with the consumers—who are they and what do they need; and so it will end with the consumers—what is their level of satisfaction; how well did we meet their needs?

While evaluation is the final step, this does not mean that evaluation only takes place at the end of a program. On the contrary, to be effective, evaluation should be built into the beginning, the middle, and the end of a program. Evaluations actually serve two purposes: to ascertain whether the consumer is being well-served, and to determine if the organization is meeting its marketing objectives efficiently.

The first evaluation process might take place after a program is researched and designed, but before it is actually launched. Such an evaluation might take the form of a pilot project (launching the program on a small scale) or employ a focus group to respond to the new program (remember the agency that planned to offer a program for recent widows).

Sometime after implementation, another evaluation should be done. Surveys or user response forms will provide useful information on program use and consumer satisfaction, and might stimulate small adjustments or re-focusing of promotional strategies to make a program more effective.

A library offering a bookmobile program learned through an intermediate evaluation that a small adjustment in schedule could greatly increase partic-

ipation. It arranged to have the bookmobile in a church parking lot on Tuesday mornings instead of Wednesday, because that was the day a senior support group met at the church. That information had been overlooked when the program was being planned.

A *sales analysis* is a method of evaluation that will help determine whether marketing objectives are being met, but it doesn't yield any information about how much better you might be doing. A *market share analysis* will give you a sense of the total possible universe and the portion that you "own." For example, a sales analysis might show that last week you served 200 meals to the homeless in your program, but how "good" is that? A market share analysis will tell you that there were 500 people that might have partaken of your free dinners, and you served 200. That makes it much easier to gauge your level of success.

Marketing expense-to-sales analysis will help you go beyond the limits of your existing budget and consider how much more you might sell if you increased marketing dollars. For example, how many additional donors would be generated by one extra mail promotion? Would the additional revenue cover the costs of the promotion and the "servicing" of the donor and still provide cash to the organization?

In addition to overall program evaluations, analyses of individual components can also be very important in determining the efficiency of a plan.

A national association hired a director of marketing to increase membership. The association had always used direct mail as the main promotional strategy, but the new director wanted to introduce telemarketing. The board resisted, saying "telemarketing is too expensive," but the director pervailed, and eventually the board agreed to a limited pilot project using telemarketing.

When the board first saw the expenses from the telemarketing project, they were appalled, saying that it proved their assertion that telemarketing cost too much. But an analysis of the cost per actual new member showed that telemarketing was actually less expensive than the direct mail they had been using.

Telemarketing is now a part of the organization's promotion, but if the board had only seen comparisons of expense without the analysis, an effective strategy would have been lost.

WHO HOLDS THE MARKETING RESPONSIBILITIES IN THE ORGANIZATION?

This chapter would not be complete without a discussion of who should be responsible for the organization's marketing activities. The discussion is most meaningful here, now that you have an understanding of how marketing operates and what it means to an organization's structure.

Organizations vary greatly in the way in which marketing is handled. In many nonprofits, each individual function area is responsible for marketing its own programs. While that's probably better than no market orientation, it's not an effective way of using marketing resources or serving consumer needs. No overall marketing calendar is kept, and opportunities for joint promotions or cross-selling are missed.

A large museum runs tours and daytrips and has a meeting department to organize and market these events. The meeting department only markets meetings, but the person who has just gone on a 10-day tour of the Roman ruins is probably not part of the market for the next trip to the Galapagos Islands. He or she is part of a market for a new publication on the Etruscan Civilization, but that book is developed and marketed by the publications department, which is independent of the meetings department.

What both departments fail to realize and exploit is that in many instances they serve the same need, though the product or service meeting that need might be different. Without that understanding, joint planning and promotions don't occur and many marketing opportunities are lost.

Some organizations go further and create a marketing department. While this is a better plan, it, too, has limitations. Frequently, unrealistic expectations are placed on the department manager, and once such a department is created, no one else expects to do any marketing. In addition, because that department manager is generally viewed as a peer by other department heads, he or she has little authority to establish a marketing orientation throughout the organization.

Because an effective marketing program requires support and commitment from the highest levels, when the chief executive staff person takes on the responsibility the chances of establishing a market-driven organization are greatly increased. The CEO has the power to hire staff and insist on a marketing approach, and he or she can channel organization resources to this effort. In addition, being at the top of the organizational chart, the CEO has a broader vision of how the marketing program is working throughout the organization.

However, this model is not always an option. The CEO may lack a strong personal commitment to marketing, or may not be trained in marketing functions. He or she might have been hired for other skills and experiences. Or, the CEO might have the interest and the ability, but lack the time to properly manage marketing activities in addition to the other duties for which he or she is responsible.

Should that be the case, the CEO might choose to hire a senior staff person to be responsible for overall organizational marketing. This position would be above that of department heads, and might carry a title such as Marketing Vice President, making it clear that the person will be a part of the senior executive team. With the appropriate authority and reporting lines, the person in this position can be as effective as the CEO in driving the establishment of a marketing orientation.

Regardless of who is ultimately assigned the responsibility for the marketing function, the success of any marketing program will depend in large part on the enthusiastic support and understanding by the entire staff—from the receptionist and the mail room clerk to the CEO—of the premise that the reason the organization exists is to understand and serve the needs of its markets and its mission.

Exhibit 4–5 is a summary checklist of the main issues discussed in this chapter.

Exhibit 4–5   Final Marketing Checklist

Want to Market? *Ask the right questions:*

- □ Whom do I want to serve?
- □ What are their needs?
- □ Can I provide a quality product/service to meet those needs cost-effectively?
- □ Are outside conditions right for my products/services?
- □ What is the most convenient way for my markets to use my products/services?
- □ What are the best ways to let my market know my product/service exists?
- □ Are my markets satisfied?
- □ How can I make things even better?

CHAPTER FIVE

Providing Needed Educational Programs

Preparing a successful educational program requires solid research, planning, and promotion. This chapter will give you an edge in creating high-quality programs that satisfy your audiences and promote the goals of your organization.

In the nonprofit world, educational programs are often the backbone of an organization's services to its constituencies. Large membership societies comprised of individuals with common interests, charitable organizations that serve the needs of society as a whole, and trade associations that represent whole industries routinely provide educational programs for their members, affiliated groups, and even the general public. In contrast, smaller nonprofits, like local civic clubs, churches, and community groups, tend to offer educational programs that are more narrowly focused, shorter in duration, and more likely to produce results that are immediately visible. Although these programs vary in sophistication, approach, and budget, they all have a common denominator: they meet an identifiable need of a target audience.

Not every nonprofit organization is in the education business, or even should be. But if yours is, you need to pay special attention to some basic rules of good marketing, planning, and evaluation. How do you determine the need for education? How do you plan a successful program? What is the most appropriate medium to use? How do you build credibility into your program? Why are promotion and easy access so important? What do you need to understand about your budget? Why is evaluation so important?

In this chapter we will offer answers to these and other important questions that you might ask yourself as you begin to plan your next educational program.

IS YOUR ORGANIZATION IN THE EDUCATION BUSINESS?

Education is a lofty goal, but not all nonprofit organizations are in the business to educate. Education is more than just providing information in the form of publications and group meetings. It is the thoughtful effort of assessing the knowledge and skill needs of a specific target audience and designing and executing an effective means of increasing the depth and breadth of the audience's knowledge and skills.

If you are in the education business, your organization's mission and strategic plan should say so. Your allocation of available resources and your program priorities should reflect a clear commitment to providing quality education based on identifiable needs. The lack of such a commitment will cloud your organization's vision of its purpose and direction. It will make it more difficult to allocate the necessary resources to quality education in the face of other interests and priorities.

The importance of having a clear mission statement and strategic plan, and using them to establish program priorities and to allocate available resources, is demonstrated in the following example.

A statewide charitable community service organization that provided financial help and counseling to needy families decided to develop a series of estate planning seminars for its constituents and the general public. The organization hoped that the seminars would encourage attendees to name the organization in their wills as beneficiaries. Much time, effort, and expense were devoted to developing the content, recruiting presenters, choosing strategically located sites in major population areas, and marketing the program. The result was disappointing. The attendance at most of the seminars was small and some even had to be cancelled for lack of registrants.

From the evaluation data provided by those who did attend, the program content and its presentation were judged to be excellent. In addition, promotion of the program was widespread and repeated through multiple direct mailings and advertisements in the organization's publications. So why did the program fail?

The answer is simply that the organization forgot that its mission did not include educating its constituents to a subject (estate planning) which was not directly related to its program mission (providing counseling and financial help to needy families). A random survey of the organization's primary donors revealed that people were suspicious of the organization's motive for offering the seminars and felt that the expenditure of valuable resources in mounting such a program was inappropriate.

Among nonprofit organizations, there are probably more examples of poorly thought out educational programs than good ones. The old adage, "If you're going to do it, do it right the first time," is especially pertinent in the area of education. If your organization is unable or unwilling to allocate the resources necessary to conduct a first-rate educational program, you would be better served to pass up the opportunity.

HOW DO YOU DETERMINE THE NEED FOR EDUCATION?

Needs assessment is the most important prerequisite of a good educational program. It can be as sophisticated or simple, as costly or inexpensive, as the program demands and as your organization's pocketbook allows. An adequate needs assessment does not require an outlay of thousands of dollars and the services of a statistician. It *does* require that you have communicated enough with your target audience in the course of day-to-day business to be aware of their perceptions of their own deficiencies in certain knowledge and skill areas. Or, as the staff or volunteer leader in your organization, you might be aware of an emerging issue that will affect your target audience. This issue might form the basis for an educational program. The more you focus your needs assessment efforts, the lower the cost.

Survey Your Internal Market

The members, donors, clients, and friends of your organization constitute your "internal" market and are closest to the issues that are most important to your organization. What do they perceive as their needs for knowledge and skills? To find out, you can distribute open-ended surveys at group meetings, mail out a simple questionnaire with one of your regular periodicals, have informal focus group discussions, poll your board of directors, or conduct a random telephone survey. These are among the most expedient and inexpensive ways of assessing educational needs within your organization.

Survey Your External Market

Your organization's "external" market might consist of many audiences. The members of other organizations with which you have common interests could be one such audience. A list of prospective donors who might be interested in (but ignorant about) supporting your organization through planned giving could be another. You might even target the general public for your assessment.

Surveying target audiences that are external to your organization requires the use of sophisticated survey instruments and sampling techniques to ensure that the results are statistically valid. Engagement of a professional to advise you is recommended. The cost of designing a valid survey instrument, surveying a large enough population to produce statistically valid results, and the interpretation of those results by a professional can be costly. Remember, however, that the success of your educational program depends heavily on a valid assessment of the needs of your target audience. If your organization is committed to providing quality education, needs assessment is not the place to save money!

Assess the Competition

One of the common pitfalls of conducting educational programs is to ignore the possibility that some other organization in the community is meeting the same educational need of your target audience. This might be another nonprofit organization, a commercial company, or the local university or community college. An assessment of this competition is vitally important to the success of your own program.

Is your target audience large enough to support more than one educational program? Is the content of your program of higher quality than the competition? Is it offered at a time that is more convenient to the target audience? Is your fee lower? Is your faculty more well-known and respected? Have you marketed your program more widely and more aggressively than the competition? These are all questions that you should ask yourself when comparing your program to the competition. The bottom line is: If you cannot do your program better and with more success than the competition, don't do it at all!

Analyze the Environment

More often than not, our societal and cultural environments present us with educational opportunities. The political arena, in particular, produces legislation and regulations that lend themselves to interpretation and analysis in the form of educational programs. This is one of the most important sources of exciting and innovative program material. It tends to be "cutting edge," causing the target audience to perceive your organization as forward-thinking, insightful, and responsive. As you conduct your needs assessment, look around for emerging issues that might affect your target audience.

HOW DO YOU PLAN A SUCCESSFUL PROGRAM?

Planning and success go hand-in-hand. Although planning will not guarantee success, the lack of good planning might lead to mediocre results or even outright failure.

Good planning begins with the development of clear program objectives. You can borrow the classic "5 Ws" from journalism to construct an excellent framework for a good program plan.

WHO? To whom is your program targeted? How do you reach them efficiently and cost-effectively with information about your program?

WHAT? What is the content of your program? Who should be recruited for the faculty, and how? How should the program be structured? Workshop? Seminar? Self-study? Should it be a single presentation or a series?

WHERE? What geographical location would be most convenient for attendees? Is there an adequate facility in the area? Is it available at a reasonable price? Is it accessible after normal business hours (for evening sessions)? Is there adequate parking and security?

WHEN? When is the best time to schedule your program? Are there competing events and activities? (Avoid scheduling near holidays or summer vacation time.) What is the appropriate length?

WHY? This is perhaps the most important question to ask. The answer provides the justification for the program. It identifies the reason why people will be motivated to attend. It ties the program to your organization's mission and strategic plan, and to the results of your needs assessment.

The program plan is your road map. It lists what needs to be accomplished (tasks), when (deadlines) and who will do the work (assignment of responsibility). Make program objectives and associated tasks measurable. This enables you to see to what extent they have been completed. Establish deadlines so you can determine whether your program planning is on schedule and whether interdependent tasks are completed in the necessary sequence. Identify resources (staff, materials, speakers, etc.) that need to be acquired and assigned to each objective and its associated tasks. Are they readily available? Is the cost reasonable?

It is only through good program planning that you can be assured that all aspects of your program have been thoroughly examined; that everything is in place at the right moment; and that you are prepared for both the expected and the unexpected.

WHAT IS THE MOST APPROPRIATE MEDIUM TO USE?

In selecting the appropriate medium for your message, remember that true education should increase the depth and breadth of knowledge and skills of your target audience, not merely inform. This requires that you have some means of validating learning of knowledge and skills once the message has been conveyed. Some media make this relatively simple. Others are designed more for presenting information only, not learning.

Workshops and Seminars

Classroom situations enable the instructor to validate learning through periodic testing and direct interaction with the target audience. They also provide an opportunity for demonstrations, hands-on practice, and other participatory learning techniques. Classroom-style teaching has yet another advantage over most other media: You can convey the latest, most up-to-date information available during these instructional sessions. One of the primary disadvantages is that to be truly effective, the size of the audience should be relatively small.

Classroom instruction is the most effective way of educating your target audience, but it can be costly. An excellent instructor is critical to the success of the program. Support materials such as textbooks, workbooks, case studies, reading lists, and examinations must be carefully selected or developed to adequately supplement the oral instruction. The preparation time is extensive, both by the instructor and by you, the sponsoring organization.

The difficulties of this type of educational program are illustrated by the efforts of the Oakland, California, affiliate of a major national nonprofit health association which sought to develop a heart health education program in elementary schools in the area. With the help of medical professionals, health educators, and teachers, the organization drafted a comprehensive curriculum that included extensive hands-on learning experiences, participatory exercises, and pre- and post-testing to validate learning. Health education students from a nearby state university were recruited and trained to conduct the program in the classroom in a compact, fast-paced, 4-hour module.

A pilot test of the instructional unit indicated that substantive learning took place on the part of secondary school students who participated in the program. On this basis, plans were made to expand the program in the local school district.

Although the program proved to be outstanding from an educational standpoint, and the initial development was relatively inexpensive due to the extensive use of volunteers, the depth and breadth of resources needed to expand the program proved beyond the capability of both the organization that developed the program and the local school district. It was simply too expensive to implement.

If your organization is committed to providing quality education and it has the resources available to do so, classroom instruction should be your first choice. But since programs of this type are usually labor-intensive, it is particularly important to be realistic about the costs and needs of staff.

Meetings and Conferences

Annual meetings, conferences, seminars, and workshops provide an excellent opportunity to educate a "captive" audience to issues that your organization and its constituents deem important. Typically, annual meetings and conferences offer a combination of general presentations for all participants and smaller breakout sessions for subgroups of the overall audience. This combination provides an opportunity to set the tone of the conference with general presentations on major themes, while using a series of concurrent breakout sessions to address specific issues that relate to these themes.

General presentations and breakout sessions that are part of a conference are more informational than educational. Typically, the number of people in attendance is so large, and the time allotment for each so small, that effective learning (and validation of it) cannot take place. The advantages are that you already have an interested audience available and the costs of meeting space and other necessities are more reasonable because the educational program benefits from the economies of scale offered by the entire conference.

If you want to present information about a variety of issues but are not concerned with validation of learning, meetings and conferences should be high on your list of media to consider. (See also Chapter 6 for ideas on planning and managing meetings and conferences.)

Electronic Media

The younger generations have been raised on video games, MTV, "Star Wars" special effects, Walkmans, CDs, personal computers, and other products of the electronic age. The technology is dazzling. The production is slick. And the advertising professionals will tell you that use of these media to educate young people is measurable in terms of results. One reason we mention this is that the electronic media are your competition.

If your organization is thinking about producing a videotaped series, a television program, or some other form of educational vehicle using the latest electronic technology, be aware that it will have to compete for attention with the products of the advertising world. Today, education via electronic media must be as good or better than commercial applications to reach and have any impact on the target audience, especially if your audience is comprised of young people. Measuring the results is tricky, at best, and doing it right is expensive.

The Seattle affiliate of a major national health association decided to educate the general public to the habits of good cardiovascular (heart) health by using a series of television public service announcements (PSAs). The PSAs had been developed as part of a research project at Stanford University and had been tested successfully in a small, central California television market. The results showed that, indeed, repeated exposure to the television messages had caused a positive and measurable change in the daily living habits of viewers.

The PSAs were reproduced by a Seattle commercial television station (as a public service to the association), with the appropriate "intro" and "extro" using the theme "Enjoy Life with a Healthy Heart." The station then distributed the PSAs to all other television stations in the state of Washington with a request that they be aired in prime time on a regular schedule, over a period of one year.

From program logs supplied by the television stations, it appeared that the PSAs were, in fact, receiving significant air time on a regular basis. However, in contrast to the controlled research project done by Stanford

University in which the audience was clearly identified and could be reached for evaluation, the extension of the program in Washington state did not lend itself to easy evaluation. To survey the general viewing audiences of each of the state's commercial television stations would have required a significantly large expenditure of funds of the association, and this was not practical. In the end, the association made the assumption that the public service campaign probably had a positive effect on the lifestyles of an unknown number of people, but there were no hard data to substantiate the assumption.

Given that the use of electronic mass media for educational purposes is an expensive proposition, if you want to reach the masses with a fairly simple message, if your organization has substantial resources to do so, and if you accept that you will not be able to measure the results with precision, electronic mass media can be a powerful and highly visible (to your constituents) means of getting your message across.

Another form of electronic media, the video cassette, lends itself well to use as an educational tool. Although still relatively expensive, video cassette programs can be used successfully, and often profitably, by organizations to educate their constituents, other special audiences, and the general public.

A local community services agency that provided job training for people with disabilities decided to take advantage of the business community's growing interest in the Americans with Disabilities Act (ADA).

With the help of its clients and the human resources departments of a few local companies, the agency developed a 15-minute videotape that illustrated, through actual case studies and testimonials, why hiring and accommodating people with disabilities is a sound business investment for employers.

A large corporation provided funding to duplicate and distribute the videotape to local businesses and other community service agencies serving people with disabilities.

In the end, the agency had served an important need of its clients (people with disabilities), had encouraged a commitment by the local business community to the spirit of the ADA, and had done it all at little cost.

Publications and Printed Materials

Printed materials seem to be at the core of educational programs provided by most nonprofit organizations. From the local church bulletin to the annual conference proceedings of a national medical professional society, the printed page has carried the burden of informing audiences large and small under the guise of education.

With publications, you have the ability to treat a topic comprehensively. Unlike electronic media, you are not constrained by time. You can use as many pages as you want to convey your message, provided the total pages fit within the overall design and construct of your publication. They also are lasting. Your publication may become a reference piece on a library shelf.

Publications can be the least expensive medium to use in informing your target audience about certain issues or subjects. But, they also can be the most *unreliable* in terms of assessing results. When the brochure, booklet, journal, newsletter, or other publication leaves your organization's office, you often have no way to be certain if it is delivered to the recipient, if it is read and, most important, if the information has any impact on the reader.

Publications serve a useful purpose as informational vehicles. But to be effective tools for education, they need to be incorporated into a more structured educational environment such as a workshop or seminar as support or reference materials. Or, they need to take the form of self-study materials incorporating a testing mechanism that ensures validation of learning.

If you are interested in providing information inexpensively, to a large number of people, you should consider using publications or other printed materials.

HOW DO YOU BUILD CREDIBILITY INTO YOUR PROGRAM?

Like value, credibility is not an absolute condition. It is more perception than substance. Is your seminar speaker a well-known and respected peer or colleague of audience members? If so, you have probably increased the credibility of your program. Is the author of your organization's new instructional manual unknown in the industry? If so, doubt about the validity of the information presented might linger in the minds of readers.

This is not to say that people outside of your organization's sphere of influence cannot do a top-notch job. Thousands of people make their living on the professional speaking circuit and they come with a long list of credentials and references which you can easily check to increase your comfort level. Even so, they are unknown quantities to you and your program's audience and they pose a risk in terms of the credibility of your program.

The important thing to remember is to check out speakers thoroughly. Talk to people who were responsible for scheduling them for their own organizations. Ask for a videotape of their presentation. (Any professional speaker worth considering has a videotape to loan.) Do everything you can to find out beforehand if this speaker can do the job you expect and give your program credibility!

What Else Affects the Credibility of Your Program?

The way it is organized, for one. Have potential attendees received notice of your program well enough in advance to enable them to schedule it along with other personal and business commitments? Have you offered your program at a date, time, and location that is convenient for your potential audience? Are the program sessions the right length? People with small children and the elderly will want an early start and a program length in the range of one to two hours. Does the price make sense given what the attendees will receive in return? People are very adept at determining the value they get for the price they pay.

Lastly, one of the most effective ways to build credibility into your program is to provide recognition within your organization by awarding *continuing education units* (CEUs). Recognition by obtaining CEUs is becoming more and more important, especially in fields where attendees need CEUs to track their professional or skills development or to maintain professional certification or licensure.

If your program is based on a needs assessment of your potential audience, identifies learning outcomes for participants, includes content and instructional objectives appropriate for the learning outcomes, is presented by qualified instructors, and is evaluated by those participating in the program, your organization might qualify for awarding CEUs. To assess your organization's qualifications for awarding CEUs, you can contact a local college or university, an association that represents the professional interests of your audience, or the founder and caretaker of the CEU, the International Association for Continuing Education and Training (IACET) in Washington, D.C.

A good example is the "Arthritis Days" seminar held each year by a local medical foundation. Rheumatologists, internists, general practitioners, physical therapists, occupational therapists, and other medical professionals from across the state attend this highly popular conference. Although the program is local in nature, the foundation arranges for persons attending the education program to receive CEUs from their own professional organizations such as the state medical society and the physical therapy and occupational therapy associations.

It is important to determine if your education program qualifies for continuing education units so you can offer this valuable benefit to your program's attendees.

If your educational program is more informational in content and appeals to a broader, nontechnical or nonprofessional audience, CEUs are not nearly as important as giving recognition to those who participate. A signed certificate of completion, notice in the organization's newsletter or bulletin, or an article in the local newspaper goes a long way toward building credibility for your program.

Credibility can make or break an educational program. It can also affect your organization's ability to mount an effective educational effort in the future. Ensure the short- and long-term success of your educational programs by doing everything you can to enhance their credibility in the eyes of your potential audience.

WHY ARE PROMOTION AND EASY ACCESS SO IMPORTANT?

The best-planned education program can fail miserably if people do not know about it. Although this sounds like common sense, often educational programs are inadequately promoted by nonprofit organizations that assume if a program is good, the audience will find out about it.

Earlier in this chapter we discussed the importance of identifying the "target audience" of your program. There are two important reasons for being able to identify this group. First, you must know who they are and what is important to them (needs). Second, you must be able to reach them with information about how their needs can be fulfilled (promotion).

Promotion

Promotion comes in three forms. First, there is paid (or free, public service) **advertising** in the media. This includes display advertising in your own publications, those of other nonprofits, companies and community agencies, or your local newspaper.

Advertising can also take the form of radio and television ads or public service announcements, outdoor display (billboard) advertising, electronic reader boards, or bus cards. But purchasing broadcast air time can be expensive unless you find a creative way to get your message across at someone else's expense.

A local children's museum in Denver mounted an effective broadcast promotion campaign at no cost. To advertise its annual "Parenting Fair," an event that included an exhibition of products, services, and educational lectures for new and expectant parents, the museum persuaded a popular family restaurant to put a tagline about the fair at the end of one of its radio commercials. The restaurant benefited from its association with the museum and the museum received some excellent promotion for its education program.

A second form of promotion is the category of **special events**. These are promotional activities that "piggyback" or make use of an existing vehicle that targets large numbers of people. Perhaps the local radio station is willing to provide free transportation to your educational workshop for the first three people who call in to its popular talk show each day. Or maybe you can strike a deal with the publisher of a national trade or industry journal so that everyone who registers for your educational program will receive a free six-month subscription to the publication.

The third form is **direct mail**. This is the most flexible form because it can be as simple or as sophisticated as you desire, and as inexpensive or expensive as your budget allows. Either way, direct mail can be one of the most effective ways of promoting your education program. If you are a local community group, sending a one-page, folded self-mailer to your prospective donors might suffice nicely. If, however, you are targeting the general public or others who are not familiar with your organization's programs and activities, you might want to develop a more interesting and eye-catching promotional brochure that will interest recipients and cause them to read and respond positively to your message.

When designing your promotional message, regardless of its form, there are a few basic concepts you should keep in mind:

- **Be hard hitting, brief, and clear** in your message. Use action words that have "punch." Think visual. Use graphics. Remember, you are competing with the razzle-dazzle of commercial television, Madison Avenue advertising, and a host of other strong stimuli in today's society.

- **Repeat, repeat, and repeat again!** This is one of the basic tenets of successful advertising. Your message will compete with thousands of other messages for the attention of your target audience. You will need to drive your message home again and again if it is to stand out among those of your competitors.

- **Promote early and often.** People in today's society are very busy. Many families consist of two working parents who have community and business activities outside of normal working hours, young children who must be transported to and from day-care, and teenagers whose extracurricular activities at school demand parental attention. Family calendars are locked up with these types of commitments months in advance.

  Get the message about your education program to your target audience as early as possible, before their family calendars are full. And, as discussed earlier, send your message more than once. Remember that you are competing with an extraordinary array of messages that your audience has to receive, process, and act on daily.

Chapter 4 of this book gives detailed information on designing and implementing a comprehensive marketing program that utilizes promotion and other means to make your target audience aware of your education program.

Easy Access

Giving your potential audience easy access to your program means that the price is right and that you make the registration process simple and easy to use.

Pricing your educational program at the proper level is not an art or a science. It is plain common sense. First, you probably want the program to be, at the very least, self-supporting (pay for itself). If so, your starting point for pricing is the program's total cost, less any sponsorship or other outside underwriting, divided by a realistic estimate of the number of customers. Now compare the resulting price with those of similar educational programs, especially ones in your geographical area. Is your price substantially higher? If so, ask yourself if the perceived value of your program justifies the higher price. If not, you should consider reducing your overall cost so you can lower the price or plan to incur a loss. If, on the other hand, your price is substantially lower than comparable programs, you should consider adding a margin that will result in a net profit to your organization. In this event, your educational program becomes, fortunately, part of your fund-raising activity. Taxes on the net profit will be due only if it is deemed "unrelated" business activity by the Internal Revenue Service.

Some organizations have a tendency to offer their educational programs at a price well below that of the competition. They do this as a community service and as a means of making the program available to a larger number of people who might otherwise not be able to afford it. But too often the organization is surprised when few people turn out for this low-priced program.

What we sometimes fail to remember is the concept of perceived value. How you price your product often reflects the value people place on that product. Thus, if your educational program is priced too low, people might question whether it is worth their while to purchase it or to attend.

Recover your costs, compare your pricing in the marketplace, and look at price from the standpoint of perceived value in the eyes of your potential audience. But most of all, use plain common sense.

The right price goes a long way in making your educational program accessible to its potential audience. But pricing is only half the challenge. You must also make it **simple and easy** for a person to sign up for the program, pay the fee and receive additional information. Although this might sound elementary, the lack of attention to details like these can produce significant barriers to the success of your educational program.

Your promotion materials should include the necessary information that will enable a potential attendee to respond:

- Title and description of the program, and to whom it is targeted.
- Date, time and location.
- Price.
- How to register and get additional information (address, telephone number, etc.).

The registration vehicle that is the easiest and simplest to use is a 24-hour, toll-free telephone number that people can use to give their name and address and to charge the registration fee to a credit card such as MasterCard or Visa. Typically, this form of registration is used when the potential market for the educational program is relatively large and scattered geographically or when the program is targeted to people unaffiliated with your organization. Although telephone registration is, by far, the easiest method for the target audience, from the standpoint of the sponsoring organization it might also be the most expensive. A careful study of the cost versus benefit of using telephone registration should be done before making a decision to proceed.

A printed registration form is commonly used for educational programs that do not rely on telephone registration. The form asks for name, address, phone, choice of program dates or elements (if the program is a series or if it has multiple parts that can be signed up for separately), the dollar amount enclosed, and method of payment. A more comprehensive form, like that for a multi-day educational conference, could have numerous options from which to choose and also ask for additional information about the registrant, such as:

- Member of your organization?
- Name preferred on name badge?
- Any special needs (dietary, access for persons with disabilities, etc.)?
- First-time attendee?
- Demographics such as age, educational level, vocation, cultural and recreational interests, etc.
- Certified through your (or another organization's) professional certification program?

The important things to remember when designing a registration form are:

- Ask only for information you plan to use.
- Arrange information on the form in a logical order.
- Leave adequate room for the registrant to enter information.
- Indicate clearly where the completed form should be mailed, and by what deadline date.

- Provide a telephone number (and hours it is staffed) for questions and additional information.
- Keep it simple.

WHAT DO YOU NEED TO UNDERSTAND ABOUT YOUR BUDGET?

Earlier in this chapter we discussed the need to price your program in the marketplace by looking at the competition and by determining what the perceived value of your program is in the eyes of your audience. We also encouraged you to consider the goal of breaking even financially or even using educational programs to raise funds. This is where a detailed and accurate budget for your program can be an important tool.

Program revenues should not be looked at in a vacuum but rather as part of an overall budget that includes a breakdown of all direct and indirect expenses that can be attributed to your educational program. **Direct expenses** are those costs of goods and services that are purchased specifically for use in planning and implementing the program. These expenses include such things as printing services, postage, telephone calls (especially long distance), supplies, speaker fees, travel and lodging, staff time, and meeting site charges for room rental, food and beverage, audiovisual equipment, and any special logistical needs.

Indirect expenses are generally referred to as overhead or management and general costs. These expenses are simply the basic costs of doing business, of keeping your organization's doors open. Examples of indirect or overhead costs are accounting, salaries and benefits of administrative staff and the executive director, occupancy (office rent, utilities, and maintenance), insurance, legal fees, and equipment. These costs are allocated, on a prorated basis, to all of your nonadministrative activities. Indirect costs also should be allocated in a logical and consistent manner, such as using a formula based on the ratio of non-administrative staff time spent on the educational program in relation to all non-administrative staff time. If uncertain about a meaningful allocation, you may wish to consult with the outside accounting firm that performs your annual audit to seek its advice about your methodology. Chapter 9 of this book, which details how to set up a meaningful chart of accounts, should also help.

Sometimes, there is a tendency to budget only direct costs for an educational program. Certainly, this places less pressure on your budget. But it also gives you an inaccurate picture, one that understates the real costs of planning and implementing the program. Having an accurate budget is especially important when you decide to evaluate the program on the basis of cost versus benefit.

Once you have developed a realistic and accurate budget, the next step is to undertake **break-even analysis,** which is simply determining how many paid attendees you need for your program in order to cover its fixed costs.

Fixed costs are expenses you incur that do not vary with the number of attendees. Generally, these are the costs of planning and promoting your educational program, such as travel and meeting expenses for your program planning committee, printing and mailing of promotional and registration materials, advertising, telephone calls, and preparing and mailing correspondence. They might also include nonrefundable deposits for meeting room rental, food and beverage guarantees, audiovisual equipment rental, and certain speaker fees and travel expenses. These are "up-front" or committed expenses that will not vary with the number of attendees.

Variable, or non-fixed, costs are those expenses that are incurred only if someone attends your program. These typically include the costs of registration, confirmation of the registration, name badge, meals, and handout materials. If a person does not attend the program, you will not incur these costs for that person.

To calculate the **break-even point** for your educational program, first subtract the per person variable cost from the registration fee. Then take the resulting figure and divide it into the total fixed cost. This will give you the number of paid attendees you will need to cover your fixed costs.

Break-even analysis can be very useful in determining "go" or "no go" in a marginal program. If you know the minimum number of attendees you need to break even, and you do not have this number of registrants by a certain date, you have the opportunity of doing some last minute promotion (perhaps via telephone) to increase the number of registrants. You also have the option of cancelling the program and minimizing your out-of-pocket costs by not having to pay speaker travel expenses and full fees, audiovisual charges, and possibly some other fixed costs.

Here is a simple example of the break-even analysis for a small workshop conducted by a nonprofit's volunteers.

Fixed Costs:

Print promotional fliers and envelopes	$ 250.00
Bulk rate postage	150.00
Telephone calls	25.00
Meeting room rental	100.00
Staff time	500.00
Total Fixed Costs	$1,025.00

Variable Costs:

Handout materials (per person)	$ 4.00
Box lunch (per person)	10.00
Morning and afternoon coffee breaks (per person)	6.00
Total Variable Costs	$ 20.00

The registration fee is $45.00 per person. By subtracting the variable cost of $20.00, you end up with a $25.00 contribution per person towards the fixed costs of your workshop. Dividing the total fixed costs of $1,025.00 by $25.00 gives you 41 paid attendees needed to cover your fixed costs.

WHY IS PROGRAM EVALUATION IMPORTANT?

The process of evaluation lets you determine whether, or to what extent, you met the objectives set forth in your program plan. This, in turn, gives valuable information that you can use in planning future educational programs. In order to be a viable tool in this regard, evaluation must meet the following conditions:

- It must be done immediately, while the experience is fresh in the minds of the audience
- The questionnaire (or other evaluation vehicle) should be simple and easy to use, and ask only what you need to know
- The questionnaire should be designed so that tabulation of the responses can take place quickly and inexpensively.

There are many different vehicles for evaluating an educational program. The questionnaire is probably the most common but suffers from the inherent drawback of incorporating the biases of the respondent. Formal testing is apt to produce less biased data but it also is more expensive. Post-program telephone surveys, focus groups, and other more personal kinds of data gathering also can be used.

Regardless of the type of evaluation vehicle you choose, design it around your program objectives and the needs of your audience, as indicated in your pre-program needs assessment. By doing so, you can accurately measure the success of the educational program against your original assumptions. As you design the questions, also think in terms of the information you want as a program planner, such as:

- Did the program's promotional materials accurately reflect the content of the program?
- Was the presenter's style appropriate for the program content?
- Was the room setup comfortable and conducive to learning?
- How far did you have to travel to attend the program?
- What topics would you like covered in future programs?

The program evaluation also provides an opportunity to "test the waters" for new ideas about program content, format, and geographical location. In addition, you can collect specific demographic information about your attendees that might be useful in developing future educational programs.

Your evaluation tool also should be designed with the total expected attendance in mind. If the education program draws a relatively small number of individuals, the evaluation questionnaire can be somewhat longer and can include more open-ended (subjective) questions. If, however, you have hundreds of attendees at your program, you should try to make the evaluation questionnaire as brief as possible (but still solicit the data you consider to be important) and limit the use of open-ended questions. Large numbers of subjective responses are very difficult to tabulate into a meaningful summary. They also drastically slow down the tabulation process and drive up its cost.

For the objective questions, stay away from those with "yes" and "no" answers and instead use ones with multiple choice answers and answers that are variable (on a scale of 1 to 5, best to worst, strongly agree to strongly disagree, etc.). These types of questions give you answers that are easier to tabulate and analyze and are more statistically valid.

Overall, a good evaluation mechanism will tell you to what extent the attendees felt their needs were addressed by your educational program, and whether or not your own program objectives were met. Along with an accurate comparison of the program's actual revenues and expenses to the budgeted amounts, you should have adequate data to judge the success of your educational program and to plan for future programs.

One last thing to remember is that putting the needs of your customer (target audience) first is expected in today's society! They are paying for something of value and it is your organization's responsibility to deliver that value with minimum effort on their part. This is just good, basic customer service and is often the key to "hooking" a person for supporting your organization or, at the very least, bringing participants back for a future educational program.

Good customer service also means that you subscribe to the notion that the customer is always right! Consider standing behind your educational product with a no-questions-asked, money-back guarantee. Remember, a good experience on the part of your target audience sets the scene for positive referrals and continued support. In contrast, bad news travels fast and can undermine the success of your organization's future programs, educational and other, in pursuit of your mission.

CHECKLIST FOR EFFECTIVE EDUCATION PROGRAMS

Determine the need for education:

- ☐ Survey your internal market
- ☐ Survey your external market
- ☐ Assess the competition
- ☐ Analyze the environment

Develop a plan:

- ☐ Identify your target audience
- ☐ Determine the content of your program
- ☐ Select a facility or site
- ☐ Determine the best time to schedule your program
- ☐ Develop a list of reasons why people should attend
- ☐ List what needs to be accomplished (tasks)
- ☐ Establish when the tasks need to be completed (deadlines)
- ☐ Draft specific objectives and make them measurable
- ☐ Identify resources (staff, materials, etc.) needed to achieve the program's objectives and complete the tasks

Choose the most appropriate medium to use:

- □ Workshops and seminars?
- □ Meetings and conferences?
- □ Electronic media?
- □ Publications and printed materials?

Build credibility into your program:

- □ Select qualified speakers and presenters
- □ Organize the program's elements well and plan for the unexpected
- □ Ensure that date, time, site location, length, and registration process are convenient for the target audience
- □ Price the program so it is competitive with similar programs
- □ Arrange for granting continuing education units, if appropriate

Promote the program and provide easy access:

- □ Choose the right promotional medium (advertising, special events, direct mail, etc.)
- □ Design your message to be hard hitting, brief, and clear
- □ Repeat your message again, again, and again!
- □ Schedule your promotion early and often
- □ In addition to pricing the program competitively, encourage early payment by giving an "early bird" discount and by accepting major credit cards
- □ Make registration simple and easy by using a printed registration form and offering telephone registration
- □ Stand behind your product by offering a money-back guarantee

Develop a budget:

- □ Calculate direct and indirect expenses
- □ Calculate fixed and variable costs
- □ Calculate a break-even analysis

Plan your program evaluation mechanism:

☐ Provide for immediate feedback at the program site
☐ Make the evaluation form simple and easy to use
☐ Design the evaluation form so that tabulation is quick and inexpensive

CHAPTER SIX

Mastering the Meeting Planner's Puzzle

With the right plan and careful execution, you can conduct a meeting that meets your objectives, enhances your organization's reputation, and even raises money. This chapter provides step-by-step guidance on developing the overall plan *and* tracking the details of a successful meeting.

Skilled executives of nonprofits put as much effort into meetings management as any other operational function. Whether the meeting is small—say, a critical gathering of the executive committee— or as large as an annual membership meeting, attention to detail and planning are essential.

Americans attend meetings. They want to participate, to contribute, to know what's going on, to network, to learn, or perhaps simply not be left out. Planners must know the needs and expectations of their audience.

Meetings are a tool for sharing information, generating ideas, hearing a presentation, planning for the future, and getting together with colleagues. The substance of the meeting must reflect your organization's goals and objectives, as well as address current concerns and challenges.

Participation is a key to the attendees' feeling good about a meeting. Think of when you've felt best about a meeting you've attended. It's undoubtedly been when you've spoken up, asked questions, and had your opinions count. Receiving a report on operations might be important, but debating a future course of action is much more satisfying. In meetings large and small, structuring the program or agenda to increase discussion is an art form practiced by the most successful.

Still, every meeting planner knows that it's the details that can kill you. Room size, seating arrangements, lighting, food, efficiencies, and comforts do make a difference.

A successful meeting is a product of good planning. Regardless of the type of meeting, its location, or its size, you will need to organize the function piece by piece as you would an elaborate puzzle, all the time paying close attention to what may seem to be an endless chain of details. Your task is to create a meeting or event that runs without a hitch and meets its goals. It's probably no exaggeration to say that everyone has sat through a meeting that has little coherence, little educational value, and no uplifting results. With the right plan, you can create a meeting that achieves your objectives, enhances your organization's reputation, and produces a surplus of income over expenses.

In this chapter we will look at the steps in planning a typical meeting of about 300 people. The same basic process applies to smaller meetings (scaled back perhaps), and can be extended to organizing even the largest of meetings.

Meetings have two basic components: the content of the meeting and the administration of the meeting. The content is the substance of the meeting, which includes speakers, panels, the venue, and the food and beverage functions. The administration of the meeting is the oversight component. This responsibility is normally assigned to one person, the chairman of the planning committee or a designee from your staff. The task will be both anticipatory and reactive, to meet the expectations and needs of the meeting attendees. Regardless of how much planning effort has been expended, there are virtually no meetings that will proceed from their opening event through adjournment and not require some tactical response to events.

DESIGNING YOUR MEETING

There are three steps to consider in designing a meeting.

1. Consider your purpose and your audience: who they are, why are they meeting at this time, what type of information they are seeking, what location is preferable, why this conference will be valuable to them personally, and what kind of social events are appropriate. Is continuing education in demand? Is raising awareness of a specific issue or issues the goal? Is the principal purpose to promote the organization and its activities

to present and future supporters? If you carefully determine these details and spell out exactly what it is that your audience will be able to take away from the meeting (both tangible and intangible), you will be well on your way to a marketable and successful event.

2. Set the specific framework for your meeting.
   - What is the desired outcome of the meeting for the organization?
   - What are the expectations of those who will attend? How will the meeting be structured to assure that those expectations are met? Participants must leave the meeting feeling it was worth their while. Know the demographics, education, career level, etc. of the expected audience.
   - Have the logistics taken into account the needs of potential attendees? Ease of transportation and timing, so that there are no conflicting events, holidays, or competing meetings, are priorities.

   It is important to clearly understand all of this information and how it interrelates. This understanding will allow you to select the appropriate site, build a functional schedule of events, present relevant speakers, attract the desired audience, and add to their understanding of the subjects discussed.

3. Designate and empower the meeting's coordinator in a role analogous to that of the conductor and the planning committee to that of the orchestra; the coordinator must be the leader, with all the details firmly in mind and on paper.

Conventions, trade shows, banquets, or any larger meeting will benefit from the services of a professional meeting planner. Often, the savings a professional can direct a nonprofit toward will more than make up the professional's cost. See Chapter 13 of this book on using consultants for ideas on how and when to consider this option.

Although the following mainly pertains to conference and convention planning, many elements are essential for other kinds of meetings.

Meeting Schedule

If planning a new meeting, look at those run by other organizations and those you have attended in the past. If, as is often the case, you are building from the model of a previous meeting, analyze what worked well and what did not. The form may be dictated by content, number of days, or how the sessions fit together. Put together a working grid or chart representing the time and length of sessions, which quickly demonstrates how events fit together and minimizes conflicts, particularly if the meeting breaks into concurrent sessions. Do not overlook adequate time for breaks, lunch, and the time it takes to move from session to session. But smaller, less complicated meetings also require a schedule. Blocks of free time should also be built into most schedules.

Regardless of length, a meeting theme or key issue should run consistently throughout the event (although a concurrent session or workshop might address other issues or include a separate value-added topic). In planning a conference, consider a general session of up to one hour to open the event, during which the keynote speaker will set the tone for the entire conference. The general session is also a chance for organization officials to make announcements about the organization, to indicate changes in the schedule, and to give a brief overview of what the time spent at the event will entail and deliver to the audience.

In a similar vein, the closing session should end the conference on a positive note. If placed at the end of the conference—after all seminars and breakout sessions—and featuring a speaker of some import, the closing session may prompt people to stay through the final day. If final sessions are sparsely attended, that lesson should be remembered for next year's conference planning.

Special Events

Special events can offer opportunities to share an experience or add a social event to the meeting. In some cases, special events can draw attendance to the conference. They must, however, be thought of in relationship to the overall meeting puzzle you are building. Consider how the proposed special event will meet the overall event objectives, sponsor(s) goals, audience expectations, budget parameters, and locale. Special events can run the gamut from a special opening ceremony to a luncheon banquet with a celebrity speaker, to a breakfast session, to a night of entertainment, to a night on the town, to a 10K run. Other possibilities are recognition from the mayor of significant accomplishments of your members or the announcement of the formation of a special task force.

When beginning to plan the special event, consider all possibilities. Be creative. The best special events are ones that engage, celebrate, create connections, and provide for dialogue among attendees. Search for ways to break the ice, to involve participants, and to create a memorable environment. Detail each component of the event as carefully as you detailed the overall meeting schedule. Tap into all available resources of both the facility you are booking and the community.

Choosing Speakers

After the design of the conference is set, potential speakers can be chosen and contacted. Speakers and panelists are often recommended by executives in your organization or by other community members. It is important for the coordinator to make sure that people recommending speakers are well informed about the theme and the goals of the meeting and how the session fits the objectives. A poor speaker can put a damper on any meeting. Many organizations will not permit a speaker to be engaged unless one of the key board or planning team members has actually heard a presentation by the speaker. You can also increase your comfort level by checking references, listening to tapes of previous engagements, or conducting interviews with potential speakers.

The keynote speaker sets the tone for the meeting and poses specific questions that participants should seek answers for during the rest of the meeting. The opening ceremony should crystalize in the attendees' minds their reasons for attending the conference, and help them shape their personal plan of action to reap the greatest benefits.

Speakers need to know:

- The audience profile and the audience expectations, as well as the potential size of the audience.

- The key points you expect to be covered in the presentation. What is really essential for your audience to get? You may even suggest some points for your speaker to incorporate.

- The total time on stage and how much time is reserved for questions and discussion. This question time, by the way, is often the most valuable and highly rated by audiences. Canned presentations are one thing, but the opportunity to ask questions of an expert on a particular issue is almost always well-received. Always "seed" a couple of questions to get this period started smoothly.

- What kind of audiovisual support will the speaker need? Will he stand at the podium or walk around a lot? (Encourage movement and obtain 30'+ cords or wireless microphones.)
- What are the fee/honorarium, travel, accommodation requirements, and what stipulations are there with regard to taping sessions? Be sure to clarify *all* expenses to avoid awkward situations later.

Similar attention should be given to panelists and moderators. For small meetings, a designated facilitator can guide the participants to accomplish their task in the time allowed.

All of the above information should be captured and confirmed in writing to all parties involved, especially the speakers. Be sure to confirm back to the speaker the date, day, length, and location of the presentation as well as any fees that were discussed, even if all the other questions have not been answered. A speaker should want to spend this kind of discussion time with you to ensure all objectives are met. It helps to also confirm to the speaker your planning objectives/theme for the event.

Early confirmation of speakers allows your organization to use the identities of the speakers in your marketing campaign; "name" speakers can draw extra attendees. Sometimes early confirmation isn't possible, particularly with politicians who are unable to predict if they will be free or not. Be aware that political speakers will sometimes cancel out. You will need to consider back-ups, just in case.

If a controversial figure is chosen to speak, the heads of the organization should be notified before the contract is signed. This could preclude any embarrassment to the sponsor; however, some organizations may value a lively discussion. Keynote speakers are generally paid an honorarium of $500 to $10,000 (superstars, such as network newscasters or other celebrities, can be even much more expensive). The honorarium for speakers for smaller sessions should be the same across the board, and lower than a keynote speaker. Sometimes, reimbursement of travel, hotel expenses, and free admission to the conference is the fee. Contracts or letters confirming arrangements should be precise on both fees and expenses.

Speaker contracts might include the following:

- Permission to release biography and photograph of the speaker to potential attendees and the press.
- Permission for the organization to tape the session.
- Request for copies of presentation, if in written form.

- Needs for special equipment.
- Arrangements for room and transportation (if rooms are billed directly to your organization, the hotel should understand that incidentals, such as long distance telephone, are not included).
- Date of final confirmation.
- Any special security arrangements.
- Contracts with an entertainer or talent agent should put in writing the agreement as to dates, fees, travel, accommodations, commissions, substitutions, staff costs, equipment costs, and stipulations concerning cancellation.

Site Selection

At first glance the selection of site may seem easy. It may appear as simple as asking: What is the site at which your members feel comfortable? Is there an unusual site that might be available to you? Which city would people in your organization like to visit? But finding the right site is not a simple task. It must take into consideration what facilities are available in a given place, what kind of atmosphere is desired, what the housing situation is, what cultural and/or sports activities are possible, and what tours are possible from the site before, during, and/or after the conference. And, of course, the projected number of attendees will determine the size of facilities needed. Check, too, availability dates of the facilities and consider weather conditions at the site for the time of year you're there. The first contact at a hotel would usually be its sales or convention services department.

In addition to hotels, there are many other places to consider as potential sites: restaurants, banquet halls, universities, convention centers, country clubs, theaters, museums, resorts.

When a particular event or speaker has been successful, do not repeat that event or presentation at another meeting of the same attendees too soon after the success. While it may be tempting to repeat a successful event, it may not work the second time and may remove some of the luster from the original event. See Exhibit 6–3 for a suggested checklist for site selection.

A nonprofit organization in Washington dedicated to helping local courts deal with rising caseloads without impairing justice held its tenth annual meeting and reception in a reserved room at the U.S. Supreme Court. The site ensured a good turnout of judges from the local Superior and District

Courts and from practicing attorneys, who were rewarded when a Supreme Court Justice welcomed attendees and spoke briefly on the role of juries. But, wisely not repeating itself, the next year the organization held its meeting at a site closer to the local courts, featuring a presentation by a local city leader.

Choice of housing—for a convention, conference, or any meeting drawing attendees from out-of-town—can depend on its cost, its location, its accessibility to physically handicapped guests, and its availability at the time you need it. Also consider the physical layout of the facility for your desired traffic flow and the type of rooms (both sleeping and meeting) to be sure you can meet your objectives.

The variety of meeting rooms available is very important. For example, a meeting of 30 people is best facilitated in a small meeting room and with a hollow square or an U-shape configuration (where long tables are set in either a U or a box shape). The opening session of a conference for 2,000 persons requires a large, auditorium-style room. Workshops may need tables set up in classroom style, so each participant has a hard surface to write on. And, if you are unsure as to the expected numbers, knowing how space can be utilized through use of airwalls (walls that can be pulled open, closed, or reconfigured to create different sizes of rooms) is a critical discussion between you and the facility manager. Consider how many concurrent sessions you will have and if there are enough rooms available. Understand how soundproof (*or not*) the walls are and what might be happening in the foyer outside of the session (light, sound, etc.). Traffic flow of the conference should be taken into consideration; concurrent sessions may cause problems. Know the number of rooms and the floorplan of the location.

And keep in mind that flexibility in timing can add greatly to your negotiating strength with hotels or other facilities. Published rates should be only a starting point for your discussion.

Budgeting a Meeting

Which comes first, the chicken or the egg? Projected income or expenses? The objective of your meeting will dictate this philosophy, but whatever it is beware of the temptation to overestimate income and underestimate expenses. Be realistic, cautious, and conservative. It is easy to overlook hidden costs (insurance liability, music licensing fees, taxes and gratuities, the cost of room rental if negotiated food and beverage or sleeping usage is not realized).

There are, of course, differences between developing a budget for a convention with an exhibit and the budget for a one-day meeting or educational seminar. While the smaller meeting may have an exhibit, it is most likely to be educational in orientation and not generate significant revenues. Consider inexpensive table-top displays if your group represents a potential market for local firms. When established and planned well, an exhibition can bring in a substantial amount of money for an organization's operating expenses throughout the year. But establishing an exhibit can be a long process during which profit is not always come by so easily. Creating a successful trade exhibition takes several years and is labor-intensive.

Corporations may be willing to sponsor luncheons or other events if they are given credit in the program or on display posters at the meeting. Without an income-producing exhibit or sponsorships, most of the income will come from fees paid by the participants, as well as in-house funding. Estimates of registration fees should take into account early-bird as well as later registration fees. Nonprofit organizations can also obtain grants from other groups or contributions from an organization joining the meeting as a cosponsor. Paid ads can be placed in the meeting's program. Food and beverage functions not included in the conference fee can be sold on an *a la carte* basis bringing in additional income; through ticket sales, you will be able to make accurate food and beverage guarantees. Local corporations or suppliers to a trade association's members will often sponsor luncheons or other events. Other potential sources of income are audio tapes, publications, novelties and mementos, and tours (although some income may be subject to taxation as unrelated business income, for which see Chapter 12).

The first budget estimates are based on general calculations, determined by site, numbers expected, days of the conference, etc. A budget can only be finalized late in the planning process and still won't be penny-exact. Although the coordinator should be the keeper of the budget, the final responsibility still lies with the executive director. The most efficiency can be gained by setting up a computer program for the budget that will recalculate expenses and income and total budget when changes are made.

Computer-generated spreadsheets offer the opportunity to conduct "what if . . ." analyses. "What will the effect be on my bottom line if I increase the program fee by $25 per person while holding my projected registration constant? What will happen if I get 25 percent fewer people than I originally projected? What will the effect be on my bottom line if I do additional mailing that results in a 10 percent increase in registration?" These are all considerations you can, and should, look at when planning the budget.

Every possible expense should be budgeted, with a contingency (5 percent) set aside for unexpected charges. It is prudent to never surprise or be surprised when dealing with financial projections. In your overall plan, set dates (90, 45, and 30 days out) where you can reevaluate and make changes. Preregistration numbers should be reviewed and the entire planning team should review the budget and possible cutbacks. It is possible no cutbacks would be desirable, but the team should give this their consideration and make a decision.

A working format for developing a meeting budget is shown in Exhibit 6–1.

Critical Dates List

An early creation of a timetable for your event is essential. The dates when actions should be completed will vary with the complexity and size of the meeting you are planning. Exhibit 6–2 is a critical dates list which can be used as a working tool toward a complete list of your own. The time frames vary, of course, depending on the size and complexity of the event: major trade shows execute site contracts five or more years in advance, while smaller meetings can be pulled together in a few months' time. Give yourself as much time as possible and be sure to add completion dates and name of the person responsible for each action.

Contracts

Solid contracts are the result of clear and documented understandings by both parties. Their importance can not be overemphasized, even for a small meeting. Contracts, or written letters of agreement, should be prepared and consigned by a qualified representative of the sponsoring organization and the providers of ground and air transportation, hotel and/or other facilities, entertainment, decorators, security, temporary personnel, and any professional speakers. As a general rule, all contracts with facilities and suppliers should clearly state:

- Day, date, to/from time of commitment or performance, to/from time for setup and teardown, location.

Exhibit 6–1   Budgeting Meetings

Income	*Expenses*
Advertising revenue	Audiovisual equipment/supplies
Audio taping royalties	Awards/gifts
Continuing education fees	Computer programming
Corporate sponsorships	Contract services
Exhibit fees	Deposits
Miscellaneous	Entertainment
Nonprofit sponsorships	Equipment rental
Program sales	Exhibit costs
Registration fees	Food and beverage
Sports day fees	Gratuities
Spouse program fees	Insurance
Suite assessments	Interpreters
Ticket sales	Labor
Tour fees	Marketing expenses
Transportation rebate	Photography
	Press room
	Printing
	Security
	Shipping/freight
	Signage
	Speakers
	Staff time charges
	Supplies
	Telephone costs
	Transportation
	Travel
	Xerox

- Compliance with hotel/motel fire safety code and applicable federal, state, and local laws, including the Americans with Disabilities Act.

- Liability and insurance coverage.

- Terms of usage or commitment (day-by-day sleeping room block, meeting space usage, special considerations).

- Financial considerations, deposit, balance due, and past due dates and penalties.

Exhibit 6–2   Critical Dates Checklist

(Revise to accommodate special requirements; size of meeting is the major variable)

Twelve months in advance:
    Select dates.
    Commit to location.
    Discuss program and contact potential speakers.
    Begin designing promotional materials.
    Establish budget.
Ten months in advance:
    Finalize program and begin speaker selection.
    Finish promotional materials and send to printer.
Eight months in advance:
    Obtain registration mailing lists.
    Identify services required, such as entertainers, special amusements, A/V,
        and begin selection process.
    Begin placements of magazine ads if used.
Six months in advance:
    Contact catering department for initial menus and confirm prices.
    Develop floor plans for meeting.
Four months in advance:
    Mail first group of registration forms.
    Request audiovisual requirements, biographies, etc., from speakers.
    Ads begin to appear.
Two months in advance:
    Begin rooming list/assignment of VIP suites.
    Reconfirm all suppliers and communicate final requirements.
One week to one day in advance:
    Give hotel, food and beverage guarantee counts (usually 48-72 hours).
    Assemble and ship registration materials.
    Check in and observe meeting room set-ups.
Supervise meeting.
Post procedures:
    Thank-you letters to hotel, speakers, and memo to staff.
    Pay invoices.
    Make master list of expenses for future reference.
    Review evaluations and start planning for next year.

- Name(s) of responsible parties who will be contacts or provide services.
- Quantities, types, and sizes of food and beverage requirements.
- Complimentary commitments to include accommodations (one "comp" sleeping room night per 50 is standard), complimentary suite for key volunteer or reduced rate staff/speaker rooms, and complimentary meeting space because of food and beverage service.
- Cancellation and/or attrition clauses should stipulate the respective responsibilities of both parties and the penalties that would be suffered if terms are not met. Actual dates, quantities, and dollars should be clearly reflected.

All items that require a contract or written agreement are negotiable. Never hesitate to seek final arrangements that meet your overall objectives and then be certain to confirm in writing.

Marketing and Public Relations

Have you ever received a brochure that piqued your interest in a meeting? If so, it was probably because the sponsoring organization had a good marketing plan. They understood that you had a need that could be met by the activities that would take place at their meeting, and they communicated that information to you in a clear and interesting way.

Marketing is essential for the planning of a successful meeting, and effective promotion is necessary to stimulate need, build attendance, and reinforce the sponsoring organization's image.

The meeting coordinator should be involved in the marketing plan for the meeting, but because the meeting will probably be only one of an array of products and services offered by the organization, promotion should be a part of the organization's overall marketing plan. (See Chapter 4 for more information on marketing and promotion.)

Public relations serves a different purpose: to publicize the organization and the special features of its conference. Public relations, however, is more than just an effort to provide one-time publicity; it transmits the image of the sponsor and of everyone involved with producing and running the conference. Like your marketing effort, public relations should be undertaken by a specialist in that area, because generating coverage by the media can be perplexing and even intimidating. It is crucial, however, that the meeting coordinator at least be familiar with the goals of public relations. In large organizations, a public relations staff will conduct the services at a conference, but that staff must remain in touch with the meeting coordinator. (See Chapter 7 on public relations for ideas.)

CONFERENCE ACTIVITIES

Registration

Registration is usually the first point of contact for your audience and remains a focal point throughout the event. When registration is efficient and friendly, it bodes well for the meeting. As a rule, a preregistered guest should not have to spend more than a minute on site to pick up credentials and be on his or her way.

Registration procedures have become much more efficient and orderly with the use of computer programming. A well-thought-out system should be planned before the registration forms are mailed. You can then collect data that is meaningful (be sure to plan for data that can track demographics for later use). Weekly reports will allow you to measure your ongoing registration pickup and the potential financial impact. (Chapter 10 discusses how to choose off-the-shelf computer packages.)

A registration system could include:

- Reminder notices to all delegates giving them the date and time of the sessions they plan to attend.
- Accurate recordkeeping and financial data.
- Accurate counts, meeting room requirements, and food and beverage guarantees.
- Valuable information for speakers and discussion leaders, such as an advance list of the people who will attend specific sessions.
- A complete, alphabetical advance registration list that is updated weekly. (Also, an exhibitor list, if appropriate.)
- A final list ready for publication and distribution at the conference.
- A prospective member mailing list that can be used for future conference announcements as well as membership promotion campaigns.

In the overall registration process, the first step is to develop a system and procedures that will work for your overall objectives.

Then, develop a registration form that will capture all needed information:

- Name.
- Business address (first name and title as it should appear on name badge).
- Telephone/facsimile numbers.
- Choice of events if additional fees are charged for optional events such as workshops, tours, banquets.
- Reservations for special events.
- Method of payment.
- Hotel registration form or guidance on hotel registration.

Forms should state the sponsor's cancellation policy. VIP registration forms should be designed to accommodate speakers, key organization members, and other special guests.

Sleeping rooms will be very important to participants in an out-of-town event. A housing form can be prepared (although all hotels listed on it must sign off on the form before it is used) and mailed along with your registration form. Another option would be to have the hotel provide reservation cards (not easily done if more than one hotel is offered as a choice) that are mailed with the initial marketing piece or along with registration confirmations. A third option would be to provide a hotel reservation phone number and have participants call the hotel(s) directly. Your objective should be to ensure that you meet contractual obligations to your hotel and that your participants are handled properly and expeditiously. You must also be sure to communicate the room rate, check-in and -out times, no-show penalties, deposit requirements, the cutoff date, and the credit cards that will be accepted. Discuss the form and the procedure with the hotel convention services or reservations manager. It will also be important to understand exactly how each room reservation will be confirmed to each guest (either by you or by the hotel).

The cutoff date is the date, per your contract with the hotel, when the hotel is: (a) no longer required to hold your block of rooms and can release any unbooked rooms to the general public; and (b) when the discounted and negotiated group rate might no longer apply and the hotel can sell the rooms at a higher rate. Be certain to take care of all speaker and VIP reservations before this date. After discussion with the hotel on their potential for sellout and your need for additional rooms, you may want to guarantee more rooms. Remember, sleeping rooms are similar to a perishable food item. If they are not consumed on a given night, they have no value. The hotel's objective is to sell every available room every night. If you receive "comp" rooms, be sure they are determined cumulatively, not daily.

On-site, the registration desk should be centrally located, with plenty of light and ventilation. The desk should be staffed with adequate personnel, either in-house or outside paid staff or volunteers. Separate preregistration lines can speed traffic flow. Prepared registration packets contain the conference schedule, as well as other information. Badges should be given out on-site rather than premailed, as some preregistrants may forget to bring them.

Be certain that you have established a solid financial control system that will pass an audit and that money handlers are bonded. Numbered forms and tickets that are assigned and accounted for are a good beginning.

The registration packet includes a program book or on-site agenda. For a small meeting this may be merely a page or two listing the agenda, speakers, and any other relevant information. For large meetings, and particularly those with exhibitions, the program book will be much more detailed to orient participants to both the meeting sessions and the exhibition floor. Work on the program booklet should begin as soon as speakers and exhibitors are contracted, but it should be printed as late as possible to allow for changes. Production costs of this book must be included in the overall budget.

Specification Sheets

Specification sheets (specs) are written step-by-step directions that are given to the hotel at least 30 days in advance of the actual event. The specification sheets should include:

- Event Name.
- Event Day, Date, and Time.
- Assigned Room Name.
- The Times Setup Begins and Doors Open.
- Food and Beverage Requirements (to include guarantees).
- Setup Instructions (Table layout as classroom or auditorium or U-shape, for example) 6' or 8' tables and number of chairs per table, water on tables or in back of room, aisles, staging, etc.).
- AV Requirements (35mm, overhead, video specifying exact type, screen size, draping, microphones specifying exact type).

- Billing Instructions.
- Contact Person at your organization.
- Any Special Instructions.

Script

A complete script adds a higher level of professionalism to banquets, award ceremonies, or other critical parts of your event. It should include a minute-by-minute dialogue including all speeches, awards, light and sound cues, who goes to the stage when, speaker introductions, etc. As a real-time guide to a successful event, it will provide an immeasurable level of comfort to all podium participants, the audiovisual support staff, the hotel, and you. The script can be the difference between a flawless performance and one with obvious glitches.

On-Site Logistics and Staff

Meeting coordinators should arrive at the conference site early, the exact time determined by the complexity of the meeting setup. A preconference meeting can resolve potential logistical problems which could start a meeting off on the wrong foot. This early time should be spent making sure all needed supplies are on hand (carefully check off a list of shipping forms to be certain everything arrived) and reconfirming specifications with the hotel. Are the room sizes still appropriate for your audience, especially if your numbers increased or decreased? You may want to change your room setups on paper before hotel staff moves staging, chairs, and tables into the positions you outlined in your specs. Will there be other groups meeting in rooms adjacent to yours or moving through public space at the same time? It isn't too late to discuss crowd and noise control with your hotel convention services manager.

A "precon" meeting with the hotel staff usually takes place on the day prior to when your event actually convenes and includes all the facility department heads and other key suppliers. Use this opportunity to review and update your specifications. This is your last chance to be sure that the instructions you have detailed were communicated to every responsible hotel department and were understood.

As the meeting planner, you need to be sure that you have enough staff on-site and have preassigned responsibilities and times when these things must be completed. Staff need to understand that if they cannot complete an assigned responsibility they must find someone else to complete it for them. (Volunteer leaders often make special requests that can pull assigned staff in other directions.)

Transportation

For a large meeting, the meeting planner negotiates with local transportation companies to provide travel to and from the airport, buses for tours, field trips, and sightseeing, and round-trip shuttle service from hotels to the meeting location (particularly used to transfer attendees from hotels to convention centers and back, which can be a significant distance.) The service records of local transportation companies may help in the decision of which group to contract with. Be certain appropriate insurance is carried by the provider and liability waivers are in order.

A staff person should be appointed the transportation liaison. If outings such as tours and field trips are planned, each bus should have a staff monitor to avoid leaving behind members of the outing at stops along the way.

Members of a professional building industry organization at a committee meeting went to Monticello, Thomas Jefferson's home in Charlottesville, Virginia, on a special tour after normal visitor hours. The tour was very exciting as the sun was setting in the west and the group explored Jefferson's masterpiece by flashlight and portable lights. Five people from the group strayed off and missed the busses when they departed for their hotel. It looked like a long—and probably wonderful—night in Mr. Jefferson's home until the group found the only curator left at the house, which, incidentally, is on a hill miles from town.

Special Guests/VIPs

Volunteer leaders of an organization donate a great deal of time and energy because of personal commitment or beliefs. There are few rewards beyond public recognition for their effort. For these dedicated and special folks, there are a few things at events that you can do for them. Be certain that there are established guidelines or precedents and that if you begin some new form of recognition, you are prepared for it to be precedent-setting. Special transportation from the airport, a hotel suite or upgrade to a corner room, or an amenity are possibilities that can be negotiated in advance from the hotel. You might also prepare advance check-in, late checkouts, or simple welcome notes.

Dealing with Problems

If the planning has been thorough, major problems are unlikely to occur. But something can go wrong at almost any meeting. Keep your calm. Most disruptions or problems can be addressed. If the meeting organizer is visibly upset, everyone else soon will be, too. If you project an image of calm competence, attendees will likely take the unexpected in stride.

Careful and complete communication with all parties involved will preclude nightmares similar to the following from happening at your special event:

- The band that you hired to play light jazz for the next 3 hours, just showed up 15 minutes late in boots and jeans and only knows country.
- The celebratory "sparklers" turn out to not be of the indoors variety and set off alarms and sprinklers.
- The after-dinner comedian's ethnic, racial, or political jokes insult someone in your audience.
- You have preassigned seating and mistakenly assigned to a table of 10, 15 people who are not happy while they stand at the table and try to figure out where the extra five will sit.
- You learn the microphone does not work just as the most senior official begins to make welcoming announcements.
- There are no vegetable or kosher plates available for special requests.
- The special awards are not to be found, and everyone is on stage expecting awards, handshakes, and photo opportunities.
- The event went very well but the final bill is 25 percent over budget.

If you have planned carefully and attempted to anticipate the foreseeable problems, you will be available to deal with unexpected events (like power outages, more people than you guaranteed showing up, the speaker's plane being delayed, or an internal political issue). With poor planning, routine issues will become problems and anything unexpected is likely to turn into disaster.

POSTCONFERENCE ACTIVITIES
Conference Evaluation

The conference is over and the participants have left for home. You wonder: How well did the meeting go? What did the participants get out of the conference? Did this meeting accomplish its objectives? What worked? What didn't? What kind of changes could be made? What did people learn? How important was this learning? The evaluation process is one that needs to be carefully thought out as the meeting is planned.

An evaluation of a meeting by the participants can be very valuable in improving subsequent meetings. Your evaluations should measure performance against your event objectives. Speakers should be measured on presentation and content (Was the material presented relative to your own organizational needs? Did you gain practical/applicable information from the presentation?). Make sure that there is a reason for the data you will be gathering, and if not, don't ask that particular question. Evaluations that are brief gather more information because more are returned than a long evaluation. There are many different kinds of evaluations. Consider cost, design, collection methods, and expertise required to format and collect the data. Ask some open-ended questions, particularly "What would you like us to do differently next year?" and "What was the most valuable event at this meeting?" Be sure to provide an address on the evaluation for sending by individuals who complete it on the plane or after they get home. Most importantly, be sure to read, evaluate, and make changes based on the feedback you receive! Evaluations can be extensive; just be sure they are accurate and reflect membership/attendees requirements.

WRAP-UP

A complete financial history of the conference should be completed within 30 days. It should include income and expenses compared to budget; food, and beverage actual consumption compared to your guarantees; types of food and alcohol consumption that may be different from what you initially ordered; and final registrant counts. This kind of history will be invaluable to your next event planning.

Thank-you letters to speakers, vendors, staff, and volunteers are in order. They should be prepared within 10 days, recognize specific efforts, and be signed by appropriate organizational representatives. Gratuities may also be given to hotel staff or suppliers for outstanding performance; if you are unsure of the appropriate amounts, a frank discussion with your convention services manager will be helpful in deciding for whom and how much.

Looking Forward

In the end, a question arises: Shall we do it again? Yes—particularly if your event met its objectives. The coming together of people for a common cause can be extremely rewarding, both for long and short term, and it can foster the beginning of positive change. Meetings, whether committees session, award banquets, educational seminars, or giant trade exhibits, can define an organization and enhance its full range of activities. The key is planning, planning, planning.

Exhibit 6–3   Suggested Checklist for Site Selection

Location:
    Is the site easily accessible by ground and air to your participants?
    Is the site positioned to planned pre- and postconference events?
    Is the climate at the site at the time of the conference acceptable?
    Is the ambience of the site appropriate for your event?

Past History:
    Check references with others who have used the site for similar events.
    Has the sponsor used this site before?
    Who owns and who manages the property?
    Are there labor negotiations that will take place anytime close to your event?

Service Facilities:
    Is a car rental service provided on site?
    What recreational facilities are provided on site?
    Does the site have any arrangements with nearby facilities?
    Does the site charge any fees for using the facilities?
    Are shops located on site?
    Are there quick copy or other office services on site?

Accommodations:
    How many rooms will the property commit for your event?
    What are the different types of sleeping rooms, how many of each, and what
        is the pricing structure?
    Will early arrivals accommodations for officers/VIPs be available?
    Do all sleeping rooms have TV, radio, clocks, coffeemakers, remote control,
        air conditioning, state of the art fire detection and alarms?
    Are newspapers, turndown, or other amenities available or standard?
    Is the level of housekeeping acceptable?
    Are some sleeping rooms designated no-smoking rooms?
    Do enough rooms meet the guideline of the American Disabilities Act and
        are they available for your event?

Exhibit 6–3 *(Continued)*

Is room service available and during what hours?

What time is checkin/checkout and will early arrivals be available for staff or VIPs?

Does the site have express checkout?

Site Personnel:

Do the site personnel need special orientation?

Are bell people appropriately dressed and responsive?

Are front desk personnel polite and efficient?

Is a concierge available to assist guests?

Are the site personnel unionized, and, if so, what is the current status of the union contract(s)?

Public Areas and Facilities:

Are there enough elevators to handle the movement of participants?

Does the site have signs to welcome participants?

Does the site have facilities for the handicapped?

Are hallways and public areas neat and clean?

Are public washrooms plentiful, clean, and well-equipped?

Are checkrooms available and staffed?

Financial Factors:

What type of financial arrangement will the site require?

Does the site provide complimentary meeting rooms based on your food and beverage and sleeping room consumption?

Does the site offer an off-season or shoulder rate?

Are rates different on weekdays and weekends?

Is a deposit required by either the organization or individual guests?

What is the site's policy on late arrivals? No-shows?

What type of currency is accepted?

Which credit cards can be used?

Are purchase orders acceptable?

What is the cancellation policy?

Are there insurance requirements?

Who has the responsibility for property damage?

Does the site have any special charge for utilities (electricity, light, labor, air conditioning)?

When will the site guarantee room rates?

What add-ons can be expected (both in additional amenities the site might have that your event can utilize and in extra charges you might incur)?

Safety:

Are site personnel safety-conscious?

Does each room have a smoke alarm and/or sprinkler system?

Does the site have a working fire alarm system?

Does the hotel post evacuation procedures?

Are exits on each floor clearly marked?

What is the system for room key assignment and replacement?

Exhibit 6–3 *(Continued)*

Are safe deposit boxes available?
Does the site maintain a 24-hour security force?
Does the site have a house physician?
How close is the nearest medical facility?
Are site personnel trained in CPR?

General:

Does the site provide transportation for site review?
Is the site planning any construction or remodeling? When and what?
Are internal communication devices available?
What other activities are booked into the site at the same time?
Is the site in full compliance with the American Disabilities Act?

CHAPTER SEVEN

Using Public Relations Tools Effectively

Enhance your image, increase participation, and support fund-raising through effective communications. Every nonprofit needs PR. This chapter introduces you to the public relations tools and techniques you need to get the word out about your organization.

Public relations is the practice of communications with individuals and groups that can influence the success of an organization and the cause, constituency, profession, or industry it represents. Nonprofit groups bring inherent strengths to the pursuit of public relations. Cause-oriented groups and charities are often identified with worthy social goals and can draw upon the enthusiasm of their followers, volunteers, and donors. Trade associations can speak for entire industries, spotlighting the services and products they provide consumers and the people they employ.

Such assets endow nonprofits with an extra measure of credibility. As a result, the news media, lawmakers, and others often seek them out for background information and for articulate positions on critical public issues. Nonprofit groups can also act as a lightning rod for controversy by speaking for their constituency and deflecting criticism from individual members.

Public relations can support many activities in nonprofit groups:

- *Fundraising*—Present the cause or service as worthy enough to merit support by documenting accomplishments and a record of service.

- *Community Awareness*—Build support by highlighting the services provided to the community, such as youth programs, education, health care, food for the hungry, housing for the poor, and environmental preservation.
- *Member Recruitment and Retention*—Communicate the benefits of membership to prospective and existing members.
- *Lobbying and Issue Advocacy*—Generate political support for positions by encouraging the news media to report the group's position and publish supporting editorials.
- *Crisis Management*—Coordinate communications during crises to help those who have been hurt and present the organization as responsible and responsive in trying circumstances.

WHAT IS PUBLIC RELATIONS?

Public relations is not merely an image-building exercise, although one of the goals is often to improve status and prestige. The most effective nonprofit organizations view public relations as two-way communications. It begins by listening to the groups or individuals to be influenced and learning their attitudes about the cause, industry, or profession. The public relations program then develops messages and initiatives that address their concerns. A truism among communications professionals holds that advertising is bought while public relations is earned. An organization can spend millions on an ad campaign that extols its greatness, but the impact will always be diminished by the fact that the praise is self-generated. Through public relations, groups set out to earn praise through good deeds, well-reasoned policies, careful work with the news media, and outreach to valuable constituencies. Trying to solicit praise or support in a self-serving manner often serves to tarnish an image. Rather than trumpeting the organization's greatness, do something that objectively can be deemed worthwhile, or simply make your case in a factual manner, keeping superlatives to a minimum.

Seek a Shared Vision

The most effective programs are based on a shared vision. It is often useful to begin with a brainstorming exercise by the leadership or a committee charged with formulating a public relations plan. Initially this group should analyze the circumstances and consider public relations options, disregarding any constraints imposed by limited resources. The agenda for this session should be as broad as possible:

- What are the strengths of the organization: size, history, committed supporters, political experience, valued products or services, important cause?
- What are the weaknesses: poor public perception, lack of awareness, weak economic condition, declining support, outspoken critics?
- How do perceptions square with realities? To what extent are perceived weaknesses accurate? Do not rush to conclude that all criticisms are unfounded. It is quite likely that some are on target; groups can build credibility by acknowledging faults and taking steps to correct them.
- How do important constituents feel about the organization? Does it elicit respect, fear, frustration, identification, excitement? How would you like them to feel?
- How would the organization operate in an ideal world? How would it be perceived? How would it work with its most important publics, such as supporters, donors, volunteers, members, the news media, lawmakers, community leaders?

The best programs find creative ways to touch a responsive public chord. For example, the campaigns in which guns are exchanged for toys or shoes trade violence for nonviolence. The Doe Fund of New York developed a program to shelter the homeless with a feature that gave it special public appeal: the beneficiaries were given jobs and required to work for their room and board. Employment helps the homeless build self-esteem and the means to support themselves, while paying for food and shelter covers 70 percent of the program's cost. Critics cannot easily dismiss this as a stopgap waste of scarce government funds.

Set Strategic Goals

The next step is to set goals, both short- and long-term, in keeping with your organization's overall strategic plan. Two years from now, how much should public perception change? If 40 percent of the public is now aware of a service or cause, the short-term goal could be to raise awareness to 60 percent, while the long-term one could be 80 percent. Goals can be fund-raising targets or legislative accomplishments. Is there a message or belief you want to impress upon certain individuals and groups? In the short term, you may want to send the message through various media, such as articles, speeches, and direct mail; and for the long term, you would search for evidence that the message was believed. It is often best to state the objectives in specific, measurable terms that lend themselves to cost/benefit analyses, such as the number of potential donors reached, funds raised, or bills passed or defeated. This makes it easier to gauge progress and help supporters appreciate the value of the public relations program.

Take a Resource Inventory

In the planning process, organizations need to take an inventory of their resources. Staff may be needed to create news releases and advisories, background pieces, issue briefs, consumer pamphlets, speeches, and other materials. Administrative support is needed to copy, collate, stuff, and mail out such materials. Other tasks include developing and maintaining mailing lists, contacting the news media, organizing news conferences, and maintaining speakers' bureaus.

For extensive campaigns, you will have to decide whether some or all of the work should be performed by an outside public relations firm. This is not an inexpensive option, but it enables the organization to continue performing its regular duties with minimal disruption. Often, the duties can be shared, delegating to the public relations firm those tasks that the organization lacks the skills or resources to perform well. It is quite possible that the optimum division of labor will change over time with changes in the staff, funding, and mission of the nonprofit group. A less expensive option is to hire freelancers to do the editorial and design work. Chapter 13, on using consultants, provides ideas on pursuing this option.

The inventory of resources should include more than a count of heads, funds, computers, and other physical assets. A nonprofit group can often receive help from its supporters; in fact, volunteers in leadership positions are often the best spokespersons for the organization. Investigate opportunities to join forces with allied organizations having common interests. Advocates for consumer and environmental causes often form coalitions, in some cases bringing in labor unions as well. Food banks often receive public relations support from supermarkets and food processors. Environmental groups find willing partners in the business community whether the cause is planting trees or recycling. Doctors support nonprofit health care agencies. If the program can be designed to offer clear benefits to partners, they may be willing to underwrite much of the costs.

Nonprofit groups can also ask supporters to contribute services or equipment instead of funds. Businesses may be willing to donate computers, software, mailing lists, reference books, and office supplies. They can design and print annual reports, consumer pamphlets, and other materials. Tax deductions may provide a financial incentive. Among your supporters may be professional publicists, reporters, writers, and editors willing to contribute their expertise to a cause they feel strongly about.

The question of resources will ultimately come down to funding. After figuring in the help available from members, volunteers, allies, suppliers, and other sources, what can the organization afford to spend? When public relations programs are considered urgent, organizations have been able to undertake a special fund-raising effort or justify a surcharge on dues. In these instances, nonprofit groups must make a special effort to articulate the benefits of the program in concrete terms—and to keep doing so as long as the program is in place. In effect, a public relations program is needed for the public relations program. All programs need such mechanisms to maintain support, participation, and funding. Groups that rely heavily on new funding sources must make a special effort.

In one of the most successful seasonal campaigns, supporters provide Christmas gifts that are requested by the needy. A church or other nonprofit group simply provides a Christmas Spirit tree and asks low-income families to list items that they need, such as shoes, warm clothes, blankets, and toys. The requests are detailed on cards and hung on the tree; then supporters select the cards and fulfill the requests.

Research Audience and Channels

With the goals and resources identified, the next step is to research the audiences that will be the target of the public relations program and the best means to communicate with them. Public relations programs can take a shotgun approach, but it is often more effective to identify the individuals, leaders, and groups that are most important to achieving the objectives. What are their views and attitudes? Their demographic makeup may be useful to know, especially in fund-raising efforts.

The research may begin with readily available materials, such as books, articles, government reports, opinion surveys and polls, Census Bureau data, and other published materials. Organizations often supplement this with their own research. This can be done through informal meetings with representatives of the target audiences. Use these sessions only to listen and gather information, not to argue with such representatives or try to win them over. You may even want to create a standing advisory council of such people to serve as a sounding board for program ideas and policies.

For a more objective reading of audience views, you can hire an outside firm to perform focus group research. The firm invites a small group of people for a meeting of several hours to discuss a list of topics set with the sponsoring organization. A moderator leads the discussion in a neutral manner, while members of the sponsoring group observe through a one-way mirror. This is the best way to learn about the range of views, the depth of conviction, and any misconceptions. In other words, it is useful qualitative research.

For quantitative research, groups often turn to polls or surveys. A common approach is to mail a list of questions on a postage-return card. The questions should be carefully worded to limit bias. Most should be multiple-choice or true-false, and the list should be short to make it easy for people to complete. The main shortcoming of this method is that it tends to eliminate the respondents who have such a negative view of the group that they throw the card away. Because of this, the survey results are often skewed to the positive side, obscuring problems or misperceptions.

For a truly objective picture, organizations turn to opinion polls in which members of the audience are surveyed by phone. If the audience is the entire public, the calls are made by random dialing. It is best to hire an outside firm to perform such polls. Nonprofit groups with limited budgets can have polling firms ask several questions as a rider on other surveys.

The research you perform at the outset serves as a benchmark by which to gauge progress over the life of the public relations program. Prepare a report summarizing the initial research, then revisit the key topics every three to six months and return to the sources to track changes. Over time, the critical issues and concerns are likely to change, especially if the group effectively engages its constituents in solving problems, allaying fears, and building enthusiasm about progress.

Identify the Best Channels

The growth of the communications industry has produced myriad channels for sending messages—from the special interest magazine and local-access cable channel to *USA Today* and "60 Minutes." The proliferation of outlets is especially helpful for programs targeting special audiences. If you operate in a specific area, develop a list of all the local magazines and newspapers—community, neighborhood, daily, weekly— and radio and television stations that have news programs. Many directories, including those below, are available that list outlets by type, city, and subject.

- *Editor and Publisher International Yearbook*—Write to Editor & Publisher Co., 575 Lexington Avenue, New York, New York 10022; or call 212-675-4380. Covers daily newspapers.
- *Broadcasting Annual*—Write to Broadcasting Magazine, 1705 DeSales Street, N.W., Washington, DC 20036; or call 202-659-2340. Covers most television and radio outlets.
- *Bacon's Publicity Checker*. Five directories: Newspaper/Magazine; Radio/TV/Cable; Media Calendar; Business Media; International Media—Write to Bacon's Information Inc., 332 South Michigan Avenue, Chicago, Illinois 60604; or call 800-621-0561/312-922-2400. Good coverage of the trade and specialty media—also lists the business/financial editors of 700 daily newspapers.
- *National Directory of Weekly Newspapers*—Write to American Newspaper Representative, 84 South 6th Street, Suite 600, Minneapolis, Minnesota 55402; or call 612-332-8686.
- *National Radio Publicity Directory*—Write to Radio and TV Publicity Outlets, Box 1197, New Milford, Connecticut 06776; or call 203-354-9361. Lists radio talk show outlets.
- *All TV Publicity Outlets Nationwide*—Write to Radio and TV Publicity Outlets, Box 1197, New Milford, Connecticut 06776; or call 203-354-9361. Lists broadcast and cable television stations.

- *Working Press of the Nation.* Five directories: I. Newspaper; II. Magazine; III. TV and Radio; IV. Feature Writer and Photographer; V. Internal Publications—Write to The National Research Bureau, 225 West Wacker Drive, Suite 2275, Chicago, Illinois 60606-1229; or call 312-346-9097.
- *Writer's Market*—Write to F&W Publications, 1507 Dana Avenue, Cincinnati, Ohio 45207; or call 513-531-2222. Includes a comprehensive list of magazines with editors' statements of editorial needs.

If the target audience has a common demographic feature, specialty magazines may be an ideal vehicle. A health care organization wanting to teach youths about good nutrition might contact the editors of *Teen, Sassy,* or *Seventeen* magazine. A soup kitchen seeking more support from local supermarkets could approach the state grocers association. Charity leaders in charge of the kitchen could appeal for help in association publications, solicit support in mailings to the members, and speak at its meetings.

The list of news media outlets should include the names of executives who make the editorial decisions and reporters who cover the issues important to the nonprofit organization. The decision makers in the print media appear on the masthead as editor-in-chief. Large dailies also have news executives in charge of major sections, such as the city editor, society page editor, editorial page editor, food editor. At broadcast outlets the people who decide the coverage are usually known as news directors. To identify the reporters, scan the publications, watch or listen to the broadcast outlet, or consult the directories listed above.

In any case, before sending material, it's a good idea to phone the outlet to verify that the key individuals still work there. Since news media outlets have high turnover rates, keeping this contact information current is essential. News media outlets are deluged with mail, and the letters addressed to no one in particular or to someone who has departed often remain in a massive pile whose size is best measured in feet or yards. Most journalists lack the time to winnow through the pile for the few nuggets of news it may yield.

Computer technology is introducing new channels for communications. Trappist monks in the Missouri Ozarks, for example, advertise their fruitcakes on computer bulletin boards, enabling prospective customers to preview the varieties and place orders. In their near future, it is quite likely that computer networks will grow as a medium for public relations messages, especially those aimed at specific audiences. Have your most computer-literate staff members watch for changes in the state of the art that might enhance communications.

COMMUNICATIONS TOOLS

The public relations field offers many methods for sending messages—from the basic news release to a news conference. These tools must be used with care, always keeping in mind the target audience and the need to have all positions and policies built on a foundation of facts and logic.

When to Send a News Release

The most widely used communications tool, the news release, is also the most abused. It should be written in a news style and carry a newsworthy message or story. Nonprofit groups have many occasions for sending out news releases:

- Report that your group expands, introduces new services, moves, or opens a new office.
- Announce accomplishments in fund-raising over a certain time period, emphasizing the number of donors or the amount raised.
- Announce an especially large contribution from a generous donor or a large grant from a foundation or government agency.
- Report the number of people served, healed, fed, or educated over a certain period.
- Provide a timely public service message, such as the clothing needed by the poor before winter or how to recycle cardboard after Christmas.
- Present the group's position on critical issues. This may accompany a recent speech or testimony that details the position.
- Describe the history of the group or its constituency when it reaches a milestone, such as 10, 25, or 50 years. This is a good time to summarize accomplishments. Contrasting your current state with conditions 25, 50, or 100 years ago often serves to

accentuate the progress and value of the group. Juxtaposing photos of the old and new can provide a vivid illustration.

- Describe a moving story that illustrates in human terms the work of the group, such as how a life was saved, a family brought back together, urban youths given career direction, any problem solved through innovation by an individual, group, or company.
- Announce the election of new directors, trustees, or officers.
- The group adopts a new mission, changing or broadening its services or focus.
- You establish an advisory council of constituents to help the group continue its tradition of good service.
- The nonprofit group receives an award, recognition, commendation, or accreditation from another organization or government or community agency.
- A member of the group is honored for outstanding performance or named to a leadership position in a community, government, or charity group.
- The nonprofit group presents an award recognizing someone who has made exemplary contributions to the ideals represented by the group. For example, you can honor a generous donor or a government official who has supported the group. You could establish an annual award in the name of a distinguished member or founder of the group.
- The group sponsors a major community event that is open to the public, such as a festival, fair, or demonstration of valuable skills.
- Report the findings of a new survey you conducted of consumers, constituents, or community residents. This can be the same survey used to track the success of the public relations program.
- In December, comment on the progress made in the year just ending and the goals for the year ahead.

By sending a news release, you advise the news media of your existence and a recent accomplishment or event connected to the group. It is generally not a good idea to follow up by phone after sending a release, unless the story is extremely important and timely. Many reporters feel harassed by follow-up calls and are likely to resent people who call with marginal leads on a regular basis. Do not despair if a release does not immediately generate a story; it may lead to a story at a later date. A steady stream of well-written and -conceived releases can help establish a group as a reliable source of news, and reporters will start calling the organization on a regular basis. As the coverage increases, so will the volume of calls.

Many nonprofits render services that make conspicuous contributions to the quality of life. News releases need only to document the contributions in a descriptive and factual manner.

Facing eviction from its 40-acre home in southern New Jersey, the Avian Rehabilitation Center publicized the fact it treated 2,000 injured birds in 1993—including 35 of endangered or threatened species, such as peregrine falcons, least terns, ospreys, and herons—and returned over 40 percent of its patients to the wild. Such publicity may prove crucial to its campaign to find a new site for operations by the summer of 1994.

Newswriting Style

Just as important as the content of the news release is the style in which it is written. The prevailing approach is based on the idea that people are pressed for time and want to learn the point of the story quickly. Newspapers are designed to be read or scanned during a 15-minute breakfast or train ride. Most broadcast stories are shorter than two minutes.

All the paragraphs in news stories are short; the first one is usually one sentence and the rest generally have no more than two sentences. They deliver the information first and the source second: instead of "ABC Charity President Joe Smith announced today that contributions tripled in 1997," write, "Contributions to ABC Charity tripled in 1997, announced President Joe Smith today." And the most important part of any news story is the beginning: the lead paragraph and the two to three paragraphs that follow. The first few paragraphs should provide a synopsis of the story or so intrigue readers that they feel compelled to read on.

The story that provides a synopsis is called hard news. The reader should be able to learn the essential facts by reading only the first few paragraphs. The second style is soft or feature news; this approach often tries to hook the reader with a human interest angle. A hard news story may begin in this manner:

CHICAGO, ILL., JAN. 5, 1998—The Air Ambulance Service saved 732 lives in 1997, more than double the number in the previous year with most of the increase coming from the blimp explosion over Soldiers Field.

"The record number of saves makes us very proud," said Air Chairman Jack McFly. "We're thankful that the special training in dirigible accidents helped us respond to the Soldiers Field tragedy."

In 1997 the service saved 312 lives in the blimp accident, another 270 from drownings, 23 from fires and 27 from other incidents.

The service was founded in 1958 and currently employs 12 full-time workers and operates four helicopters. A nonprofit group, it is supported by public donations, along with contributions from area hospitals. . . .

A feature story on the same topic might read like this:

When Bruce Leonard first heard about the plan to receive special training in blimp rescues, he scoffed, "We haven't had one of those since the Hindenburg. You've got to be crazy."

Leonard's opinion changed dramatically less than two months later when he was holding his chopper 50 feet above a blazing blimp rescuing 18 terrified passengers—an act of valor that earned him a commendation from the city of Chicago.

The service rescued 312 people in all from the blimp accident over Soldiers Field. This one incident accounted for nearly half of the 721 rescues in 1997—a record and more than twice the number in the previous year. . . .

News releases written in either style should make liberal use of quotes by leaders of the organization. Quotes add color, emphasis, and human interest; and if news outlets do not publish the release, they may pick up some of the quotes.

All releases should observe the conventions of capitalization, abbreviation, hyphenation, and usage that prevail in the news media. The most widely used convention is AP style, as set forth in *The Associated Press Stylebook* (available in many major bookstores or from the Associated Press, 50 Rockefeller Plaza, New York, N.Y. 10020; 212-621-1824). The publication also offers useful grammar guidance.

News Release Format

All news releases must carry certain elements. The first page should appear on the group's letterhead or special letterhead designed for news releases. Special letterhead should include the word NEWS prominently across the top or side, and the name of the group or its field of expertise, such as NEWS FROM ABC CHARITIES or NEWS ABOUT THE HOMELESS. The other necessary elements are described below.

Release Date and Time—Above the headline, advise the news media when they may publish or air the information. In most cases, the instruction will be FOR IMMEDIATE RELEASE. If, for example, you are sending out a release before an event takes place, the instruction should be FOR RELEASE ON (the date and time the event is to occur).

Contact Person—Underneath or across from the release date, provide the name of a person the news media can contact for more information, and type a telephone number under the name. You may also want to provide the contact's home telephone number if calls are anticipated at night or over the weekend.

Headline—Summarize the highlights of the story, drawing from the points made in the first few paragraphs. This could consist of a main head and a kicker above or below. View the headline as an opportunity to sell the story, to encourage the editor or reporter to read on.

Dateline—Most stories should begin with the city and state from which the release is coming (either where the group is headquartered or the site of the event being described) and the date. For example: PEORIA, ILL., AUG. 3, 1999—. . . . Note that AP style requires that the names of states and months be abbreviated except for those with four letters or fewer. A dateline is not needed on feature stories that are not time-sensitive.

Body—Leave several inches of white space above the headline to give news editors room to edit the copy, revise the headline, and insert type specifications. Do not break sentences or paragraphs from one page to the next. Number pages at the top, using either the standard numbers or the traditional news format (ADD ONE for page two, ADD TWO for page three—along with a one- or two-word slug line for the story, for example ADD ONE—RESCUE). Type MORE at the bottom of each page except the last; at the end of the story, type ### or -30-.

Standard Description of the Group—It is good practice to end releases with a three- to four-sentence description of the organization, its purpose, scope of activities, number of supporters or members, and any other information that would help an outsider quickly grasp its reason for being. This statement can appear on all materials published by the organization: consumer brochures, research reports, testimony, newsletters, journals, and even the back of business cards. This helps ensure that the essential facts about the group are disseminated in a consistent manner.

A final news release would then look like this:

Exhibit 7–1   News Release from ABC Charities

NEWS FROM ABC CHARITIES

CONTACT: Jack Collins   FOR IMMEDIATE RELEASE
999-111-0000

RECORD FUND-RAISING IN 1998 ENABLES ABC TO BUILD NEW SHELTER FOR BATTERED WOMEN AND CHILDREN

PEORIA, ILL., DEC. 31, 1999—After raising a record $805,000 this year, ABC Charities plans to build a new shelter for battered women and children just north of the downtown area, announced ABC President Janet Sullivan today.

"We are especially grateful to the Land of Lincoln Foundation, the Peoria United Way and the Midwest Savings and Loan for this record year," said Sullivan. "The first two accounted for half the contributions, while Midwest spearheaded the holiday drive that put us over last year's record of $743,000."

ABC is already laying plans for the new shelter with donated assistance of local architects. "We're designing a facility that can care for up to 120 women and children," she said. "It will have a well-equipped medical center on the premises staffed with a full complement of physicians, social workers, and nurses."

The shelter would be the most ambitious undertaking in ABC's 10-year existence. It contributed to the expansion of the Peoria Youth Center two years ago and the opening of Martha's Soup Kitchen in 1994.

The shelter will fill a significant community need. Peoria police received more than 700 reports of domestic violence against women this year, said Police Chief Brian Ames, adding, "The actual number may be more than twice that since most incidents are unreported.

"A new shelter would become a welcome refuge for hundreds of suffering women and children. I can't think of a more valuable contribution to this community."

ABC Charities was founded in 1987 by several prominent Peoria families. Its mission is to work "for the betterment of the community and the well-being of its citizens." ABC's annual operating budget has grown from $100,000 to more than $800,000. It contributes to youth programs, soup kitchens, health care agencies, and housing projects.

(###)

Broadcast News Releases

News releases may also be sent to radio and television outlets in forms suited for those mediums. For radio, the releases are narrated onto cassettes and sent to news directors. The most costly variation is the video news release designed for television outlets. These are sent either in cassette form or by satellite. The length should fit the short television news format. The video release should be packaged whole and in parts so that producers can easily extract quotes and visuals for use in stories they develop. It is common to send broadcasters a "B" roll of images that can serve as background visuals for the coverage. Only the most well-endowed organizations can afford video or audio news releases. It is best to retain a public relations firm to produce these and tend to the technical details.

Background Materials

In many communications activities, you will need to distribute background information that provides a broader context, essential facts, historical perspective, or the status of the issue at hand. At a minimum, you will want to present the basic information about the organization, as described above, although it is common to develop a more detailed description running one or two pages.

Background materials help establish a nonprofit group as an objective, credible source of information. This is not the place to make emotional appeals. It is best to present the facts in a neutral manner, acknowledge opposing views, and refute them in a dispassionate manner. Save the purple prose for speeches, testimony, colorful quotes for the news media, and opinion pieces in newspapers and magazines. Several formats are commonly used:

Question-and-Answer—Think of the questions that members of your target audience are most likely to ask, and provide brief, straightforward answers. Oftentimes, the piece is structured to begin with the most basic questions and progress to the most complex and controversial. Some subjects lend themselves to a chronological approach.

Issue Brief—This format is best for legislative issues. In one section, present the background: the circumstances that gave rise to the issue, problem, or difference of opinion. In another, describe the status, such as where the bill stands in the lawmaking process and the steps that remain before it becomes law. Finally, the brief should state your position on the issue. Issue briefs should run no longer than two or three pages. These serve primarily to give public officials, journalists, and other interested parties a quick read on the issue and where the group stands.

Fact Sheet—Use this format to present the basic information about your organization, cause, profession, or industry. Charts and tables are often helpful. Summarize the services and programs and whom they benefit; the dimensions of the problem that the group is trying to solve; or the economic performance of the industry or profession. Fact sheets can be copied onto standard-sized sheets or printed in pamphlet form.

Fact Card—You can also condense the essential information onto a wallet-sized card as a convenient handout or print it on the back of a business card.

The News Conference

The news conference is an overrated tool perhaps, overused because we see prominent public figures meeting the press so often on television. Few events or issues are large enough to warrant a news conference. Save this tool for dramatic announcements on matters of great public concern. The plan to build a shelter for battered women is dramatic enough. Research revealing public health hazards might also qualify, although the group should make sure the research is strong enough to withstand scientific scrutiny. Whether a news conference is successful also depends on the size of the city and the intensity of competition for news coverage. What plays in Peoria may not in New York City.

News conferences are also useful for responding to emergencies. They provide a timely and efficient way of disseminating vital public information. During disasters, emergency response agencies can use news conferences to request blood, blankets, food, water, four-wheel drive vehicles, and other items.

There are many logistics in planning and conducting a news conference:

Whom to Invite—Letters or news advisories should be sent to all reporters who regularly cover the group or the issues to be covered at the news conference, along with the news directors and newspaper editors. Ask the local Associated Press bureau to include the conference in the Day Book, the list of events circulated each day to all news organizations. When reporters come to the news conference, have them sign a log to provide a record of who attended.

Where to Hold It—Carefully select the site, considering the image that will appear behind the speakers. For example, to emphasize the importance of citizen response to jury summonses, the Council for Court Excellence held a press conference in Washington just outside the entrance to the D.C. Superior Court. Beyond visual considerations, the site should be centrally located, such as a downtown hotel or press club, and have a large room equipped with chairs, a podium, sound system, and enough electrical capacity for the broadcast media.

When to Hold It—The best time is often about 9 or 10 a.m. to give the news media ample time to meet their deadlines, especially evening broadcasts and newspapers.

How Long—Generally, limit the duration to one hour or less because reporters lack the time to stay longer. A large portion of the time should be reserved for reporters' questions.

Who Should Represent the Group—In nearly all cases, the nonprofit's chairman or top executive should serve as the principal spokesperson. Minimally, this individual should welcome the news media and make an opening statement about the issue at hand before turning the forum over to people with more detailed knowledge of the subject. All the senior executives in the group should be on hand to answer questions that the top executive cannot.

Handouts—Provide the news media news releases, background materials, and copies of the statements. These are often placed in a press kit with the group's logo and pockets inside for the materials. Releasing the statements in print form does not eliminate the need to present them at the news conference since television reporters must film them.

Rehearse—Not only should the speakers rehearse their remarks, but also the answers to the questions that reporters are likely to ask. Focus especially on the most difficult questions.

Consumer Information

One of the best ways for nonprofit groups to build goodwill is to educate consumers about matters that affect their health and well-being. Many subjects are suitable:

- How to recycle and otherwise help the environment.
- Methods for storing food and preparing it safely.
- First aid information.
- Preparing for emergencies.
- Vacation ideas.
- Recovering from natural disasters.

The information can be provided in numerous forms. Ambulance services can provide their phone number on a pressure-sensitive sticker to be placed on the telephone. Brochures are probably the most popular format; announce their availability to news organizations, saying you will send one free to any consumer who sends the group a self-addressed and stamped envelope. Other formats:

Public Service Announcements (PSAs)—These are like broadcast news releases described above, except that the message is public service–oriented. However, the competition for time is intense in most cities and most outlets reserve the times that command the greatest audiences for commercial advertisements, airing PSAs during the late night and early morning hours. Although the sponsoring organizations do not have to pay for the air time, only the most interesting and professionally produced announcements are likely to be broadcast.

Programs for Schools—An excellent way of looking after the long-term interests of a group is to educate those who will be your supporters, donors, and consumers in the future. Offer the organization as a resource for teaching classes; veterans in the group may enjoy such an opportunity. Groups can also produce films and videos and other instructional materials. Some organizations prepare instructional kits, including a guide suggesting how teachers can present the subject and booklets for the students. A creative alternative is to design games that children can play in school or at home and learn valuable information in the process.

Annual Reports

It is customary for organizations of all kinds to publish a year-end report summarizing activities and accomplishments. Such reports are a tailor-made answer to the question, What have you done for me lately? Fortune 1,000 corporations invest large sums designing works of graphic art intended to impress current and would-be investors. Such glitzy reports can be counterproductive for nonprofit groups, for they leave the impression that funds are being squandered on style rather than substance. Thus, nonprofit groups can save money and produce a more effective report at the same time.

Groups that rely heavily on donations will need to publish some kind of accounting of funds raised and spent. Other small nonprofit groups can dispense with an annual report, perhaps devoting the December issue of their newsletter to a review of the year's achievements. Larger groups should view the report as a means to recruit and retain supporters and as a background piece for journalists, public officials, and community leaders.

Use the annual report to document accomplishments and new programs. Shine the spotlight on those who support the organization and benefit from its services. This is not the place for gratuitous praise or for ego-massaging the group's leadership—features that tend to undermine the credibility of organizations that rely on a large quotient of public trust. As with all background pieces, stick with the facts.

The structure of such reports is open-ended. Think of half a dozen accomplishments or programs over the last year, and devote a section to each. With photos, charts, and several pages of financial information, you should have enough material for a 16-page report—the most economical length for printing. Groups may also conserve funds by publishing reports every other year.

Speeches

The speech is one of the most effective public relations tools because it is a news event unto itself. To make a statement in a public forum carries more weight than including the same statement in a news release. The news media are inclined to give it more coverage, and the audience may be deeply moved if the speech is well-conceived and -delivered. Speeches are an especially powerful means for group leaders to strengthen their standing.

Speeches differ from other types of writing. They are written for the ear, not the eye—meaning the style should be conversational, the structure explicit, and the scope narrowed to a few key points. The ideal length is 20 to 30 minutes. Narrow the topic by asking what action you would like the audience to take in response to the speech or what beliefs you would like them to adopt.

In some cases, videos, slides, and other visuals can enhance the presentation. Such props also introduce the opportunity for technical problems. You must rehearse any presentation relying on visual props and have a contingency plan in case the system fails. Group leaders should also bear in mind that visuals distract the audience's attention from the speaker. If one purpose of the speech is to strengthen the leader's stature, visuals should be minimized or eliminated altogether.

Leaders of nonprofit groups are likely to receive many invitations to speak. Local civic clubs—Lions, Rotary, etc.—offer valuable forums for nonprofit charitable organizations. Seek out forums where you can address the key audiences identified in your public relations plan. Invite the leaders of key constituencies to speak at one of your meetings as an act of reciprocity. After you deliver the speech, broaden the impact by sending copies to the news media.

COMMUNICATIONS TACTICS

Nonprofit groups bring formidable resources to the practice of public relations, but these must be carefully used. Important audiences may be skeptical, and the news media and public officials may assume adversarial postures in some instances. The rewards for adept actions are as great as the penalties for ill-conceived ones.

Media Relations

No institution is more independent than the media. This quality gives news an air of authenticity—like a third party ruling on the facts. Nonprofit groups should cultivate relations with the reporters that cover their issues. The best approach is to act as a valuable source, providing accurate and timely background materials, articulate positions, and colorful quotes. Do not attempt to wine and dine reporters. Most news organizations prohibit this, and reporters resent the implication that their favor can be bought.

This does not suggest that you should act as a passive participant in the news gathering process. View the news media as a vehicle for disseminating messages to important audiences while supplying the information requested. Groups should set up a system with the following elements for fielding media calls:

Identify a Spokesperson—To avoid confusion and contradiction, groups should clearly define a spokesperson and discourage others in their group from talking to the news media. The top executive will usually be the primary spokesperson. Larger groups may designate another executive, usually the highest ranking communications official, to share the role.

Build in Time to Reflect—Whenever possible, find out the reporter's topic ahead of time so you can respond in a calm, intelligent manner. The easiest way to buy time is to have someone else answer the phone and inquire about the subject before relaying the call to you. If the subject is especially complex or controversial, you may elect to call the reporter back.

Respect Deadlines—Reporters from daily newspapers and broadcast outlets often have only several hours to complete a story. An excellent way to cultivate good media relations is to respect their deadlines by responding promptly to all press calls. If the spokesperson does not know the answer to the question, offer to find out and call the reporter back. Be sure to follow through on that promise; call-backs help build a source's credibility with reporters.

Stick With Your Field of Expertise—Resist the temptation to comment on subjects outside the purview of your group. You may be treading on the territory of other groups that could serve as important allies.

Don't Comment on the Business of Supporters or Members—Nonprofit groups exist at the pleasure of their supporters or members. Spokespersons should play up the positive features of their constituency but never offer opinions on the troubles of individual supporters or members. Obviously, this does not apply to professional groups that have mechanisms for censuring members for ethical breeches. Even in these instances, it is best to let the action speak for itself.

Broadcast Interviews

Broadcast media, especially television, pose special challenges. The impact can be powerful while the format limits the time allotted to sources literally to a few seconds. It is common for half-hour on-camera interviews with a source to be reduced to two 15-second clips in a two-minute story. Thus, you have to make every word count. In television the visual dimension adds another challenge. You may say the right words, but your fidgeting hands, tense facial muscles, and gaudy clothes undermine the message. Here is a broadcast interview checklist:

Preparing for the Interview

- Find out the program slant (consumer, business, hard news, interview, etc.) and how the interviewer's position compares with yours.
- Within the theme or format of the show, determine two or three important points you want to make during the interview. Anticipate responses to questions that can be legitimately asked.
- Make certain that facts supporting your position come to mind easily and are up to date.
- Before the interview, check the morning newspaper and radio and television news shows for late-breaking stories that affect the issues to be discussed.

Physical Setting and Body Movements

- Keep your hands off table microphones, don't drum your fingers on tabletops or tap your feet on the floor or the side of a chair.

- Don't look down or breathe heavily into microphones hung around your neck or clipped to clothing.
- Avoid sudden body movements (standing up, learning back in a chair, etc.) that might take you out of camera range.

Personal Appearance

- Dress conservatively. Men should wear dark suits, solid color shirts, and long socks. Women should wear a business dress or suit, preferably a solid color.
- Remove loose jewelry and prominent rings (except wedding bands). Women shouldn't wear heavy necklaces or bracelets, diamond and rhinestone jewelry, large earrings, or pins.
- Don't wear sunglasses or polar-gray glasses. Remove name tags, lapel pins, and all extraneous items attached to jackets.
- When seated, don't slouch or lean to one side. When standing, don't rock back and forth or place hands in your pockets.
- Keep your head up so as not to look guilty when listening or talking. Avoid casting your eyes toward the ceiling.
- Try to match your facial expressions with the seriousness of the matters under discussion. Do not smile at the wrong time because of discomfort.
- Ask for makeup on your face to control perspiration and reduce light reflection.

Oral Presentation

- Answer questions in 10- to 20-second sound bites. Give the headline first, then document the answers if time permits. Avoid time-wasting phrases, such as "That's a good question . . ." or "I'm glad you asked me that . . ."
- Take a second or two to frame your answer if you need it rather than thinking out loud. Do not repeat the question, especially if it's hostile. Do not repeat negative words.
- Answer only one question at a time.
- Work in your two or three key points, using conversational techniques. You might acknowledge a related question as a bridge or answer a question in such a way that the interviewer must ask a question related to one of your key points.

- Avoid using large dollar figures or other complicated statistics; percentages are better. Where possible, round off numbers or use small ones.
- Don't be defensive. Enjoy taking the offensive. Above all else: be positive.

Community Relations

The benefits of community relations are self-evident. Purely charitable organizations promote community relations to raise funds, while others reinforce their value as an institution worthy of support. Community relations activities are virtually immune from criticism. The possibilities are endless:

- Health fairs offering free tests of cholesterol and blood pressure levels.
- Fun runs in which either the entry fees are donated to charity or sponsors for each runner donate a certain amount for each mile run.
- Rubber ducky races in which the entry fees go to charity. The ducks are placed in a local river.
- Tailgate cookouts before football games in which local grocers and restaurants donate the food and the proceeds go to charity.
- Publishing a cookbook of recipes from local leaders or celebrities. *Cooking With the Stars*, released in 1993 by the Center for Science in the Public Interest, features 200 health-conscious recipes from celebrities and politicians.
- Litter clean-up days coordinated with local youth organizations.
- Building homes for low-income families.
- Distributing blankets and sleeping bags to the homeless.
- Sponsoring sports leagues for youths.
- Mentoring youths to help them stay in school and off drugs and alcohol.
- Support for local food banks and soup kitchens.
- Demonstrations of your group's services in public forums.
- Raffles and lotteries to raise money for worthy causes.

Community relations programs require the same attention to detail needed in all public relations programs. Especially when programs involve more than one group, begin coordinating activities months before the joint activity is to begin and clarify the division of responsibilities. This practice builds trust and avoids awkward encounters in which leaders of the sponsoring groups present conflicting messages.

At the start of every flu season, the Visiting Nurses Association of America sends an army of nonprofit nurses into supermarkets, drug stores, and health clubs to vaccinate people. The group buys the serum in bulk and nurses donate their time to reduce the cost to about $10 per shot. The program started at the local level, and success has turned it into a national program that administered 800,000 flu shots in 1993.

Political Action

One oft-overlooked application of public relations is its role in lawmaking. To the extent that elected officials are moved by public opinion, public relations can influence the legislative process. A newspaper editorial, a creative demonstration or televised testimony can sometimes win more votes than conventional lobbying techniques. For this approach to work, however, groups must show how their legislative goal serves the public interest: how it will help consumers, save money for taxpayers, create jobs, promote health, serve the needy—in other words, the broad causes that public officials champion when they run for office. If a legislative goal cannot be expressed in broad terms, public relations will not be an effective tactic.

A campaign in 1986 helped defeat a measure known as the Beer Baron Bill, which would have exempted beer wholesalers from certain antitrust laws. The supermarket industry was the lead opponent, represented by the Food Marketing Institute (FMI). The beer wholesalers had advanced the measure well over a four-year period, convincing several hundred members of Congress to sponsor it. FMI had managed to block the beer bill in the past, but this time the proponents had attached it as an amendment to budget legislation that had to pass.

FMI took an inventory of the groups supporting its position: the Consumer Federation of America, Association of State Attorneys General, U.S. Department of Justice, Federal Trade Commission, the association repre-

senting tavern owners, and many others. FMI sent a packet of information to the editorial page editors of the nation's 300 largest daily newspapers. The packet portrayed the Beer Baron Bill as an irresponsible measure that would increase the price of beer and ultimately other consumer products. The packet contained the following elements:

- *One-page cover letter describing the issue, noting the urgency of the situation, and asking the newspaper to provide editorial support.*
- *An issue brief providing the technical details of the bill, the legislative history and current status, FMI's position, and a summary of scholarly research documenting the inflationary impact of exclusive territories.*
- *A list of groups for and against the beer bill, showing only two proponents, beer wholesalers and brewers.*
- *Copies of letters and statements from other groups opposing the measure.*

More than 40 newspapers published editorials opposing the beer bill, including the Los Angeles Times, Chicago Sun-Times, New York Times, Washington Post, Detroit Free Press, Cleveland Plain Dealer, Baltimore Sun, *and* Des Moines Register. *FMI created posters displaying the editorials and distributed copies to every member of Congress.*

When effectively applied, public relations can affect legislation in a strong and enduring manner. It is best to reserve such campaigns for issues in which nonprofit groups can clearly align their goals with the public interest.

Crisis Communications

Occasionally, events may threaten the integrity of the group or its constituency. Industry trade associations may have to respond to consumer or regulatory issues; a charitable organization may be called on to explain the cost of a fund-raising campaign. In these situations, effective communication is paramount. A group under fire that speaks with many voices or runs for cover may find its reputation irreparably damaged. Those that communicate well that the group is meeting the challenges will find their stature enhanced.

When a story breaks affecting either your nonprofit organization itself or the industry or profession which your group represents, you will need to determine whether and when to talk to the news media. Often you will not have the luxury of not responding or delaying a response. It may be best to initiate contact to avoid suspicion that you're hiding something. This also puts your spokesperson in a position to control the flow of information.

All communications in crises should be limited to verified facts. Speculation is never a good idea and especially not in a crisis when theories are often disproved.

Crises often present certain logical intervals in which to communicate:

1. Immediately upon hearing of the incident or controversy, announce your availability to respond to inquiries and plans to gather additional information, where appropriate.
2. After a preliminary investigation, provide an initial assessment of what happened.
3. When new, significant facts are uncovered, issue progress reports.
4. After completing the investigation, give a full account of the incident, what you learned, and how you will avoid future crises of this nature.

You should also inform supporters, members, and other constituents in a timely manner. Share with them any statements you are making and positions on issues raised by the crisis. This will help them frame responses that are consistent with the group's.

After the Crisis. Once the emergency has subsided, the crisis communications team should review the experience and consider the need for follow-up actions. You may want to thank publicly any individuals who were especially helpful, and send a word of thanks to members of the news media as well.

Handling Adverse Publicity

Every group with a high public profile is likely to receive criticism from time to time. Several national charitable organizations have had to answer charges in recent years that they were overcompensating executives or using funds unwisely. Resist the temptation to accuse the news media of conspiring to destroy the organization. Reporters do hunt for controversy, but most are bound by ethical codes that require balance and objectivity. Make good use of the opportunity to provide your side of a story; and if you learn of an investigation that could be damaging, it may be wise to preempt it with a news conference or interview with a competing news organization before the adverse material is published or aired. If some of the charges are on target, you may want to announce corrective measures ahead of time.

When considering whether or how to answer an adverse report, you have to weigh several factors. First, your response may keep in the news an issue that you'd rather have disappear. Dignified silence is often the best course for matters of secondary importance. Second, you could limit the response to correcting factual errors in the spirit of setting the record straight. This approach is wise if the issue is likely to arise again. An aggressive response should be reserved for matters that threaten the integrity of the organization or its constituency. In all cases, the response should be built on facts and reason; emotion tends to be counterproductive.

If a group's constituency is being investigated, the group can play a valuable role by speaking for its supporters and serving as a lightning rod for criticism that might have been directed at them. The group can also develop broad-based programs to resolve problems.

Occasionally, groups may want to work with critics to correct problems that they've cited. The critics can be invited to debate issues in public forums with articulate spokespersons from your group. This can provide a full airing of all sides, giving the news media a more sophisticated understanding of the issues, which may improve coverage in the future.

Communicating with Constituents

Almost every nonprofit organization has a core constituency. This will vary by the type of organization: for a university, it may include all graduates; for a church, its parishioners; for a charity, recent contributors; for a membership organization, its members. To this group, communication must be frequent and in tune with the basic mission and principles of the organization.

Internal communication differs from public relations in the breadth or extent of the audience you are attempting to reach. Public relations is concerned with a wide audience: the men and women who read newspapers that carry stories about an organization's activities, the radio programs that broadcast listings of public performances or activities, or those outside your usual group of supporters who receive direct mail pieces. Although communications designed for your core constituency may have wider uses as well, the distinguishing feature is that they are written and designed primarily with your constituent audience in mind. That audience must feel, when reading your newsletter or other communication, that it was created specially for them.

Communications vehicles vary from the most direct of memoranda to high-technology. Often, the choice of how to communicate itself tells much about the organization. Marshall McLuhan wrote, "the medium is the message." An organization that communicates through a two-page front and back newsletter creates a different image from one that uses an electronic bulletin board. One that uses academic language, with complex sentences or a specialized vocabulary, creates a different image than one written in journalistic style.

The possibilities—some of them obvious, some more specialized—include:

- Periodic written reports from the president or other executive staff;
- Special reports on recent organization activities or analyses of issues affecting the organization or its members;
- Regular newsletters, whether short (two to four pages) or more elaborate;
- Magazines or other more "glossy" publications, usually including advertising;
- Scholarly journals, brochures, or even books sponsored by the organization;
- Audio or even video tapes designed to communicate information about the organization;
- Electronic bulletin boards or E-mail designed to let members or your constituency dial in for information.

Internal communications activities evolve as the organization grows or changes. At the earliest stage it may have been sufficient for the executive simply to telephone his key board members frequently to tell them how the organization was progressing. Soon there comes a time the number of individuals who should receive information makes this impractical. Printed communications fill this role and also speak to the organization's role in its community or profession.

The first step, often, is a two-page newsletter photocopied on the organization's letterhead. This should be printed on a different masthead, perhaps two-color, to set the newsletter off from the stock used for letters or memoranda. A professional graphic artist can give this a touch of professionalism. A complex creative design is unnecessary, but the organization's name or acronym can be laid out in a modern, professional manner; the apparent savings from doing this yourself risks the price of an amateurish presentation. If your organization is a true charitable 501(c)(3) with limited funds, a local graphics designer might even waive or reduce fees.

Any outdated newsletter design—probably any design more than ten years old—should be redone. An old newsletter design will show its age, as clearly as a ten-year-old dress or automobile. If you choose to stay with the old, do this consciously, not just by default.

Newsletter stock, whether for the two- or the four-page format, should be preprinted, usually with two colors on the masthead. The newsletter can then be printed in one color (usually black, occasionally dark blue or brown if the stock has been designed for that) and will still have a lively, colorful effect on the first page.

Design and production get more complicated for the four-page format. Usually, the copy is laid out in columns. Headlines have to fit and the layout of stories beginning on the first page and continuing to other pages has to be organized and easy for the reader to follow. The length of the stories should fit the space available—whether four pages or eight—to avoid excess white space. Since the larger formats won't fit on an office copier, the camera-ready copies will have to go to a quick printer. Along with the additional professionalism of appearance, the writing will require more care.

Modern information technology has made the writing task easier than it used to be. The ease of correcting and rewriting copy on a word processor, and checking for typing or spelling errors with error-checking, makes it easier for non-professional writers to produce clear articles. Simple layout can be done with software programs that make "desktop publishing" possible. The laser printer produces camera-ready copy that is of sufficient quality for most newsletters.

Although the substance of articles must come from staff administering the projects or following the issues of concern to the nonprofit, it may not be cost-effective for the executive director to write and rewrite stories, or for the director of membership services to learn to use the layout features of a desktop publishing program. Professionals will do these jobs faster and usually do them better. Issues to consider in deciding whether to hire new staff or use outside consultants for these or other projects are covered in Chapter 13.

Costs of production will vary from one part of the country to another. Staff time for a newsletter is usually covered in staff salaries. Out-of-pocket costs can be projected carefully. A format like that shown in Exhibit 7–2 will make estimating easier.

Exhibit 7–2   Newsletter Cost Estimate Form

Newsletters

Preprints—based on 2 color (Blk & PMS), preprinting on page 1 of a 4-page newsletter.

Number of Copies	Preprint Cost
2,500	
5,000	
10,000	
20,000	

Imprint with black ink only, folds to #10.

	500	1,000	2,500	5,000
4 pages				
6 pages				
8 pages				

Additionals

• any applicable sales taxes
• type from disk (desktop publishing)
• design and layout
• photos
• mailing and postage

Magazine publishing is best left to organizations with a very large membership. Moving from a newsletter to a magazine is tempting. With a magazine, an organization may be able to sell ads. This may permit greater use of color, sometimes even four-color covers. The magazine can be circulated to prospective contributors or to a wider audience that the organization wants to reach, becoming a public relations tool. But the costs go up geometrically. Unless there is the potential for circulation in the tens of thousands (and where that large a market exists, there is usually a competing for-profit publication), writing, editing, production, and distribution costs are likely to be far greater than can be offset by advertising revenues.

Membership organizations sometimes strive to increase the proportion of "non-dues income" without realizing that a magazine or other publication actually costs more than it brings in. The figure you need to focus on is the "bottom line," not the top-line income from advertising or sales. If staff costs are covered in other line items—and it can be difficult to allocate executive time to a publication—the nonprofit organization may not realize how much a magazine is really taking of its resources. If it is not "carrying itself" in the fullest sense, including a realistic analysis of how much time and attention it is taking away from other activities, it's time to step back and ask: Is this really helping us achieve our mission? Is communication in this form necessary? A publication decision should be shaped by the strategic plan, rather than shaping it.

FORWARD-LOOKING PUBLIC RELATIONS

The ultimate goal of public relations is to anticipate change so the group can have programs in place when it comes. Groups that listen carefully to their constituents can identify emerging trends and needs. If you take action to resolve a problem at the neighborhood level, you'll be prepared to address it at the city or state level—or perhaps your action will prevent its spread. At its best, public relations is a means for engaging constituents in constructive dialogue, a catalyst for change that keeps groups a step ahead of their critics. The discipline endows groups with a vision of their broader purpose, providing inspiration for all who are touched by their actions.

SUMMARY

- Public relations can support many activities in nonprofit groups: fund-raising, community awareness, member recruitment and retention, lobbying and issue advocacy, financial relations, and crisis management.
- The most effective programs view public relations as two-way communications with groups and individuals important to the group.
- The group should set strategic goals for the program based on a vision shared by the leadership and supporters.
- When searching for public relations resources, the group should see if supporters can contribute professional skills, equipment, and other items.
- Audience research will help nonprofit groups develop appropriate messages and track the success of the program.
- Nonprofit groups have many occasions for sending news releases, from announcing the introduction of new services to commenting on the accomplishments of the year just ended.
- Releases should be written in a news style in which the first four paragraphs provide a synopsis of the story or so intrigue readers that they feel compelled to read on.
- News releases should include a release date and time, contact person, descriptive headline, and a description of the group, among other features.
- Mailings to the news media must often include background materials, such as question-and-answer pieces, issue briefs, and fact sheets.
- News conferences should be reserved for dramatic announcements of great public concern or responses to emergencies.
- News conferences must be carefully planned and orchestrated, from the invitation list and site to the time, duration, and the people who speak on behalf of the group.
- Nonprofit groups can build goodwill by educating consumers about matters that affect their health and well-being, such as how to recycle, prepare for emergencies, shop for products and services, and recover from natural disasters. The formats range from brochures to public service announcements on radio and television to educational programs for schools.

- Nonprofit groups should publish annual reports to provide an accounting of funds raised and spent and to document accomplishments and new programs. The most economical length for printing is 16 pages.
- Speeches are especially effective at sending messages because they are a news event unto themselves. The speaker should develop a strong, simple message and deliver it in 20 to 30 minutes.
- Since the news media are an excellent vehicle for disseminating information to key audiences, groups should set up a systematic method for handling media inquiries.
- Broadcast interviews pose special challenges, requiring spokespersons to consider their appearance, along with the message they want to communicate.
- Nonprofit groups can reinforce their value as an institution worthy of support by improving community relations. There are many ways to do this, from sponsoring health fairs to supporting youth groups.
- Nonprofit groups can use public relations to pursue legislative goals when their position is clearly aligned with a broad public interest. The methods include urging newspapers to publish supporting editorials and providing dramatic displays in testimony.
- Crisis communications can often make or break a group's reputation since its every move in such a situation will be scrutinized.
- Even a nonprofit group may experience adverse publicity. In some instances, no response is needed. In cases where the integrity of the group or its constituency is threatened, the group should respond aggressively, always limiting the response to facts and logic.
- The best public relations programs serve as an early warning system for emerging trends and concerns and endow groups with a broader vision of their purpose.

CHAPTER EIGHT

Getting Political Support for Your Cause

Whether it's a campaign to the local school board or the U.S. Congress, your nonprofit can be a power advocate for your donors and constituents. This chapter explains what it takes — organization, research, patience, persistence, and enthusiasm — to have an impact on government.

Getting political support for your cause is an attempt to persuade members of a legislature—whether city council, county commission, school board, planning commission, state legislature, or the United States Congress—to enact legislation, take action favorable to a cause, or defeat or repeal a measure. In response to such a targeted effort or government relations program, a legislative body or government official may set up a new program, change an existing one, guarantee certain rights, appropriate funds, or maintain the status quo. These efforts are also called lobbying.

America is a nation of advocates. Individually and collectively, we seek to influence our government to set its priorities in accordance with our own concerns. A government relations program is an organized effort to influence your government.

The term "lobbyist" was coined in 1870 by President Grant, who would often go to the Willard Hotel in Washington, D.C., for an evening drink. The Willard is just a few blocks from the White House. The many groups and individuals who wanted to influence the President learned of this habit and would wait for him in the hotel lobby. When President Grant walked through the lobby, these individuals would attempt to engage him in conversation to request help with their issue of the day. President Grant, not always pleased with these individuals, called them "lobbyists."

ESTABLISHING A GOVERNMENT RELATIONS PROGRAM AT THE LOCAL LEVEL

People speak out at town meetings or city council sessions for improved highways, and they talk to school officials about changes they believe are necessary in the curriculum. They call town hall to say they want more frequent garbage collection or to ask for more tennis courts or soccer fields. This is lobbying for government to meet the needs of the people. This process is a part of our American tradition of free speech and the right of citizens to seek redress from their government.

Sometimes people will join forces to advocate for specific legislation on topics or programs of interest to them. They may form a permanent organization, or unite temporarily to pursue a single, time-limited goal. Many groups that advocate changes in legislation or fight to maintain the status quo have familiar names: National Education Association, Sierra Club, American Medical Association, AFL-CIO, American Nurses Association, National Organization for Women, National Wildlife Federation. These and many other organizations have well-established government relations programs at the national, state, and local levels. What gives them purpose is their agenda or mission. They want to accomplish some purpose, create an initiative, or defeat a program that is counter to their mission.

Nonprofit organizations at the community level attract membership and support for—in fact, usually owe their very existence to the appeal of—their mission. A Parent–Teachers Association (PTA) is formed to ensure that the voices of the parents and students are heard by the school administration. A civic association is formed to protect a neighborhood from unwanted development and to improve a neighborhood by upgrading government services and programs for the neighborhood. A charitable organization serving the elderly may need support from the local city council.

A government relations or lobbying program of a nonprofit organization seeks to influence the local, regional, state, and/or national elected and appointed officials and government agencies. The program needs to be organized and planned with a clear understanding of the timetable of the decision-making process and of the key people that need to be reached. While nonprofit organizations at the community level may focus on local officials and agencies, often your member of Congress can be of great assistance in a variety of ways.

THE IMPORTANCE OF A GOVERNMENT RELATIONS PROGRAM

Government action reflects what the people want only if enough citizens take the trouble to let decision makers know what they think. Americans are becoming more sophisticated about focusing attention on the issues about which they are concerned. If you do not take the initiative in lobbying for the causes in which you believe, citizens with views diametrically opposed to yours may see their agenda adopted, while yours fails for lack of attention. Simply being organized and prepared to respond to actions and decisions that are adverse to your organization's interests can be a deterrent to decision makers from making those adverse decisions. If elected or appointed officials know that you can marshall a letter-writing campaign or a public testimony campaign to support your interests, they are more likely to be cautious or mindful of your views. Often a government relations campaign is initiated to respond to one issue and is disbanded once the issue is resolved. Keeping an ongoing government relations program in place will help your organization marshall a quick response to new issues and signals your clout to decision makers. This should help create a more positive environment for your organization and its interests.

Individual citizens can have an impact on public policy, but groups of like-minded people and coalitions of groups can be an even stronger force. Many lobbyists are volunteers; others are the paid staff members of organizations.

To be effective, you must know how the government works and be aware of who is involved in the decision-making process. Knowledge of the best timing for advocacy can add greatly to your success.

The Council for Court Excellence in Washington, D.C., provides one example of a successful government relations campaign by a local-level nonprofit corporation. Concern had been growing for some time that, because jury duty took several weeks, people were less and less willing to serve on juries when called and voluntary compliance with jury duty was diminishing.

To reduce the amount of time a person had to serve, the Council for Court excellence decided to advocate a "one day/one trial" system where if chosen as a juror, the citizen would serve for that trial only and complete his/her service in one to three days. Advocacy before the City Council and the U.S. Congress (which oversees the District) was necessary to accomplish this, and the success created a new level of esteem for the Council in its constituency.

PARTICIPATION IN YOUR GOVERNMENT RELATIONS PROGRAM

It is important to create a government relations steering committee to work with staff in designing the strategy for your campaign. If possible, appoint people to this committee who know the key decision makers and who are politically active, particularly in support of the elected officials who are making the key decisions on the issues important to your organization. Bipartisanship is important and can be accomplished by having on your steering committee people who are politically active in support of both Democrats and Republicans. Try to include some individuals who are intimately familiar with that portion of the government and the programs that you are trying to influence.

Once the steering committee has mapped out the strategy and has prepared the documents that will represent the key arguments or positions, the broader membership can be enlisted to help provide testimony, contact key people, and help write letters. It is most helpful, in order to enlist this broader support, to include as much of the membership as possible in the decision-making process.

The individual citizens you include in your campaign do not need to be polished professional lobbyists. They will often be more effective if they are not. They do need to be both committed to the cause and direct, genuine, and enthusiastic in their presentation. Every American carries political weight because each individual can help vote someone in or out of office. In addition, your elected officials may need you as much as you need them. Since most elected officials are generalists, they rely on the expertise and experience of their constituents to help them make informed decisions.

STARTING A GOVERNMENT RELATIONS CAMPAIGN

A government relations campaign is started when you realize that your interests and those of others in your organization are at risk. While a well-established organization should be constantly monitoring relevant issues, a local organization's campaign is often traced back to a discussion over coffee or a meeting in someone's living room. The campaign begins as you map out your strategy and plan how to maximize your effectiveness. You should know as much as possible about the person you are attempting to influence, as this will help you tailor the presentation to that individual.

You should know something about the decision makers you are planning to contact.

- What are their interests?
- What are their backgrounds?
- What is their record of support on the issue you are advocating?
- On which committees do they serve, and what positions do they hold?
- Who chairs the committee that will be considering the proposal you support or oppose?
- Who is leading the opposition?

You should also know as much as possible about the groups and individuals who are arguing against your position, as the decision maker will also hear their arguments. If you know the position and arguments of your opposition, you can address those points or concerns in your presentation to the decision maker. It is better to address these issues and offer counter-arguments than to let them go unanswered. The decision maker will appreciate your honesty and efforts to help him or her make a balanced decision.

If you want to know an elected official's position on a specific legislation, pick up the telephone and ask that official's staff member. Most elected officials have offices that may be contacted easily. Let the elected official's staff know you want a copy of a pending bill, study, report, or hearing record, which can be obtained without cost for constituents.

A successful government relations campaign must have clear, easily articulated goals. When possible, the campaign should express values of importance to the public—justice, fairness, equality, and truth—as well as the importance of the issue being advocated. Try to frame the issue to appeal to prevailing public opinions and beliefs. For instance, conquering disease enhances productivity, improving schools helps strengthen the economy of the nation, controlling commuter traffic through our neighborhoods improves safety for our children.

An appeal is most effective when addressed to the widest possible group of potential constituents, not just a narrow body of supporters. Instead of talking about the excitement of cancer research, discuss your concern for the people who have the disease and for their families.

Remember that advocacy is a long-distance race. Battles rarely are won or lost with a single effort. Successful advocacy requires persistence, organization, research, patience, and enthusiasm.

THE IMPORTANCE OF FACTS FOR A GOVERNMENT RELATIONS CAMPAIGN

To be effective, you need to know the subject and what impact the decision will have on lawmakers and their constituents. With accurate information, a lobbyist becomes a helpful and concerned citizen. Without it, he lacks credibility.

You need to know:

- What will the action, position, or legislation you are advocating accomplish?
- Why is it important that it be done now, instead of next year?
- What will occur if what you are advocating does not happen?
- How much money will it save?
- How much money will it cost?
- How much will not doing it cost—in dollars spent, in lost productivity, or reduced quality of life?
- What will it do in terms of jobs, impact on the economy, or the health and welfare of the local population?

It is important to understand and explain, in as much detail as possible, the impact of your proposal. You should be able to explain how the proposal will affect the interests and priorities of the decision maker you are attempting to influence. For example, an elected official will want to know how the proposal affects his or her constituents. How many people in the official's district will be helped by it? A representative whose constituency consists of many young families may be most interested to learn how your proposal will affect the health and safety and education of children in the district.

FACTS ARE NOT ENOUGH FOR A GOVERNMENT RELATIONS CAMPAIGN

Facts are vital for the staff and volunteers of an organization with a government relations goal, but they are not enough. Conviction also is essential. Once your decision makers and their staffs begin to recognize your name and say, "Oh yes, you're with the Friends of the Library group," you know they are paying attention to you. When they realize that you are personally committed to the issue, they will pay more attention to your views. Of course, always remain calm and professional in your presentations. Coming on too strong can be a turn-off and may hurt your cause.

A LETTER-WRITING CAMPAIGN IS IMPORTANT

Writing letters, and often lots of them, is important. Often officials on the state or federal level and in large cities are too busy to read every piece of mail that is sent to them. However, they do get regular staff briefings on how many letters they have received, what topics the letters address, and the position taken by the writers. Even the busiest decision makers will insist that all the mail be answered, approve of the response made, and personally read representative samples of the mail on the major issues. Of course, elected officials and decision makers with a smaller volume of mail may read and personally answer all their own mail.

In today's environment, personal attention by the decision makers to each piece of mail is unusual, but they will read mail from friends and recognized community leaders. Communications from the elected chair or executive director of a nonprofit organization, speaking for the organization, carry special weight. Sometimes, a single thoughtful letter can change an official's mind or at least convince him or her to review an opinion. Informative letters on an issue can provide a good understanding of the thinking of constituents and insight into specific problems. Exhibit 8–1 contains a checklist of suggestions to ensure that your correspondence is as professional, efficient, and effective as possible.

Presenting Your Case

The first time you meet with a key decision maker face-to-face can be exciting, even if you are nervous. Good advance preparation may help to calm your nerves and will make the visit more effective.

1. **Call for an appointment**. Explain that you are a constituent and that you would like to meet with the decision maker to explain your position on a specific topic or issue. It is preferable that you have credentials as the chairman or president of a group or organization and can say that you would like to also bring with you a few of the other leaders of your organization. Explain briefly why you think the decision maker will want to meet with you. For example, a vote or decision is coming up in the very near future and this matter is of vital importance to

Exhibit 8–1   Checklist for a Letter to a Key Decision Maker

---

1. **Address your letter properly.** Be sure your name, address, and phone number appear on the letter so that the legislator or official can respond. Be absolutely certain that names are spelled correctly.

2. **Identify the issue clearly.** Be as specific as possible so the reader will know exactly what action you want taken. For example, "I am writing to request your support at the October Board meeting for the continuation of HB Middle School in its current location on Vacation Lane."

3. **Be clear.** Leave no doubt in the reader's mind where you stand on the issue.

4. **Be brief.** Letters should be a single page. If more must be stated, enclose a fact sheet elaborating on your single-page summary.

5. **Be personal.** Form letters do not have the same impact as those written by someone who cares enough to take pen in hand or sit down at the typewriter. Give your own reasons for taking a stand.

6. **Use facts and figures.** Select those facts and figures that best present your case, but also facts and figures that will refute your opposition's arguments.

7. **Be respectful,** even if you disagree with your decision maker's position. Explain why you hope that he or she will reconsider.

8. **Ask specifically for what you want, and ask if the decision maker will help.**

---

your group and to a large number of the decision maker's constituents.

2. **Mention shared political values.** If appropriate, mention that you are a member of the same political party and that you supported him or her in the past or contributed to campaigns.

3. **Be prompt and be brief.** Plan to cover your topic in five minutes if possible, ten minutes at most. Do not linger unless your decision maker or the staff member makes it clear that a longer visit is welcome.

4. **Emphasize facts.** If you cannot answer a question, admit it and plan to follow up as soon as possible by letter or phone call with the information. Within 24 hours, send a single-page summary of your position and the most important facts to answer the questions for which you did not have answers. Be sure your address and phone number are on the summary sheet, so that you can be contacted for further information.

5. **Aides *are* influential.** Even a "firm" appointment with a decision maker may result in a conversation with an aide instead. Although it may be more exciting to meet an elected official in person, an interested aide can be an asset to your cause. Present your case just as if the aide were the decision maker.

6. **Limit your group**. Do not bring someone along who is not prepared to provide important information in support of your position or someone who is not as enthusiastic as you are about the issue.

7. **Say "thank you."** Thank your decision maker for his or her time when your leave the office. Follow up with a note when you get home. Also write to say thank you if the decision maker takes the action you requested. Most congressional mail asks for favors or expresses complaints, so a thank you letter makes an impression. Be sure to thank the staff person as well.

MAKING THE CAMPAIGN MORE EFFECTIVE

Whether you will be writing a letter, calling on the phone, sending a telegram, or making personal visits to your elected officials, the following tips will make your lobbying more effective.

- Always learn as much as you can about the process, the people, and the issues before you state your case.

- Clearly state the purpose and subject of the communication.

- Do not threaten elected officials (even if only to vote against them) because this never works in an advocate's best interest.

- Explain why you are interested. If you are concerned about funding levels for education because your family has children in the school system, share this information.

- Limit the scope of your letter to one, or at most two, topics.

- State the message in your own terms. Mass-produced letters save time, but they are less effective and will receive a mass-produced response.

- Build long-lasting relationships with your decision makers and do not destroy the goodwill you build over a single disagreement. Decision makers will understand if you do not agree with them on every issue.

- Be timely with responses. Learning about the decision-making process will give you clear ideas about when letters and visits will be the most useful and will be given the most consideration.

COALITIONS

Coalitions are formal and informal alliances of organizations formed to accomplish a common goal. Some coalitions are permanently established to work toward a long-term goal. Informal or ad hoc coalitions are usually formed to defeat a single law or encourage the adoption of specific policy; once the goal is accomplished, an informal coalition disbands. As long as a group of organizations and individuals can put aside their differences and focus on the single goal they all share, coalitions can be a most useful lobbying instrument.

Coalitions are effective because they can marshall the energy of a large number of people through the organization they belong to. Usually a coalition will establish a steering committee to coordinate and agree on the overall strategy and tactics of a campaign. Coalitions are also effective because they demonstrate to the decision makers that many groups, not just one isolated group, support a particular view. For example, in many larger communities there are federations of civic associations and federations of PTAs. When these federations take a position it often carries more weight in the minds of decision makers than would one civic association or PTA.

Creating a Coalition

All it takes to start a coalition is to recognize a common interest. A coalition of PTAs could be formed in support of increased state funding for local schools or of having elected instead of appointed school board members. A coalition of civic associations could be formed to stop the construction of a major highway through their communities.

Coalitions are effective because they demonstrate that you are not speaking from a narrow position of self-interest. Coalitions help by activating more people to support your cause. Coalitions speak of unity and numbers of people committed to a cause. These facts impress key decision makers, particularly those who are, or who work for, elected officials. Organizing your own government relations campaign or program should be the first priority. But once that step is taken, think about organizing or creating a coalition.

LOBBYING

Grass Roots Lobbying

The term "grass roots" was first coined at a political convention, when a speaker from Kansas described rural citizens who were closest to the earth as being our nation's "grass roots." Since then, grass roots lobbying has come to mean the efforts of individual citizens to influence key legislators and policy decisions. Grass roots lobbying can often help your government relations campaign by demonstrating the broad level of support that exists for your cause.

There are two cautions that should be considered before attempting to mount a grass roots campaign. First, it can be counterproductive if the broader membership of your organization does not have all the facts and information necessary to lobby effectively on an issue. If your broader membership is well informed through meetings and mailings, they may well be able to aid your cause.

Second, government relations campaigns can easily reach the point of overkill, and you may do more harm than good by annoying the key decision makers whom you are attempting to persuade. Often, key decision makers will appreciate being relieved of responding to a thousand pieces of mail when a visit and a few letters would have made the point.

Hiring a Professional Lobbyist

Organizations contract for consulting services when they do not have the time or the skills to do the job properly themselves. Professional consultants are hired when those individuals have special contacts or relationships with the decision makers and when they have the special in-depth knowledge of an issue that is necessary for a successful campaign. Professional consultants are skilled at keeping track of the progress of an issue; can tell you when a meeting with your decision maker would be most effective; and may suggest the best time to organize a letter-writing campaign.

Consultants cannot win every time, nor can they work magic. Consultants cannot invent good reasons for your cause if you do not supply adequate facts or generate enough enthusiasm. A good lobbyist will be able to help *you* make the most effective case to the right people at the best time.

One major advantage of hiring a lobbyist is gaining access to important information before it becomes general knowledge. Often lobbyists can do this because they maintain close day-to-day contact with the programs and decision makers you are trying to influence. The services of someone who monitors government agencies and legislative bodies can help an organization's volunteers maximize their effectiveness by knowing when, how, and to whom the case should be made.

Lobbying expenditures, particularly at the state or federal level, may not be tax-deductible. Your government relations consultant should be able to explain the issues involved in tax deductibility.

Government Relations Campaigns Make a Difference

The effectiveness of a lobbying campaign is often directly related to the time and energy invested, although one effective meeting, letter, or telephone call with a key decision maker can equal months or years of passion and effort. Always survey the key decision makers and/or their staff or those around them to determine how interested they may be in a particular issue to gauge the level of effort required.

One local school organization mounted a campaign in Arlington County, Virginia, in 1992 to convince the school board to keep an alternative middle school open. The campaign was initiated and developed following a school board's unanimous vote to consider whether or not to close the school. It was clear from their discussion that the school board members were all leaning toward closing the school.

The PTA notified all parents of the middle school students and its companion high school of the school board vote and then held several large meetings. So as not to distract itself from other activities, the PTA decided to establish a special committee to lobby for the continuation of the school. The PTA elected a committee chair who was well known in the county, particularly with key decision makers. Members of the committee were selected based on their knowledge of the schools, school bodies, curricular issues, school board members, and county board members. A lobbying campaign was planned which included the following elements:

- *A quality document was written and developed that answered the opposition's arguments and advocated the continuation of the school. At a key time before the vote, the document was provided to each of the school board members, the superintendent, and key staff in the superintendent's office.*

- *Members of the steering committee made appointments with, and visited, each of the school board members and key staff.*

- *Recognizing that the school board had asked staff to study the issue, the steering committee met with the research team and presented information to them throughout the year.*

- *Successful efforts were made to form coalitions with other alternative schools, the Association of PTAs, and the Federation of Civic Associations.*
- *Members of the steering committee took several of the more outspoken school board members to lunch for a more social, less formal exchange of views.*
- *Three individuals (always including one student) testified throughout the year at each board meeting, outlining arguments in support of continuing the school.*
- *Because the school board members were appointed by the county board, the steering committee met with the chairman and several members of the county board, which had expressed support for alternative schools. Because the county board was in the process of selecting a new school board member, the candidates were surveyed on their attitudes toward alternative schools. The results of the survey were distributed to the county board.*
- *Throughout the year, the steering committee reported to the PTA, held several large full membership meetings, and sent out frequent mailings to the parents to keep them informed and to urge them to write to the school board.*
- *Finally, in June, at the school board meeting where the decision was made, 25 parents, school staff, and students testified. The testimony was polite, well researched, and effective.*

The school board voted unanimously to keep the middle school open. All five members had started in February leaning toward the view that the school should be closed. By June, because of a well-organized, fully committed, and enthusiastic effort, the school board was turned around. They were impressed with the presentation of the faculty and the steady flow of information, letters, and meetings throughout the year; they appreciated not being overwhelmed at the final meeting by 50 or more witnesses and a large crowd of supporting parents, students, and faculty. It was a successful campaign, tailor-made to the situation, the history of the issue, and the position and personalities of the key decision makers.

Government relations campaigns at the local, state, and national levels make a difference. The example just stated was at the local level. At the national level, consider the successful campaign of James and Sarah Brady in getting the Brady Gun Control bill passed. This took several years of sustained persistent effort, but eventually the five-day waiting period before the sale of a handgun was signed into law.

Legal Limitations on "Lobbying"

The right to petition our government is basic to democracy. The First Amendment to the Constitution of the United States specifically states that "Congress shall make no law . . . abridging . . . the right of the people peaceably to assemble, and to petition the Government for a redress of grievances."

Congress has, however, limited the use of tax-deductible dollars for lobbying. It is important to note that, in this context, "lobbying" is not synonymous with "government relations." For the purposes of tax law, "lobbying" is the attempt to influence state or federal legislation or the decisions of the President, the Vice President, or the top two officials of U.S. Cabinet agencies—such as the Department of Commerce or the Department of Health and Human Services. Other government relations activities—such as advocacy programs directed at the regulatory or administrative arms of government—fall outside the legal definitions of lobbying.

Because all contributions to 501(c)(3) organizations are tax-deductible charitable contributions, these groups face the strictest limitations. Federal law provides that these organizations should not engage in any "substantial" use of tax-deductible contributions for lobbying.

Because "substantial" was never defined, most tax-exempt organizations stayed clear of lobbying until the law was clarified in 1976. Congress at that time removed all doubt as to the legality of lobbying by nonprofit tax-exempt organizations and permitted 501(c)(3) organizations to replace the subjective limitation with a sliding-scale monetary limitation (described in IRC §501(h)). Now, according to section 501(c)(3) of the Internal Revenue Code, these organizations have the same right as other organizations (within the limits of sliding-scale monetary limitations) to voice their political concerns.

Keep in mind that none of these limitations applies to personal advocacy before any body of government by volunteers or non-salaried members of the organization. The most effective advocates for your cause are usually your board members and other supporters. Unless government relations becomes a major focus of your organization, providing information to your members to use in their personal advocacy work will not put your tax status at risk.

But 501(c)(3) organizations should not hire a lobbyist or a lobbying firm (including a law firm to work on legislation) or expect any paid staff members to devote the majority of their time to legislative affairs without consultation with legal counsel. Some large 501(c)(3) organizations have established 501(c)(6) organizations—to which contributions are not deductible as charitable gifts on the contributor's own tax form—to carry out their legislative advocacy and other government relations work. This requires sophisticated legal counsel.

Are Some "Lobbying" Expenses Deductible?

501 (c)(6) organizations do not face any similar limitations on lobbying activities. Government relations, including lobbying, is the principal reason for some organizations' existence. Although lobbying, no matter how extensive, will not threaten the basic tax-exempt status of a 501 (c)(6) organization, the tax deductibility of the portion of dues used for lobbying was limited by law passed in 1993.

Members of 501(c)(6) organizations can no longer deduct the portion of their dues used to influence the federal or state legislatures or top federal executives. It is not considered lobbying if no attempt is made to influence legislation and the contact is made only for the purpose or research and monitoring of legislative activities. Contact with the Executive branch is lobbying only if it is directed to the President, Vice President, or top officials of Cabinet offices or if the purpose was to influence legislation. But local activities are exempt: any portion of dues used for local government relations activities remains tax-exempt to the extent that dues to the organization are otherwise deductible as a business expense. Expenditures for work with regulatory agencies—as opposed to legislative bodies—also remain fully deductible.

Under the revised law, any 501(c)(6) organization engaging in state or federal legislative advocacy should notify its members that the portion of dues used in these activities is not deductible on the member's tax return. (Alternatively, the nonprofit organization may itself pay a "proxy" tax on its lobbying activities at the marginal tax rate for corporations—currently 35 percent.) While the revised tax law increases the cost of some "lobbying" activity, it should not affect a government relations program that is efficiently administered and important to the mission established by your members.

Details of the application of these laws to nonprofit organizations which engage in significant government relations activities are complex and will require advice of legal counsel. But these are not typical situations for many small and medium-sized nonprofit organizations. Don't be afraid to present your case to local officials and, when necessary, to state and federal officials. Often, your donors or members will expect it of you.

CHECKLIST FOR CREATING A GOVERNMENT RELATIONS PROGRAM

1. Clearly identify the outcome you wish to accomplish through your government relations program or campaign.
2. Identify staff responsible for the program and establish a steering committee of officers and other key members of your organization to manage the program or campaign.
3. Members of the steering committee should include those with program expertise as well as those with knowledge and good relations with the key decision makers you need to reach.
4. The facts need to be collected, analyzed, and developed into a position paper that best presents the case for your issue. This needs to include arguments that counter any arguments being used by those who oppose your position.
5. Develop the campaign strategy. The following elements should be considered:
   - All the key decision makers need to be visited and presented with your key arguments and the position paper. Do not forget the staff associated with key members.
   - A letter-writing campaign needs to be launched.
   - The broader membership should be kept informed and included in the process insofar as they can be helpful.
   - Coalitions should be formed with organizations that have similar views.
   - Opportunities to testify before public bodies should be taken.
   - Public relations campaigns to support your campaign goals should be undertaken.
6. The success of the campaign needs to be monitored and modified as appropriate as the campaign proceeds.
7. You may need to hire a professional lobbyist for selected parts of the campaign.

8. Include only those people in your campaign who share your full conviction and enthusiasm. While enthusiasm is critical, it is important to remain calm and professional in your presentation.

9. Say thank you and do not burn your bridges. Remember that not every key decision maker can agree with you on every issue, but they may well be with you on the next issue.

CHAPTER NINE

Financial Management

Money isn't everything, but without it (and proper financial management) your nonprofit could suffer. You need timely, accurate, and meaningful financial information to assess today's results and plan for the future. This chapter provides an overview of accounting issues to help you better manage your financial resources.

Regardless of its size or type of organization, every nonprofit, from a university hospital to a local charity, needs to maintain accurate financial books and records. The purpose of this chapter is to explain what is required to maintain the books and records for a nonprofit organization with basic bookkeeping needs. Large organizations with complex transactions, income from multiple sources, or large payrolls, will need more complex accounting systems than those described here. However, basic accounting concepts are pervasive. Executives, even of nonprofits with their own accounting staff and outside auditors, should understand what their accountants do and why. It is the responsibility of the nonprofit executive, recognizing that the needs of each group are different, to identify those topics that are relevant to the organization's administrative and operational requirements.

This chapter does not attempt to teach you how to invest your organization's funds. It does cover the basic requirements for establishing an accounting function, from implementing an accounting system to generating financial statements. Along the way, practical guidelines are provided covering:

- Banking;
- Staffing;
- Establishing a chart of accounts;
- Accrual and cash basis accounting;
- Budgeting;
- Financial statement preparation;
- Internal accounting controls;
- Audits;
- Tax returns;
- Policies and procedures.

The accounting system is the foundation for understanding your fiscal responsibilities. It does not have to be complex. In fact, it can be quite simple and straightforward, whether you have substantial or limited resources. Nevertheless, accounting is an important function that measures and reports the effectiveness of your organization's operations.

WHAT IS THE ACCOUNTING PROCESS?

The accounting process encompasses the recording and reporting of transactions affecting the financial status of an organization. Regardless of the size of your nonprofit group, your leadership expects that processes and procedures will be implemented to generate useful financial statements and to secure the assets of the organization. Meaningful financial data cannot be produced without a mechanism to capture, record, review, summarize, and report information. This entire process is called accounting.

Bookkeeping is simply the recording of transactions. While accounting and bookkeeping are often used interchangeably, their differences are significant. Bookkeeping is just one facet of the accounting and financial management of your nonprofit group. Accounting refers to the entire process of recording and reporting and requires that systems (automated or manual) be in place to facilitate bookkeeping and to produce accurate, meaningful financial statements and management reports.

The accounting process can be described as an ongoing, monthly cycle consisting of:

- Cash receipts and disbursements;
- Accrual entries (unless maintaining the records on a "cash" basis);
- Other journal entries;
- Closing procedures;
- Financial statement preparation;
- Review and analysis.

The ultimate goal of an accounting system is to generate accurate and timely financial statements that provide meaningful financial data to the readers. These readers may include the leadership of your organization (the governing board), the executive director, donors, lenders, and the public. While the bookkeeping function may end when the monthly financial statements are issued, the accounting process is not complete until a thorough review and analysis have been performed. The remainder of this chapter will describe some of the key steps in the accounting process.

GETTING STARTED: OPENING A BANK ACCOUNT

If you do not already have one, you must open a bank account so funds can be deposited and vendors paid. Most nonprofit organizations have relatively simple banking needs. This does not mean that the decision to use a particular bank should be taken lightly. First, you must identify your organization's basic service needs. They usually encompass deposits, withdrawals (usually issuing checks but sometimes using wire transfers), and obtaining bank balances.

Sometimes, more extensive banking services might include: direct deposit for payroll, investing available funds, debit and credit transactions processed through the Automated Clearing House, lockbox services, merchant account (credit card) transactions, loans, and on-line access to bank account information via your personal computer.

Most banks can provide all of these services, and many large brokerage houses have money market accounts that can be used like checking accounts. Assuming that all banks appear to be the same, how can you find the bank that is right for you? One way to start is to contact other groups of a similar size that might have the same service needs as your organization. Using references from other nonprofits is an excellent way of identifying a bank that offers services that meet your needs. The bank that you use personally or that serves for-profit firms may not be the best for serving nonprofits. Visit the bank and discuss your expected needs with the bank officer. Consult with your attorney or accountant for recommendations, too.

Use the following criteria when searching for a bank:

- *Financial strength*—Although this is not the pressing topic it once was, knowing that your bank is financially stable is important. Although you may not want to investigate capital ratios and liquidity, you can obtain quarterly and annual reports (assuming that the bank is a publicly traded institution) directly from the bank. You can also read analysts' reports on the financial strength of the bank.

- *Quality of service*—Ask your references if they would choose the bank again if they were starting over. Does the bank process transactions accurately the first time? Is the bank responsive to their needs?

- *Clearance*—All banks are now subject to the Expedited Funds Availability Act which mandates the maximum length of time that checks can "clear" through the system and be made available to the customer. Many banks have implemented processes and procedures that reduce this time. This could be an important factor for organizations with severe cash flow restrictions that need immediate use of deposits. If the source of your funding is national or international, be sure to check with the bank to find out how long it takes to clear checks.

- *Location*—Although not critical given that so many banking services can be performed remotely, access to a bank branch is an important criterion for those organizations that may need to make daily deposits. Sometimes, it is necessary to visit with bank personnel, and a nearby branch can save time. Inquire about the availability of a night depository so that deposits can be made after the close of business.

- *Experience with other nonprofit groups*—Even though your needs may be simple, your banker may be better equipped to address your concerns and banking problems if he or she is attuned to the particular issues of nonprofit groups. If your organization grows, it may become an important consideration as your service needs change.

- *Banking personnel*—It is usually incumbent upon the customer to establish a working relationship with the branch manager. Meet with the manager and determine if he or she will be responsive to your needs.

- *Lending*—Does the bank make loans to nonprofit organizations? If you anticipate the need for borrowed funds, you might want to identify some of the criteria used by various banks for extending credit. Of course, most banks will want to see a history of solid financial results and strong cash flow and will review your organization's credit history with vendors. However, collateral requirements and the approval process vary from bank to bank. Decide whether or not you can establish a long-term relationship with your banker that will someday facilitate such borrowing.

- *FDIC Insurance*—Most institutions have government insurance provided by the Federal Deposit Insurance Corporation. Make sure the banks you are considering carry such insurance. Should you need to maintain in the bank more than the maximum amount covered by FDIC insurance, ask your banker for suggestions that would help diversify and thereby protect your group's money.

- *Fees*—Service fees can vary significantly from bank to bank. Make sure the banks you are considering have a clear understanding of your service needs. Banks are entitled to make a profit, but it is your responsibility to ensure that the fees assessed to your account are reasonable and competitive. Review them every six months in case circumstances have changed. If your volume for particular services is high, the bank may be willing to extend volume discounts. However, most small nonprofit organizations are not initially in a position to negotiate deeply discounted fees.

Banks usually charge fees for maintaining the account and for transactions. For example, transaction fees may be assessed for each check cleared, each stop payment, each deposit, and each wire transfer. You can pay for such costs by maintaining a predetermined balance in a non-interest-bearing account (paying with "soft" dollars) or by paying monthly fees out of an interest-bearing account (paying with "hard" dollars). Your banker can help you determine which method is most suitable for your organization. Be sure to ask about special accounts that might be available only to nonprofit organizations with a limited number of transactions.

Nonprofit groups can establish the following types of bank accounts:

- *Demand Deposit Account (DDA)*—This is a transaction account or a basic checking account that pays no interest. It can be appropriate for organizations that want to pay for bank services with "soft" dollars.
- *Interest-Bearing Checking Account*—Available to nonprofit groups, this account simply pays interest on available funds. The interest rate is usually not as high as that paid on money market accounts and savings accounts. However, keeping operating funds in an interest-bearing checking account can eliminate the need to "manage" these funds by transferring dollars in and out of interest-bearing and non-interest-bearing accounts.
- *Money Market Account*—Excess funds can be deposited into a money market account that usually pays a higher interest rate than an interest-bearing checking account and savings account. Money market accounts provide liquidity, but there may be restrictions on the number of monthly checks or disbursements drawn on this account.
- *Savings Account*—The same accounts available to individuals are also available to nonprofit organizations. Once again, there may be monthly restrictions on the number of transactions.

Your bank may also be able to assist you in investing excess funds in Certificates of Deposit (CDs), Treasury bills, commercial paper, or other investments in accordance with your investment policy approved by the board of directors.

Your bank should be financially stable, offer a variety of services, and have strong ties to the community. While banks are certainly entitled to make a fair profit, you have an interest in minimizing transaction costs and maximizing services.

STAFFING THE ACCOUNTING FUNCTION

Finding the right level of staffing for your nonprofit organization is a challenging task. Determining whether or not a separate bookkeeping/accounting function is necessary is also a difficult chore. The size of your operation should give you some guidance in deciding if a bookkeeper is necessary.

Small organizations can usually maintain the books by assigning this responsibility to a volunteer, part-time staff person, or full-time administrative assistant who has other responsibilities. Although bookkeeping experience is helpful, it may not be required if sufficient guidance is provided and the accounting system is simple. This arrangement may be appropriate for groups with relatively small budgets and limited check-writing volume.

An alternative to staffing this position is to outsource this function to an independent bookkeeper, accounting firm, or management firm. Such outsourcing can be cost effective and efficient because direct supervision will not be required, there are usually no payroll issues when using independent contractors, and presumably the person or firm performing such services has the resources and the expertise to meet your particular needs.

Organizations with larger budgets may require an accounting staff consisting of (1) a chief accountant with nonprofit experience to oversee the operation and (2) assistance from one or two bookkeepers who might separate the accounts receivable (cash receipts) and accounts payable (cash disbursements) functions.

ACCOUNTING SYSTEM

Establishing an accounting system, while not directly fulfilling the nonprofit organization's mission, is nevertheless a critical administrative task. A well-designed system, even if it consists solely of manual ledgers, can mean the difference between timely financial information and incomplete, unsupported records.

The accounting system is really just the mechanism that facilitates the recording of transactions into (in the case of computers) or onto (in the case of a manual ledger) various files or ledgers that can be used to generate financial statements.

Usually, the number of transactions (deposits, checks, and journal entries) will determine whether or not it is cost-effective to automate the accounting process. A manual system may be the most appropriate choice for a small operation with a limited number of transactions. Small groups with no paid staff and limited assets may simply "keep the books" in a checkbook supplied by the local bank. Some groups may write enough checks to warrant the purchase of a check register accounting system whereby checks are manually recorded in a ledger at the same time they are prepared. This combination checkbook-and-expense-distribution journal provides a simple way of recording receipts and disbursements while maintaining your checkbook balance.

Some organizations may maintain manual ledgers and then send the ledgers to an accounting firm each month. The accounting firm, often certified public accountants, will input the data into its own system and generate financial statements for the organization. This process may work well for groups that have a close working relationship with their accountants. However, it can give a false sense of security. The fact that the statements are printed from a computer system on a laser printer does not mean that they are accurate or complete.

An automated system does not have to be a complicated system. There are numerous accounting applications available that do not require any previous accounting or bookkeeping experience. Such systems can be installed and maintained by the nonprofit's paid or volunteer staff. Typically, accounting packages include a general ledger, an accounts receivable subsidiary ledger, an accounts payable subsidiary ledger, and sometimes a payroll module.

Payroll is a function that many small (and even some large) organizations prefer not to handle because they do not have staff experienced in this area. The task of paying employees, withholding taxes, filing state and federal forms, and paying state and federal taxes is an onerous one. Taxing authorities are usually unforgiving so penalties and interest accrue quickly if payments or filings are late. The payroll function can easily be contracted out to a firm that specializes in such services. A payroll service can establish direct deposit and arrange for automatic payment and reporting of all taxes at reasonable prices.

Automated accounting systems will run using the most basic personal computers available. They are easily installed and maintained. It is important, however, that particular attention be paid when establishing the chart of accounts (see the section below). When identifying an automated accounting package, be sure to consider the following criteria:

- How easy is it to use?
- How easy is it to install?
- What hardware capacity is necessary to process adequately all anticipated transactions?
- What reports can be printed?
- Can data be uploaded and downloaded to diskettes for use in other applications (such as Lotus 1-2-3 or Excel spreadsheets)?
- Is the vendor reputable?

- Do you know of other, similar organizations using the software?
- Is the cost reasonable?

CHART OF ACCOUNTS

Once a system is identified, you must establish a chart of accounts, the account numbers your organization will use to record and report financial transactions. The chart of accounts can be very simple and easy to use as long as it is not too detailed. A separate account number is not needed for every type of revenue and expense anticipated. Ask yourself what is important to monitor and whether or not this information should be specifically identified in the financial statements.

There is one complicating factor that must be addressed when establishing the chart of accounts. Nonprofit organizations should report their results using functional classifications as well as natural classifications. Functional reporting reflects revenue and expenses by major programmatic activities or functions, such as research, community services, membership services, or public relations; and supporting activities, such as general and administrative and fundraising. Natural accounts are those that can be used across functional categories. Natural account numbers can refer to specific accounts including both income—such as contributions, membership dues, or other income—and expenses, like those for meetings, salaries and fringes, printing, rent, telephone, etc.

When devising the chart of accounts, use a numbering or lettering scheme that refers first to the functional classification. Programmatic activities and supporting activities are functions that are usually two or three digits long. They are usually assigned numbers so that they print in numerical order. See Exhibit 9–1.

Exhibit 9–1 Sample Functional Category Table

Function Number	Function Description
001	Balance Sheet
100	Research
110	Community Services
120	Membership Services
130	Public Relations
200	General & Administrative
210	Fund-Raising

Natural account numbers are usually three or four digits long and can be used throughout your chart of accounts in the appropriate functional categories. Be sure to use the same natural account numbers throughout the functional categories. You should use a series of numbers that group the natural account numbers by financial statement category, as shown in Exhibit 9–2.

Exhibit 9–2 Sample Natural Account Table

Natural Account Number Range	Financial Statement Category
1000 - 1999	Assets
2000 - 2999	Liabilities
3000 - 3999	Net Assets
4000 - 4999	Revenue
5000 - 9999	Expense

The chart of accounts provides a location for posting all transactions within the general ledger. For example, based on Exhibits 9–1 and 9–2, an organization could record postage expense for a membership mailing to 120-7760. Or, cash received could be recorded in 001-1010. Fundraising revenue might be recorded in 210-4200. Both the function and the account number are used when coding transactions.

The chart of accounts is important because it is the basis for generating your monthly financial statements. Most accounting packages will print reports that are based on a combination of functions and account numbers, so it is important to develop the chart of accounts with reporting in mind.

ACCRUAL AND CASH BASIS ACCOUNTING

Although not required, many nonprofit organizations follow generally accepted accounting principles—rules promulgated by the Financial Accounting Standards Board—in their financial statement presentation. One of the basic tenets covering financial statements is that accrual basis accounting shall be followed.

Under accrual basis accounting, revenue is recognized when earned rather than when received, and expense is recognized when incurred rather than when paid. Using accrual basis accounting can produce prepaid expenses (when goods or services are paid for in advance) and prepaid or deferred income (revenue received for goods or services that have not yet been performed). Additionally, revenue relating to the current year but not collected until the next year would be reflected on the statement of financial position as accounts receivable and on the statement of activities as revenue. Expense relating to the current year but not paid until the next year would be reflected on the statement of financial position as accounts payable and on the statement of activities as expense.

At year-end, your group should perform a thorough review for items that should be accrued as revenue or expense. Generally, revenue that is expected but not received before the end of your fiscal year will be recorded as a receivable. Examples of such accruals are advertising income or publication sales. Additionally, expenses that are incurred but not yet paid will be recorded as a payable. Recording such entries before the books are closed for the year will minimize the number of audit entries that must be posted retroactively. The year-end statements will provide a more accurate picture of your organization's net assets if accruals are made. Accrual basis accounting allows for a better matching of revenues and expenses within the accounting period.

During the year, however, your organization may determine that keeping the books on a cash basis is sufficient. If your financial reporting needs are not significant and you have limited staffing for the accounting function, it is easier to record revenue when cash is received and to record expense when disbursements are made. Conversion to the accrual basis of accounting can then be performed at the end of the year. During the year, however, you should be aware of expenses that have been incurred but not yet paid to avoid overspending your budget or cash position.

CASH RECEIPTS

The accounting process starts with cash receipts, a function common to all organizations regardless of size or purpose. In accounting terminology, cash also means funds from checks, travelers checks, credit card payments, or wire transfers. Nonprofit organizations receive cash for dues, conference registrations, contributions, grants, investment income, advertising income, sales of merchandise and special events, or any services to members or the community from whom they obtain fees.

For most nonprofit organizations, checks are mailed directly to the office where they should be recorded or logged in by one person and deposited by another. This segregation of duties helps mitigate the risk of loss or misappropriation. Recognizing that some groups do not have enough staff to segregate these duties, it is incumbent upon the leadership to develop a mechanism that helps ensure that all checks received are deposited into the correct account on a timely basis. Rotate certain functions among the staff, assign the responsibility for opening mail to different people throughout the year, review the journals or logs periodically and compare these subtotals to the deposit slips and entries recorded in the general ledger in order to address the lack of segregation of duties. All amounts received should be deposited promptly; do not hold back any cash for the petty cash fund. When that fund needs replenishing, a check should be cashed for the amount needed.

All checks should be restrictively endorsed upon receipt. A rubber stamp can be readily obtained from the bank. Cash and checks should be deposited the same day they are received or secured overnight in a fireproof safe.

If the volume is significant, you can establish a lockbox system with your bank or with a third-party vendor that specializes in customized processing. Checks can be sent directly to the bank in your organization's name. The bank will deposit those checks and send you batch totals with supporting documentation. The benefits of this system include the timely deposit of funds, enhanced internal accounting controls, and convenience. Of course, these services can be costly as there are usually fixed and variable bank fees associated with lockbox services. Your banker can tell you whether or not such a service is appropriate for your group.

Documentation should be available for every deposit made. A copy of the deposit slip and copies of checks or other notations should be filed in chronological order. As the deposits are made, code them in accordance with your chart of accounts and organize them so they can be entered into your accounting system.

CASH DISBURSEMENTS

Cash disbursements include the processing of checks, wire transfers, and petty cash. This function is a critical one because it entails direct access to one of your organization's most valuable assets, cash. Even if your staffing resources are limited, your group needs to implement internal accounting controls to safeguard your funds and to ensure that disbursements are authorized and appropriate.

Ideally, the cash disbursements function includes the following:

- Approve invoice for payment.

- Authorize that a check be issued.
- Prepare and record the check.
- Sign and mail check to vendor.
- Reconcile bank account.
- Review bank statement, bank reconciliation, and check register.

The critical internal control feature inherent in this function is that the person authorizing and signing checks is not the same person preparing the checks and recording them in the general ledger.

For those groups with limited staffing, there are steps that can be taken to enhance controls even if you cannot segregate the duties as suggested above. First, pay from original invoices only. Do not pay from statements because you increase the likelihood of duplicate payments. Next, authorize the invoice by signing and dating the invoice and circling the amount to be paid. Mark or stamp it paid once the check is issued. Insist that approved supporting documentation be attached for every check so you are assured that the expenditure is authorized and legitimate. In some cases, it may be appropriate to require more than one signature for disbursements in excess of a predetermined amount. An extra precautionary step in a small organization is to have the bank statement sent directly to the executive director or another senior person who is not an authorized signer. The executive director will then have a chance to review the cancelled checks and deposit listing for any unusual transactions. Periodically, the bank reconciliations should be reviewed in detail and tied into the general ledger to ensure that no unauthorized transactions have occurred.

When the disbursement is made, it must be coded and recorded in the general ledger. File a copy of the check with the supporting documentation by vendor.

ACCRUAL ENTRIES AND OTHER JOURNAL ENTRIES

Posting accruals and adjusting journal entries is a standard process within the accounting cycle. As noted previously, accruals are made to record revenue and expense in the proper period, whether or not funds have been received or disbursed. After month-end, review the files to determine if revenue collected in the subsequent month should be recorded as a receivable the month before. Advertising and royalty income are two examples of items that may require accruals.

On the expense side, review the open payables file and record invoices that have been received but not yet paid. Also, if the expenditure is material (significant), accrue for items or services that have been received but have not yet been billed. Recording these entries in the monthly financial statements will generate a more complete financial picture of your organization's assets and liabilities.

CLOSING PROCEDURES

Closing procedures entail a review of key asset and liability accounts. Each month, a series of accounts should be reconciled against subsidiary ledgers and other supporting documentation. It is possible that during the month, entries are miscoded and misposted and therefore ending balances will not be accurate. Closing procedures include the process of posting balances to the general ledger and performing an internal control called the analytical review.

Cash is the first account that should be reconciled or "closed" as part of your organization's closing procedures. Cash can be closed by preparing a bank reconciliation and having it reviewed by someone other than the person posting entries to the general ledger. You may have an accounts receivable subsidiary ledger that must be reconciled and posted to the general ledger. Other asset accounts that may require special attention include deposit accounts, clearing accounts, and prepaid expense accounts. Make sure that all account balances have support or some type of corroborating documentation that ties into the numbers on the statement of financial position.

Liability accounts should also be reconciled as part of the closing process. Many accounting systems use an accounts payable subsidiary ledger that must be closed and then posted to the general ledger. This closing procedure may include the recording of last minute invoices and the crediting of payments after issuing checks. The accounts payable ledger should tie into the general ledger each month. Other liability accounts that may require some type of reconciliation include clearing accounts and prepaid income.

While analytical review procedures are especially appropriate for large organizations with more complex financial reporting, you should know what they entail and how you may be able to benefit from them. Analytical review is the review of current account balances as measured against some other criteria. Your closing procedures can include a comparison of current results with those from the same period last year. Balances can be compared to your budget and ratios can be computed and monitored from month to month. Results can even be measured against industry standards as a means of identifying potential problems. Numbers should be reviewed to see if they make sense given your knowledge of the organization's activities. These steps can be performed as part of the review and analysis procedures described later in this chapter.

BUDGETING

Budgeting is a process that must be tailored to the individual needs of your organization. No matter how unique your organization is, however, there are some practical considerations that are common to all groups. Keeping in mind that a budget is a benchmark for measuring the results of your operations in fiscal terms, you should develop a budget based on historical information, trends, industry conditions, and the economy.

Normally, the executive director will develop the annual budget and submit it to the board for approval in accordance with the nonprofit's by-laws. As this approval process usually takes a few months, many association executives begin to prepare the budget three or four months before the end of the year.

First, examine last year's results and this year's most recent financial information in order to identify trends and changes from your expectations. In projecting revenues, identify the most likely income sources first and the period of time over which this revenue will be recognized. Membership dues, publication sales, and investment income are some revenue categories that are usually more predictable than others. Fund-raising receipts, other donations, grant income, and in-kind contributions are more difficult to project. The budget for these categories is based more on historical information and the executive director's specific knowledge of these areas.

There should be a direct relationship between projected revenues and expenses that will be incurred to carry out the nonprofit's mission. Preparing the revenue side of the equation first will make it clear to what extent programs and services can be rendered. Ask the appropriate association employees or volunteers to estimate expenses and to identify when they will be incurred. You might want written explanations for amounts over a certain percentage of last year's budget or actual numbers.

Budgets should be prepared on a "calendarized" or seasonal basis. If operating under the accrual method of accounting, reflect revenues and expenses when earned and as incurred. Under the cash method, show in each month the projected cash receipts and disbursements. Reflecting the budget in this way will make the monthly financial statements more meaningful when results are compared to the budget.

Don't forget to develop a capital budget: one that encompasses the purchase of fixed assets such as computer equipment and furniture. Although they are usually not recorded as expenses within the financial statements, these purchases can entail a significant amount of money and are therefore subject to the same kind of approval and review as other expenditures. Capital expenditures can be more easily predicted because the number of such transactions is small compared to your day-to-day operations.

While the budget is often considered a working document, its purpose is to make estimates of future revenues and expenses and to serve as a management tool. There are usually no right or wrong budgets. Because it will never be perfect, those who prepare it should do the best they can with the information available, be prepared to defend it, and then utilize it as one measure of the success of your nonprofit's programmatic activities. Understanding and responding to significant variances from the budget is probably one of your most important fiduciary responsibilities.

FINANCIAL STATEMENT PREPARATION

The accounting cycle is almost complete as financial statements are generated and then reviewed. Financial statements should include a statement of financial position (balance sheet), a statement of activities (income statement), and a statement of cash flows.

Recently, the Financial Accounting Standards Board issued Statement of Financial Accounting Standards No. 117, *Financial Statements of Not-for-Profit Organizations*. This statement governs the presentation of financial statements for nonprofit groups of all sizes (although implementation for small organizations is delayed until 1996). This pronouncement states that the results of operations shall be reported by identifying changes in permanently restricted net assets, temporarily restricted net assets, and unrestricted net assets. Both the statement of financial position and the statement of activities will report the balances in these classes of net assets.

A statement of financial position (see Exhibit 9–3) reports the assets and liabilities of an organization at a particular point in time. It usually includes three sections: assets, liabilities, and net assets. The assets section will include your checking, savings, or money market

Exhibit 9–3   Sample Statement of Financial Position

The Food Distribution Network, Inc.
Statement of Financial Position
As of November 30, 19XX

Assets:	
Cash	$55,600
Accounts receivable	2,750
Investments	59,900
Fixed assets, net	32,375
Total assets	$150,625
Liabilities and net assets:	
Accounts payable	$16,250
Accrued liabilities	2,400
Total liabilities	18,650
Net assets:	
Unrestricted	131,975
Temporarily restricted	0
Permanently restricted	0
Total net assets	131,975
Total liabilities and net assets	$150,625

accounts; investments or reserve funds, if any; the organization's fixed assets, including furniture and fixtures; and accounts receivable and other items of value to the organization.

The liabilities section will include trade payables (amounts owed to vendors), deferred income (income to be recognized in a future period), and other obligations that the group has incurred.

The net assets section will report the cumulative net worth of the organization, consisting of the difference between total assets and total liabilities.

The statement of activities (see Exhibit 9–4) measures, in fiscal terms only, the effectiveness of your organization's ability to carry out its mission. It reports revenues and expenses and shows the change in your net assets from one year to the next. Exhibit 9–4 is an example of functional reporting.

You can also combine a functional and natural report as shown in Exhibit 9–5.

Exhibit 9-4 Sample Statement of Activities (functional basis)

The Food Distribution Network, Inc.
Statement of Activities (unrestricted class only)
For the 11 Months Ended November 30, 19XX

	Current Month Actual	Current Month Budget	Current Month Variance	Year-To-Date Actual	Year-To-Date Budget	Year-To-Date Variance	Annual Budget
Revenues							
Contributions	$9,200	$9,000	$200	$111,000	$99,000	$12,000	$108,000
Fees	900	1,000	(100)	8,000	11,000	(3,000)	12,000
Fund-raising	4,000	5,000	(1,000)	58,900	55,000	3,900	60,000
Investment income	225	200	25	3,050	2,200	850	2,400
Other income	1,100	1,000	100	8,000	11,000	(3,000)	12,000
Total unrestricted revenues	15,425	16,200	(775)	188,950	178,200	10,750	194,400
Expenses							
Restaurant pick-ups	4,400	4,000	(400)	46,500	44,000	(2,500)	48,000
Hotel pick-ups	2,000	3,500	1,500	31,600	38,500	6,900	42,000
Distribution facilities	3,150	2,500	(650)	24,200	27,500	3,300	30,000
General & administrative	4,750	5,000	250	56,850	55,000	(1,850)	60,000
Fund-raising	400	500	100	4,900	5,500	600	6,000
Total unrestricted expenses	14,700	15,500	800	164,050	170,500	6,450	186,000
Increase in unrestricted net assets	725	700	25	24,900	7,700	17,200	8,400
Net unrestricted assets at beginning of year	—	—	—	107,075	107,075	0	107,075
Net unrestricted assets at end of period	—	—	—	$131,975	$114,775	$17,200	$115,475

Exhibits 9–4 and 9–5 reflect column headings that are appropriate for monthly financial reporting. Audited financial statments would differ by showing yearly results only.

A supplementary statement of activities (see Exhibit 9–6) is an additional report that can (must, for certain types of organizations) be included as part of your audited financial statements. It reports revenues and expenses by natural categories. This statement can be useful in comparing common types of expenses across functions or programs.

The statement of cash flows (see Exhibit 9–7) is a required statement that accompanies the audit opinion, other financial statements, and footnotes as part of the annual audit. This statement is generally not prepared on an interim basis (monthly), but it does reconcile how your organization generated and used its cash during the year.

REVIEW AND ANALYSIS

It is incumbent upon your organization's leadership, usually the treasurer, to review the monthly financial statements in order to identify errors, trends, and unusual transactions. The following items should be considered:

- Examine the cash balance to ensure that balances maintained in checking accounts are adequate but not excessive.
- Note the investment balance, if any, and identify any significant changes from month to month.
- Examine the balance in prepaid expenses and prepaid income to ensure that increases or decreases in balances are appropriate given the timing of your group's activities.
- Examine the balances in fixed asset accounts and make sure there are no significant increases or decreases without prior knowledge and approval.
- Ensure that the accounts payable balance remains in line with expectations.
- Examine the payroll liability accounts for unusual increases.
- Examine major sources of income to determine if actual results are in line with the budget. Obtain explanations for significant variances.

Exhibit 9-5 Sample Statement of Activities (functional and natural account basis)

The Food Distribution Network, Inc.
Statement of Activities (unrestricted class only)
For the 11 Months Ended November 30, 19XX

	Current Month Actual	Current Month Budget	Current Month Variance	Year-To-Date Actual	Year-To-Date Budget	Year-To-Date Variance	Annual Budget
Revenues							
Contributions	$9,200	$9,000	$200	$111,000	$99,000	$12,000	$108,000
Fees	900	1,000	(100)	8,000	11,000	(3,000)	12,000
Fund-raising	4,000	5,000	(1,000)	58,900	55,000	3,900	60,000
Investment income	225	200	25	3,050	2,200	850	2,400
Other income	1,100	1,000	100	8,000	11,000	(3,000)	12,000
Total unrestricted revenues	15,425	16,200	(775)	188,950	178,200	10,750	194,400
Expenses							
Restaurant pick-ups							
Meetings	45	100	55	1,105	1,100	(5)	1,200
Miscellaneous	1,800	1,750	(50)	18,745	19,250	505	21,000
Postage	75	70	(5)	895	770	(125)	840
Salaries and benefits	1,600	1,500	(100)	18,750	16,500	(2,250)	18,000
Telephone	225	200	(25)	2,055	2,200	145	2,400
Travel/transportation	655	380	(275)	4,950	4,180	(770)	4,560
Total restaurant pick-ups	4,400	4,000	(400)	46,500	44,000	(2,500)	48,000
Hotel pick-ups							
Meetings	0	40	40	810	440	(370)	480
Miscellaneous	945	1,735	790	13,050	19,085	6,035	20,820
Postage	75	80	5	1,355	880	(475)	960
Salaries and benefits	560	1,095	535	7,800	12,045	4,245	13,140
Telephone	110	155	45	1,935	1,705	(230)	1,860
Travel/transportation	310	395	85	6,650	4,345	(2,305)	4,740
Total hotel pick-ups	2,000	3,500	1,500	31,600	38,500	6,900	42,000

Distribution Facilities						
Meetings	80	65	(15)	385	715	330	780
Miscellaneous	40	50	10	365	550	185	600
Postage	95	70	(25)	495	770	275	840
Rent and utilities	500	500	0	5,500	5,500	0	6,000
Salaries and benefits	1,550	1,400	(150)	14,355	15,400	1,045	16,800
Telephone	110	125	15	835	1,375	540	1,500
Travel/transportation	775	290	(485)	2,265	3,190	925	3,480
Total distribution facilities	3,150	2,500	(650)	24,200	27,500	3,300	30,000
General & administrative							
Audit	0	175	175	2,100	1,925	(175)	2,100
Bank charges	65	50	(15)	650	550	(100)	600
Depreciation	45	45	0	495	495	0	540
Insurance	100	100	0	1,100	1,100	0	1,200
Miscellaneous	1,200	1,300	100	15,590	14,300	(1,290)	15,600
Postage	50	70	20	675	770	95	840
Rent and utilities	700	700	0	7,700	7,700	0	8,400
Salaries and benefits	2,400	2,400	0	27,500	26,400	(1,100)	28,800
Telephone	65	60	(5)	545	660	115	720
Travel/transportation	125	100	(25)	495	1,100	605	1,200
Total general & administrative	4,750	5,000	250	56,850	55,000	(1,850)	60,000
Fund-raising							
Miscellaneous	65	50	(15)	520	550	30	600
Postage	135	160	25	1,795	1,760	(35)	1,920
Telephone	175	200	25	1,905	2,200	295	2,400
Travel/transportation	25	90	65	680	990	310	1,080
Total fund-raising	400	500	100	4,900	5,500	600	6,000
Total unrestricted expenses	14,700	15,500	800	164,050	170,500	6,450	186,000
Increase in unrestricted net assets	725	700	25	24,900	7,700	17,200	8,400
Net unrestricted assets at beginning of year	—	—	—	107,075	107,075	0	107,075
Net unrestricted assets at end of period	—	—	—	$131,975	$114,775	$17,200	$115,475

Exhibit 9–6   Sample Supplementary Statement of Activities

The Food Distribution Network, Inc.
Supplementary Statement of Activities (unrestricted class only)
For the 11 Months Ended November 30, 19XX

	Restaurant Pick-Ups	Hotel Pick-Ups	Distribution Facilities	General & Administrative	Fund-raising	Total
Audit	$0	$0	$0	$2,100	$0	$2,100
Bank charges	0	0	0	650	0	650
Depreciation	0	0	0	495	0	495
Insurance	0	0	0	1,100	0	1,100
Meetings	1,105	810	385	0	0	2,300
Miscellaneous	18,745	13,050	365	15,590	520	48,270
Postage	895	1,355	495	675	1,795	5,215
Rent and utilities	0	0	5,500	7,700	0	13,200
Salaries and benefits	18,750	7,800	14,355	27,500	0	68,405
Telephone	2,055	1,935	835	545	1,905	7,275
Travel/transportation	4,950	6,650	2,265	495	680	15,040
Total expenses	$46,500	$31,600	$24,200	$56,850	$4,900	$164,050

Exhibit 9–7   Sample Statement of Cash Flows

The Food Distribution Network, Inc.
Statement of Activities (unrestricted class only)
For the 11 Months Ended November 30, 19XX

Cash flows from operating activities:	
Change in net assets	$24,900
Adjustments to reconcile change in net assets to	
net cash provided by operating activities:	
Depreciation	495
Increase in accounts receivable	(1,050)
Increase in accounts payable	5,775
Decrease in accrued liabilities	(600)
Net cash provided by operating activities	29,520
Cash flows from investing activities:	
Purchase of equipment	(3,500)
Proceeds from sale of investments	10,250
Purchase of investments	(4,050)
Net cash provided by investing activities	2,700
Cash flows from financing activities:	0
Net increase in cash	32,220
Cash at beginning of year	23,380
Cash at end of period	$55,600

- Examine all expenses for costs that exceed the budget. Obtain explanations for significant variances.
- Examine programmatic activities and obtain explanations for significant variances.

You should also review the check register each month in order to note readily identifiable unauthorized disbursements. Review the listing for unusual payees and identify those payees that are not familiar. Also, review the listing for unusual amounts, including even dollar amounts, and obtain explanations for such disbursements.

Periodically, the executive director should review the bank reconciliation to ensure that reconciling items are researched and resolved on a timely basis.

DOES YOUR ORGANIZATION NEED AN AUDIT?

Although your organization may not be required to have an audit, it is generally recommended that an audit be performed, even if your operating budget is less than $100,000. An unqualified audit opinion stating that the financial statements present fairly the balances and results of operations is sometimes critical in fund-raising, borrowing, and accepting government grants. Within your organization, an audit will help provide assurances that the financial statements are accurate and complete.

An audit of your organization's financial statements can give the leadership confidence that the fiduciary responsibilities have been fulfilled. Your auditor will perform tests of your accounting system, review the internal accounting controls, examine corroborating documentation, perform analytical review procedures, and confirm cash accounts and other balances in order to render an opinion on the financial statements taken as a whole. The auditor will review the accounting principles being followed and the financial statement format to determine whether or not they comply with generally accepted accounting principles.

Generally, the board of directors chooses an auditor after receiving a recommendation from the executive director. When choosing an auditor, consider the auditing firm's experience with nonprofit organizations, the firm's resources, the individuals assigned to the audit, their availability, their commitment to advising your organization on a variety of business matters, and the anticipated fees (you may be able to negotiate a lower fee if the work is performed during the "off season"). Check their references and ask them what differentiates their firm from others that provide the same service.

You should be aware of the various types of audit reports that can be issued by your certified public accountant. The most comprehensive audit includes procedures that test the organization's compliance with generally accepted accounting principles. These procedures are performed in accordance with generally accepted auditing standards which require that the auditors satisfy themselves that material transactions are properly reflected in the financial statements and are disclosed in the footnotes. This results in a complete audit.

An audit includes an opinion, a statement of financial position, a statement of activities, a statement of cash flows, footnotes, and sometimes a supplementary schedule reporting results by natural accounts as well as by functional areas. The footnotes are an integral part of the audited financial statements. They disclose the nature of the operations, a summary of significant accounting policies, a description of significant events, the nature of any related party transactions, and detailed information on the organization's commitments and contingencies.

Upon completion of the audit, your auditors will require a management representation letter addressed to them that acknowledges management's responsibility for the fair presentation of the financial statements. Typically, the executive director and selected board members (usually the treasurer and president) are asked to sign the letter. If you are not familiar with this procedure, ask your auditor for a copy of the letter that must be signed before issuance of the financial statements. In addition to the audited financial statements, the auditors should provide you with a management or internal control letter in which they discuss any suggestions that they have for improvements in your policies and procedures.

An auditor's review of financial statements includes procedures that are not as comprehensive as a complete audit. A review report indicates that the testing performed is less than that of a full audit and that only analytical review procedures were applied. Corroborating evidence, including confirmations, are not a part of review procedures. A review provides only limited assurances that the financial statements are complete. It may be appropriate when an organization cannot afford an audit or when an audit is not necessary given the limited scope of its operations.

A third type of service that auditors can perform is a compilation. A compilation report states that the account balances presented are those provided by management. The auditor will take absolutely no responsibility for any of the numbers or for the adequacy of the footnotes or other disclosures. Compilations may be appropriate for organizations that retain CPA firms to prepare their monthly financial statements or for those groups that want a professional presentation without any assurances that the numbers are correct.

TAX RETURNS

If your organization's gross receipts are in excess of $25,000 per year, IRS Form 990, Return of Organization Exempt from Income Tax must be completed and filed by the 15th day of the fifth month after year-end. A penalty totaling $10 per day will be assessed by the Internal Revenue Service if the tax return is late or incomplete. However, IRS Form 2758 may be used to obtain an extension if necessary.

Some of the information that must be completed in the tax return includes the following:

- Details of the revenue and expenses in the year to recalculate the final net assets at the end of the year.
- Details of expenses by program services, management, and fund-raising.
- A description of activities related to your organization's exempt purpose.
- A statement of financial position at the beginning and end of the tax year.
- List of officers, directors, and trustees, including compensation paid to them.

If your group is exempt from federal income taxes under section 501(c)(3) of the Internal Revenue Code, you must also complete Schedule A of Form 990. Schedule A requests other information including the five highest paid employees other than officers and directors, the five highest paid persons for professional services, and further detail of revenues for the four years preceding the audit year.

You may be required to file IRS Form 990-T, Exempt Organization Business Income Tax Return if your organization has $1,000 or more of gross income from an unrelated business, such as advertising revenue or the sale of lists and labels to for-profit organizations. This income, net of allocable expenses, is subject to Federal tax (and possibly state tax). The 990-T and related tax payments are due by the 15th day of the fifth month after year-end.

Your nonprofit is required to maintain a copy of your Form 990 tax return on file and available for public inspection.

You may want to ask your auditors to complete the annual tax return and extension request if necessary. They can also advise you with regard to unrelated business income tax and local tax filing requirements.

POLICIES AND PROCEDURES

Finally, to ensure that the accounting cycle is completed as directed by management, your organization should develop and maintain a fiscal policies and procedures manual. Such a manual does not have to be lengthy but it does have to be formalized and the staff should be instructed to follow it at all times. The manual should include the following topics:

- Financial statement presentation.
- Distribution and timing of the financial statements.
- Chart of accounts.
- Bank account reconciliation procedures.
- Investment policies.
- Check-signing procedures.
- Travel expense policy.
- Revenue collection and recording.
- Payroll policies.
- Insurance.
- Controls over fixed assets.
- Controls over inventory, if applicable.
- Budgeting.
- Corporate tax filings.
- Conflicts of interest.

Not all of these topics are appropriate for the day-to-day operations of small organizations. The fiscal policies and procedures manual can be an evolutionary document that expands as your group's operations become more complex. If followed and maintained, such a manual can help mitigate some of the inherent internal control problems prevalent in many small nonprofit organizations. It should help define the responsibilities of those involved in the financial affairs of your nonprofit organization. It should also promote operational efficiency, which will in turn permit you to concentrate on providing services and carrying out your organization's mission.

CHAPTER TEN

Choosing and Nurturing an Information System

You can save time and money with the appropriate computer technology and information systems. Cutting through the computer lingo is only half the battle. You also need to identify what you want to achieve and what you can afford. This chapter will help clarify what you *really* need to know to automate your operations.

Nonprofit organizations are prodigious producers and consumers of information. Financial reports, contributor records, and meeting minutes are generated in the normal operation of any nonprofit organization. The development, management, and dissemination of information may even be the primary purpose and function of some nonprofit organizations.

Modern technology has developed information *systems*, based upon computers, which enable us to manage and use information more accurately and efficiently than ever before. In order to succeed, the executive of a nonprofit organization today must be familiar with these tools. This chapter is aimed at both providing you with some basic concepts on the management and use of modern information systems, and sharing lessons gleaned from experience with such systems in a nonprofit environment.

SELECTING AN INFORMATION SYSTEM FOR YOUR ORGANIZATION

There are very simple rules for creating an information system which will stay within your budget and will keep the work flowing.

Remember that technology is a tool for performing work tasks. It is not an end in itself.

Appropriate information systems must flow from a clear operational plan. Lacking a thorough assessment of operations and goals, some nonprofit organizations wind up using large and complex systems to accomplish very straightforward and simple tasks. The converse is true for organizations trying to do complex tasks with small systems pushed beyond their limits. With a good, clear operational plan, the information system (and the technology used for it) can be properly selected for your particular needs.

Let's say that one of your goals is to track information about your organization's membership. Information for each member would include the usual, such as name and address, but would also include some statistical information. Some large nonprofits, such as the American Association of Retired Persons, require very powerful computer systems, because the organization has hundreds of thousands of members and keeps detailed information on each. Smaller organizations may be able to keep all of the information they need on a single personal computer.

The ability to translate an operational plan into a technology plan and then into a working system requires a particular expertise. This can be gained over time with study and on-the-job experience, but it is easier for a nonprofit executive, once his organization has moved beyond basic word processing, to purchase the services of experts. The major hazard of using consultants is getting locked into their view of the future and what your capabilities should be. This is where the operational plan must be clear. Information system decisions should spring from practical, operational decisions and not from someone's new toy wish list.

No one can predict the future, particularly in technology; but neither can you predict the services that your organization will be providing five or ten years from now. Purchase your system for the functions that you are performing now and will be performing in the near future. Here again, the operational plan should spell out the services that you are currently performing. The technological tools required to perform them will flow from the plan.

The Basic Tools

There are some basic information system services that every nonprofit organization should have available. These include:

- Word processing for letters, minutes, and other documents;

- A spreadsheet for budget preparation and cash flow projections;
- An accounting program for regular financial reports; and
- A database program for maintaining membership or other types of records.

Large nonprofit organizations might also use desktop publishing programs, graphics programs, electronic communications programs, and other tools which are becoming more and more common in the workplace.

A Glossary of Terms

In order to be sure that we understand the terms used in modern information systems technology, let's go over some of the basics.

Hardware is the physical wiring and machinery that make up the computers and their systems. This includes central processing units (CPUs), monitors, keyboards, network interface cards (NICs), and the assorted cables. Peripherals are other devices that may be considered optional, such as printers, joysticks, plotters, etc., that can be attached to the CPU.

Software is the instructions that tell the computer what to do. Computer programs such as word processors, spreadsheets, and other common business applications are all based on software developed to accomplish certain tasks.

There is also **Firmware**, which is hardware that has software instructions imprinted or embedded in it so that the instructions become firmly built into the hardware. An example would be the computer chip that contains the instructions that the computer uses to "wake itself up" when you first turn it on. This chip instructs the computer how to access the various drives and cards that are contained in the CPU.

A **LAN** is a Local Area Network, a **WAN** is a Wide Area Network, and a **MAN** is a Metropolitan Area Network. These are groups of computers that are connected together in order to communicate. The major function of a network is to allow computers in different physical locations, say two offices side by side or separate installations on each side of the globe, to share information.

Networks vs Stand-alone

With a stand-alone personal computer, a user learns the system and then can refine it constantly, either in small increments or larger portions. A small increment might be learning to use a single keystroke where a number of keystrokes had been used for the same result, such as in creating a "macro." A large increment might be the addition of a whole new software program that allows data to be manipulated in completely new ways. Stand-alone systems provide an individual user with a personal tool for information management.

Networks, on the other hand, impose some limits on the ability of the individual user to customize the tool to his or her own use. Networks of individual computers tied together were originally created to share expensive resources such as hard disks and printers. Since the price of these resources has come down precipitously, networks are now primarily used for sharing software and to facilitate communication between computer users. Most office organizations, even those with small staffs, can benefit by the use of a network. Some nonprofit organizations with as few as four persons on the staff work so closely together that a network adds to their efficiency.

In recent years, one of the greatest expansions of computer use has been for electronic mail. Most LANs have the capability of sending messages between users with files or other information attached. This is a common way to communicate and has completely replaced executive memos in some offices. With connections outside the local network to public networks such as Internet, CompuServe, MCI, and Prodigy, electronic mail can be passed to anyone who has an electronic mail box. Some nonprofit organizations use these facilities for communications among their officers, committees, boards, or members in disparate locations.

Centralization

One of the philosophical questions which must be addressed in the development of an information system is whether to model the system on a centralized information flow or to decentralize. The benefit of centralization is control. With a centralized system all of the information is kept in one place and is, therefore, more secure. The downside is that users of the information may have more difficulty in accessing relevant data and less control over how the information is used.

A decentralized model, such as a LAN, allows for greater information flow. It offers less security and data integrity, but with this type of system the actual users of the information have greater access to the data. The decision regarding the centralization of data should be based upon such issues as the sensitivity of the data, the requirements for accuracy, and the efficiency of accessibility.

The 80 Percent Rule

A trap that has put many nonprofits into large holes is the creation of custom software. The 80 percent rule is that if a piece of software does 80 percent of what you want it to do and is the best you can find for those tasks, buy it! It is much easier to change employees or to change how they operate than to create a piece of software that works and does 90–100 percent of the work to be performed.

For example, a nonprofit organization with a complex Unix multi-user system developed a customized membership software program. This system was created and supported by the vendor of the hardware. But when there was a change in the business to be performed by the organization, the software had to be changed also and the vendor was the only source with the expertise to do it. The organization faced these choices: invest the money to train one of its employees to the level of expertise necessary to make the changes; hire a programmer to do the job; or keep on paying the consulting firm whenever they needed a change. What they ultimately did after several false starts was to scrap the customized system and buy off-the-shelf software to do what they needed.

A subsidiary problem to the limits of customized software is the customization of off-the-shelf software. One nonprofit purchased a membership package and proceeded to write programs to make it do exactly what it needed. Within one year the program was so customized that when the original company published an upgrade, the nonprofit could not make use of it.

When you purchase software you are buying a partner in your business. Make sure that you will get the training and support that you need. This is why many organizations will only purchase "industry standard" off-the-shelf software. These software programs will typically do 80–90 percent of the information processing that a nonprofit organization requires, and should be the first option for a nonprofit executive to consider.

If you think you have a process that cannot be performed by off-the-shelf software, find a consultant and have him or her do a thorough market search. With the rapid development of new, sophisticated software tools, numerous niche markets are being filled by software companies. Most software tools are gaining such flexibility and power that they can perform almost all organizational processes without the organization resorting to large customization projects.

One nonprofit with a large membership base had a system with 15 terminals working off one CPU. This included a custom membership package, which could be used for fund-raising appeals, fast word processing, and an excellent operating system, but which was very complex. The operators of the system had a difficult time maintaining it because all of the commands were learned by rote. The operators did not have full understanding of why they were doing what they were doing. As a result, anytime there was a problem the consulting firm was called in to fix it. This is an expensive way to go.

STAFFING YOUR INFORMATION SYSTEM

Computers are able to do any repetitive task extremely fast and with incredible accuracy. The problem is that they must be instructed to perform their work in exceptional detail and with exact precision. This is where the difficulty lies with modern information systems and where the challenge begins.

The use of information system computers takes skills that can be learned, but they are different from other business skills. The availability of the new computer-based information systems has literally redefined work in the modern organizational setting. Technology should give you more options, flexibility, and power. It should not paint you into a corner and constrict your abilities. When it does, it is inappropriate technology.

Training is vital for efficient information flow and your investment in training should equal or exceed your investment in capital equipment. Presently, high schools and colleges do not teach their students the "industry standard" software programs, nor do students often learn them on their own with any degree of competence. Your organization must take it upon itself to ensure that your workers know how to use the tools that you are providing them. This is part of the continuous process of keeping up with technology, providing a modern workplace, and ensuring productivity and a high level of worker morale.

There are numerous ways of providing training, and the process of education does not need to be expensive if it is spread out over time. Large leaps can make training extremely difficult, so you should plan to make change gradually and constantly so that it is the norm rather than the exception. Another benefit of this constant change is that your staff does not become habituated to one and only one tool. They should learn to generalize, to understand the principles behind the tools, and thereby to adapt to a different tool merely by changing keystrokes to accomplish the same task.

For example, there are many different word processing software packages, but they all perform the same functions using different keystrokes. If your staff learns by rote they cannot adapt to a new tool. If they learn through principle, they can.

Cross-Training

There are two major information assets in your business: the information in the computer system and, more important, the information in your staff. If there is only one individual in your organization who knows how to use your information systems, you are in for trouble. Because the information systems skill level of many entry-level employees is minimal, training in the systems that you install is very important. Equally important is the cross-training of several individuals in your organization on the same tasks.

Ongoing training and cross-training keep morale up and workers interested as well as making your whole staff stronger. A professional development plan should be created along with the strategic technological plan, and the two should run parallel with each other.

Once you have trained your staff, be prepared for changes. If you have trained your staff well, they will be coming up with ideas for processes, software, and hardware that will make your organization more efficient. It is impossible for one individual to track the myriad changes occurring with technology, but if your staff are alert to watch for new tools, they can have a great effect on their own work environment. Systems do best when they are growing and changing.

PREPARING FOR CHANGE

One of the basic aspects of any "system," whether it is an economic system, a company, the biosphere, or an information system, is that it grows and changes constantly. Systems are not static entities needing only maintenance, like a building. The strength of a system is that it is "self-learning." In other words, it accepts constant feedback and responds to the changing needs of its environment.

It Will Be Out Of Date!

Many people worry that their systems will be out of date before they can become expert in using them. With the speed at which technology is currently developing, that is probably true, but that is not a reason to purchase a system that is more powerful, and therefore complex, than is necessary. With adequate training and support, a simple system will perform the functions it was designed to do until the scope of the functions changes. Follow your operational plan!

Version Upgrades

If you have purchased off-the-shelf software for your information system, you will inevitably be faced with the option of upgrading your software to new and improved versions. You do not need to examine your present software every time a new version comes out, but you do need to know when your present version of software has been superseded by another generation that truly performs better. Upgrades are justified not by simple improvement in degrees, but in kind.

An example is the move from WordPerfect 5.1 to either 5.2 or 6.0. A move to 5.2 would have been advantageous only if there were bugs or severe limitations in 5.1 that were keeping your users from performing vital tasks or slowing them down significantly. A move to 6.0 is justified because there is a useful change in the way word processing is performed. A new industry standard has been set by Microsoft with Windows and with the use of the Graphic User Interface (GUI, pronounced "gooey"), which provides users with pictures or graphics to aid them in manipulating the machine. Other companies will have to meet or exceed this standard to compete with Microsoft, and users will have to learn this new standard (in the software of their choice) to perform the tasks that will be asked of them.

How to Plan Ahead

A clear operational plan, updated frequently with tactical technology changes, has a sweeping effect on how an organization's activities are conducted. As a new technology emerges—say, video conferencing—each nonprofit organization should periodically look at the possible problems and opportunities that it represents.

Organizations change, but very few organizational processes actually disappear. The development of the fax was expected to cut into the postal service. It has to a degree, but not to the extent expected. Electronic mail was supposed to cut down on the number of phone calls, but phone calls are ever-increasing. People make use of any and all communication channels that they have available. The idea is to make sure that you understand the cost-effectiveness of each service and use the appropriate one for the job.

Emerging information technologies illustrate a principle described by Buckminster Fuller as "ephemeralization." Fuller's premise was that progress is the doing of more with less. In computers the principle is manifested by the geometric increase in computer power with each generation of equipment, while the size and power consumption continue to decrease dramatically. Each technological step gives the user more capabilities for a lower cost.

The "ephemeralizing" technologies are enabling workers to become independent of time and space. A simple example is the use of electronic mail instead of the telephone. With the telephone, both parties must be present on the same line at the same time to have a conversation. With electronic mail the information is passed *asyncronistically*, meaning that each party gives and receives information at a time independent of the other. An example of space independence is telecommuting, which enables workers to dial into their company's network from anywhere.

How Do I Deal With The Complexities?

If you have a good, well-trained staff and expert advice from a consultant, you can keep the issues very simple. The overall technology plan will come directly from the operational plans and the goals contained in it. The complexities will be worked out by the installer, the maintainer, and the users. The evaluation of how well the system is working is simple: Is it meeting the business needs that it was intended to meet?

MAINTENANCE

Like any system, your information system will require regular and periodic maintenance. Once again the maintenance strategy must be determined by the operational plan and a good look at what your resources are. For example, if you have a very knowledgeable user community, your own staff may be able to diagnose and solve software problems. If you have a large enough group you can afford to train a particular staff person to diagnose and solve hardware problems. If everyone is covered by other work, an outside company can be brought in for hardware maintenance or software support.

On this issue in particular, be careful of who gives you advice. Hardware is extremely inexpensive to purchase when compared to a maintenance contract on a number of machines. The purchase of an extra workstation as a "hot spare" which can be swapped out at a moment's notice is cheap insurance. The defective unit can be shipped back to the manufacturer and fixed. A maintenance contractor might not advise you to put in spare equipment, suggesting that your machines and your staff time are too valuable and if you have a system failure it should be up and running within four hours. With a hot spare, you can be up and running within a half-hour.

Software companies usually have free (1-800) telephone support lines, and while these are crowded and you may be on hold for a long time, you generally get the right answer. There are also computer user network forums that can be connected to the manufacturers that will give out advice and answer questions. Sometimes, these manufacturers will go so far as to put software upgrades and fixes onto a user network for customers to download. As you can see, with adequate training, you can be self-supporting.

Disaster

You must have a competent support network as well as a complete disaster recovery plan to take care of any contingencies. Backups should be made and kept on a planned schedule. Large nonprofits may use a daily backup that is kept for two weeks, a weekly full system backup that is kept for a month, and a full system monthly backup that is kept off-site. With such a system, the most data that could be lost even in a complete "meltdown" of the systems would be one month. This is an example of how you should think through your entire system.

A disaster recovery plan would permit you to keep operating if your building had a fire or became uninhabitable for some reason and you had to recreate your complete system in another location quickly. What would have happened to your operation if your non-profit had been housed in the World Trade Center? With a complete backup of data off-site, you could rent or buy new systems, restore the information, and be up and running as fast as the new machines could be set up. Think through what you would need in such a situation and keep it off-site.

SUMMARY

Begin with an operational plan. Make it as clear and complete as possible. Move constantly and consistently into the future without extreme leaps forward, by following careful planning.

Start with the simplest system that will meet your needs and build on it. It will inevitably become more complex, but as it grows so will the expertise of your users and support staff. Just remember, the care and feeding of your system is the training and professional development of your staff and the addition of hardware and software when the need arises.

Consult with experts and your staff to create a complete strategic technological plan based on your operational plan. Have goals and time lines with demonstrable milestones. Be prepared to change and modify as the organizational climate changes and different services become available.

Enjoy the new technology. With all of the changes in efficiency and increases in productivity, there should be the time to appreciate the labor saved, the quality increase in the output, and the added ability to be creative. Allow your staff the freedom to explore this new way of doing business. With an adequate and appropriate information system, the management of your organization should get easier all the time.

CHAPTER ELEVEN

Your People and Their Environment

Your organization will thrive with proper management of its most important resource: its people. This chapter provides a summary of human resources principles and practices that will improve your organization's working environment.

Most nonprofit organizations start out small and are preoccupied with identifying their mission and establishing programs and plans to carry it out. The founding member of a children's health clinic situated in a church basement, for example, will probably be more concerned with fund-raising and public relations than with managing staff and office resources. This young nonprofit will most likely have a small staff and scant office needs. That, however, can change quickly.

For example, what happens when the willing lender of a computer needs the equipment back? Or if the neighbors who graciously let you use their copying machine move away? Or when a professional, full-time staff member is needed to do a job that volunteers have so far handled? Soon that church basement doesn't have sufficient space for you and your staff and office equipment and for your meetings that inevitably conflict with church activities. Your organization is growing and your needs changing. It is time to take on a more professional profile.

It is in making this jump that promising nonprofit organizations may falter. The stumbling block for many is generating sufficient funds to grow, either through program revenues or community support. But often the basic activities of managing the office and directing the staff can place unnecessary stress on that growing nonprofit.

If managed properly, both the staff and the environment can reinforce the nonprofit's goals. Given an awareness of the principles of human resources and office management, those tasks can evolve along with the organization. Who ultimately supervises these activities varies with the size of the office. These duties will likely be spread among a small staff; a large office will have individuals specifically responsible for human resources and office management. And there is a wide range inbetween these two situations.

The important thing is to proceed methodically, maintaining the spirit of the organization without letting the administrative tasks overwhelm you. Managing human resources and the office environment are, of course, means to achieve the organization's goals; they should not become goals in themselves. To put it another way: the measure of a successful organization is not how large a staff it supports or how well decorated the offices are, but whether or not the people, equipment, and surroundings are the right ones to help move the organization forward to achieve its strategic objectives and fulfill its mission.

Certain principles of personnel management (now generally called *human resources*) and office management apply to all organizations regardless of their size. Each is addressed below, in separate sections, from the perspective of a growing nonprofit organization.

HUMAN RESOURCES

A nonprofit organization succeeds because of its people—because of their commitment, enthusiasm, intelligence, and drive. Therefore, it is crucial to find and choose the best employees possible. To act otherwise is to invite failure. Human resources is concerned not only with finding good leaders but also with forming a group of people with different skills who work congenially together for a common good.

Once the staff is hired, trust must be built between employer and employee, manager and worker, to heighten chances for success.

If such trust is elusive, the nonprofit's goals are impossible to meet. Managing your human resources will also involve promoting creative responses to challenging work, as well as guarding against unethical or unlawful practices.

Human resources activities revolve around five broad tasks:

- Hiring and placement.
- Fair and equitable compensation.
- Communication between staff, management, and volunteers.
- Compliance with local, state, and federal employment laws.
- Maintaining and enhancing an organization's image.

START-UP AND GROWTH

As mentioned earlier, the start-up of a nonprofit may be more reflex than planning. But as your organization grows it will be necessary to identify the tasks and staff needed to reach its goals. This is true even if your organization can't yet afford the entire projected staff. Begin to construct an organizational chart that can be your guide to growth. How large is the staff now? In five years in the future? Who is responsible for which tasks? What is expected from each individual? How will the team interact? How might growth affect the organizational chart? Will some work be farmed out to consultants or performed by volunteers?

At the same time, realistically assess how far the funds budgeted for staff will stretch. Some members of the staff initially may need to take on duties that ultimately may be given over to new employees as the organization grows. Sometimes, it may be impossible to predict growth patterns, but it is useful to document the realistic and the ideal. Ultimately, as your organization grows, it will be more important to establish clear and precise descriptions of what is expected from each individual in order to avoid confusion. For smaller groups, however, tasks may shift among the workforce depending on the issue.

Let's assume that in the beginning you realize that with your limited resources you can't hire all the full-time staff you need. There are other ways to get services done. Part-time employees may be appropriate for specific tasks, but because benefits are not always given to them, part-time employees may be hard to attract and keep. Volunteers can be an extremely important pool of labor. Nonprofits, such as museums, homeless shelters, soup kitchens, advocacy groups, and others, would not be able to function without their volunteer armies. Maintaining a good volunteer troop, however, takes attentive management, positive interaction, and strong leadership. The larger the number of volunteers the greater the need for a volunteer coordinator as a full-time, paid staff member.

To find loyal volunteers, an organization needs to effectively promote the altruistic or educational endeavors of its mission. A small museum, for example, can offer volunteers in-depth training and easy access to knowledgeable staff members. A soup kitchen offers an unique opportunity for volunteers to get involved with the community. Once involved, volunteers need recognition, some kind of thanks for the contribution they make to your organization. They won't be receiving paychecks, so their worth should be acknowledged through other activities—special awards, certificates of merit, mention to the local press, an annual luncheon. Volunteers should be encouraged to contribute to the larger whole—i.e., their suggestions and observations should be solicited and taken seriously by the staff.

Another source of labor and expertise is independent consultants who can be called on to accomplish tasks that the staff cannot perform, due either to lack of expertise or time. For instance, you might decide to mail a bimonthly newsletter to your supporters. A consultant may be called in to design the newsletter and produce it, too. Tasks for consultants can range from the production of newsletters and brochures to public relations projects to fund-raising (see Chapter 13 on using consultants). Some consultants, particularly those seeking to make a name in your community or who are committed to a cause, may be willing to volunteer services. The qualifications of the consultants should be carefully checked, and most jobs (if not volunteered) should be bid out to three contractors before a contract is signed. If projects are continuous, it is sometimes less expensive to enter into a long-term contract with a particular consultant. Such an arrangement can also bring continuity to the special projects. For some tasks, especially those such as data processing, equipment maintenance, cleaning, and food service, look to larger service-providers.

FINDING AND HIRING STAFF

Job Descriptions

Finding and hiring staff starts with a clear, concise job description. If there is no written job description, the hiring process is handicapped from the beginning.

At a minimum, the job description should include the following:

- Basic skills required, both technical and educational.
- Duties and responsibilities.
- Any other information that defines the scope of the job, particularly any indications of multiple duties.

Job descriptions later become a barometer for employees and the employer, for such activities as performance appraisals, promotions, and salary raises. Job descriptions should be reviewed once a year, and also in the event of a significant shifting of responsibilities.

Cause-related nonprofits may theoretically find two very different kinds of candidates: those with an empathic feeling for the cause but, perhaps, without managerial or technical skills needed to fill the position; or candidates with the desired skills and experience but less personal commitment. (Actually, there is a third kind of candidate, who combines the best of the two preceding types—but skilled *and* committed candidates can be hard to find.)

Each organization establishes its own style, as regards official documents. For job descriptions, Exhibit 11-1 can be used as a guide.

Getting the Word Out

Ads placed in the local newspaper's classified sections may bring a slew of responses. Professional journals are useful for highly specialized positions, although the typical monthly format may not offer timely announcements and responses. For certain positions, posting ads at community centers can be effective. The least structured, but sometimes useful, method is word of mouth, say, an employee to a friend, etc. Sometimes a job seems crafted for a specific person known to the organization. Or a professional network can provide likely candidates. As with the job description itself, any ad-

Exhibit 11–1   Job Description Format

JOB TITLE

JOB SUMMARY
The job's responsibilities and duties. Its supervisory, technical, or administrative scope.

SKILL AND EDUCATIONAL REQUIREMENTS
Experience, educational background, and training desired.

ACCOUNTABILITY
Title of person to whom this employee reports. Relationships within and outside of the organization.

SPECIAL ATTRIBUTES
Any specific talents that apply to this job.

vertisement or announcement of an open position should be accurate and concise.

Reviewing Resumes

As resumes arrive, develop a fair and systematic process to review them, always keeping in mind what skills are required to fill the position. With experience, each reviewer will develop his or her own rating system. Obviously, the guts of the resume are all-important—the education, experience, skill levels, and any demonstrable communication and interpersonal abilities. Interest and commitment to an organization's mission should be noted.

Start judging a candidate as soon as you open the envelope. Does the resume look like it is written with care? Are there typographical or spelling errors? Is it orderly and easy to read? Is the cover letter direct and cogent or rambling and ineffective?

To uncover more intangible qualities in a candidate look for evidence of:

• Sustained interest in a job or cause.
• Loyalty to an organization.
• Ability to be a team player.
• Ability to communicate.
• Ambition.

- Detail-oriented skills.
- Knowledge about the job being pursued.

Interviews

Conducting good interviews is a learned skill and requires careful preparation, execution, and follow-up. It's perhaps hardest to master the techniques of putting applicants at ease. Proceed with the general understanding that applicants will be nervous. Try to remain objective rather than subjective in reaction to the applicant's appearance, personality, or background. Someone who may not fit the image you have could turn out to be an excellent employee. During the interview, address administrative issues, such as compensation and benefits, travel requirements, starting date, and special job requirements.

In order to make objective and fair comparisons, ask interviewees a common set of questions that can help determine the candidate's job-related skills and experience, general intelligence and aptitude, attitudes and personality. One expert interviewer, Robert Half, suggests the following questions in his book *Finding, Hiring, and Keeping the Best Employees*:

"What was your single most noteworthy achievement or contribution in your current job?"

"What specific strengths do you bring to this job and this organization?"

"How do you make important decisions?"

"Why have you decided to leave your present position?"

"What risks did you take in your last few jobs, and what was the result of having taken those risks?"

Obviously, the overall goal is to learn as much about each candidate as possible, as well as determine if that candidate's resume is accurate. Generally, an interviewer should try to determine the candidate's ability to do the following:

- plan tasks.
- prioritize.
- delegate.

- work on a team.
- solve problems.
- apply knowledge.
- know limitations.
- take initiative.
- learn on the job.
- communicate with associates.

Versatility is a sought-after attribute to nonprofit organizations.

Your interviewing technique is significant. Candidates should not be rushed into answering questions and should not feel threatened when asked to explain some point further. Pay attention to the individual applicant by soliciting small talk and tailoring questions to previous answers. Remember, you are trying to sell yourself as well as hire an employee. Don't lead the candidate to a short "yes" or "no" answer without an explanation, if an explanation is what you are seeking. Be cautious with a candidate who appears overqualified. It is possible that soon after employment, that person may become disenchanted or bored.

Secure a candidate's approval to your soliciting references. The candidate may wish that his or her present boss not be called but rather someone on the staff of his or her current organization or a former employer. And realize that references often can be subjective.

Choosing the Candidate and Making the Offer

One candidate may stand out as the final choice for a position. It is likely, though, that no one person is the perfect candidate, but that some compromises have been made. If the hiring process has been carefully considered and executed, however, the odds of making a mistake are minimized.

Once a candidate has accepted the job offer, it should be confirmed by a letter accurately restating the job offer, for the letter can be used in a court of law as an official document.

A personnel checklist should be filed for each new employee and contain:

- Employment application.

- Formal job offer letter and employee acknowledgment.
- Social security number.
- Completed I-9 Form (for all employees).
- Federal, state, and local tax withholding forms as applicable.
- Insurance forms—health, group life, disability, other.
- Record of the job description and performance evaluations.
- Retirement plan application.
- Receipt for benefit plan options, where applicable.

Compensation — Salary and Benefits

Setting salary levels is a difficult task for any type of organization. You need to research what comparable salaries are elsewhere. One avenue is to look to salary surveys of nonprofit industries. You can also contact other organizations like your own and inquire about their salary structure. Traditionally, nonprofits have had a reputation of offering low salaries. That, however, may be misleading in the 1990's, as many of the best employees seek salaries that are more competitive with the for-profit sector.

The type of benefits offered may provide an extra incentive for a candidate to join the organization—benefits such as medical and dental health care insurance, disability, life insurance, and retirement tax-deferred plans. Where full-time employment is concerned, it is unusual to find an organization that does not offer what are called "absorbed benefits," such as vacation leave, sick leave, and bereavement time off, as well as holidays. Sometimes a lower salary can be offset by an attractive benefits package or a shorter work week.

For budgeting and planning purposes, it's helpful to list the salary range of each position, even though you may not afford the top ranges. When salary and benefits are set, you can then document the true cost of keeping a staff member, by combining salary with health insurance costs, unemployment insurance costs (in some jurisdictions), worker's compensation, and pension plan contributions—any cost that the employer pays for the employee. On the other hand, staff members should be aware that their pay will reflect federal and state tax withholding and FICA contributions. Every position needs to be classified as exempt or nonexempt to comply with the Fair Labor Standards of 1934. (Exempt employees are exempt from overtime payment. Nonexempt employees must be paid time and one-half for time worked over 40 hours in a calendar week.)

ON THE JOB
Manager/Employee Relationship

An organization's executives set the tone for the office environment. Human resources, however, has a role in promoting practices that respect, motivate, and reward employees and retain their interest in the organization. If the revolving door turns too fast, the staff loses a sense of continuity, especially a small staff.

Employees should be respected for their dedication, creativity, innovation, ideas, and individuality, even if it is often easier for managers to negatively critique performance than acknowledge gains. If harsh criticism is necessary, try it first in private rather than as a public rebuke. Encourage enhanced performance whenever possible and reward an employee who is responsible.

Challenge is an important part of one's job. Employees more and more often seek opportunities to advance ideas, to be part of the greater good, to contribute to important decisions and projects. It's called "risk-taking" or more recently "empowerment," and, if handled correctly, ultimately can be of great value to an organization.

Performance Appraisal

When communication between you and your employee is strong, performance evaluations are a tool to review past performances, as well as to discuss future activities. Performance appraisals run from the informal to the very structured and usually are held once or twice a year. As a nonprofit grows, these reviews will be more formal. Regardless of its style, the evaluation should be objective and fair.

Basically, the appraisal starts when an employee is hired. The job description becomes the basis against which an employee's performance is evaluated. How well has the employee reached these goals? Each time an employee is evaluated, new performance goals are set, in agreement between employee and employer. In six months to a year, these goals are checked, with the process continuing onward. If an employee has performed badly or not lived up to your expectations, you can emphasize the need to correct this in the future.

There will be instances when management will find an employee's inadequacies too great. A negative review should be forthright and clear. A dismissal will call for documentation.

Performance appraisals are often used to justify salary increases. However, discussions of salary can dilute the appraisal objectives and should be handled separately.

Promotions, Raises, and Rewards

A reassignment can be beneficial if an employee grows complacent and needs a new challenge. Promotions can also be used to reward a good employee, overcome salary caps, and honor seniority. Generally, organizations set a salary range for a particular position, but allow some growth within and above that range. Raises are definitely awards, but mean less when the raise simply meets a cost-of-living allowance. Budget realities, however, may temper your desire to monetarily reward even your best employees. In lean years, those committed to your organization's mission may agree to delay personal salary expectations.

Special recognition, rather than financial rewards, will have to satisfy your cadre of volunteers. Such recognition can take the form of special awards, certificates of merit, mention to local press, or an annual luncheon.

DOWN . . . AND EVENTUALLY OUT

Stress and Burnout

Unrealistic expectations—and the work that can come with them—may place undue stress on your employees. Sometimes, stress levels rise and fall with a particular project. If problems remain after completion of that project, if there is a loss of caring, lack of interest, and negative attitude by an employee, you may need to reshuffle responsibilities or further investigate the nature of the stress. Burnout will turn that revolving door.

I Quit/You're Fired

Reasons for an employee's resignation can include: limited opportunities for advancement, lack of recognition, unhappiness with management, inadequate salary or benefits, boredom with the job, or a need to try something different. Resignations can be countered with new job responsibilities, but may eventually have to be gracefully accepted by you.

Firing an employee is unquestionably a difficult task and needs substantial backup. Employees can be fired due to failure to perform, insubordination, or embezzlement and other crimes.

Budgetary or programmatic changes may bring the need to reduce your workforce, even for the most successful organizations. Sometimes as a consequence of success, for example, environmental organizations attract fewer funds and contributions if the government is perceived as more sympathetic. Laid-off workers may receive some kind of compensation or out-placement services (such as employment counseling) and will be eligible for unemployment benefits. Firings and layoffs should be done in private, supervisor to employee.

PERSONNEL POLICIES AND PROCEDURES

An organization must have official documents on hand. Personnel policies and procedures should be documented in a manual that is available to current and prospective employees. Small nonprofits may not have a formal presentation of these policies and procedures but must somewhere have policies and procedures written down. The information should be as up-to-date as possible. Exhibit 11-2 is a sample table of the contents of a personnel policies and procedures manual.

Compliance with Local, State, and Federal Employment Laws

In our litigious society, the legal ramifications of personnel policies and practices are significant. While lawsuits have been thought to be a problem of the for-profit world, nonprofits are covered by the same laws; even a small or mid-sized nonprofit organization could be severely affected by legal action of a present or former employee. Therefore, it is important that an attorney knowledgeable in em-

Exhibit 11–2   Sample Table of Contents

Table of Contents
Personnel Policies and Procedures

THE ORGANIZATION
  Introduction
  History
  Mission
WORK SCHEDULE
  Workday
  Workweek
  Lunch Period
  Holidays
  Personal Days
  Vacation
  Sick Leave
  Family and Medical Leave
  Leave of Absence
  Bereavement Leave
  Severe Weather Conditions
  Jury Duty
  Time Off Without Pay
COMPENSATION
  Paydays
  Overtime & Compensatory Time
  Change of Employee Status
  Salary & Performance Reviews
EMPLOYEE BENEFITS
  Social Security
  Workers' Compensation Insurance
  Unemployment Insurance
  Retirement Plan
  Benefits for Part-Time Employees
CODE OF CONDUCT
  Bulletin Boards
  Business Attire
  Emergency Procedures
  Harassment
  Housekeeping
  Personal Conduct
  Security
  Smoking Policy
  Visitors, Vendors, Suppliers
RECRUITMENT
  Equal Employment Opportunity
  Employment of Relatives

ployment law review the organization's personnel policies and procedures, hiring practices, firing practices, rules of employee conduct, workplace safety and security, performance reviews, salary increases and promotions, and other actions or documents with legal implications.

At least the implications of the following should be well known:

1. **Federal minimum wage.** The Fair Labor Standards Act sets the minimum wage, pay for interns, and the status of exempt and nonexempt employees.

2. **Equal employment opportunity.** Title VII of the Civil Rights Act of 1964 outlaws discrimination in employment practices toward individuals based on age, race, religion, sex, color, or national origin.

3. **Job safety and health.** The Occupational Safety & Health Act requires each employer to comply with safety and health standards in the workplace by maintaining the workplace free from recognized hazards.

4. **Accessibility.** The Americans with Disabilities Act of 1992 forbids discrimination against disabled workers in hiring, compensation, and advancement and mandates accessible office space for the handicapped in offices with more than 15 employees.

THE OFFICE ENVIRONMENT

Don't be intimidated by the sound of the term "office management." The most important requirements are that the office environment be pleasant and functional, that equipment and supplies meet the employee's needs, that the communication system is reliable, and that the mail is properly handled. Efficiency and cost-effectiveness is the goal of a well-organized office system and can translate into significant savings for nonprofits.

Nonprofit organizations can benefit significantly from two concepts: in-kind services and competitive bidding. In-kind is any supply, equipment, or professional aid that is donated or offered at a very low cost by for-profit organizations. The donor gets the benefit of a tax deduction and saves the cost of disposal of old furniture or equipment.

Purchases, and especially equipment and furniture, should be thought out in terms of the entire office needs. A good rule of thumb when purchasing is to use a bidding system, in which the purchaser, if possible, bases the decision on the bids of three vendors. The vendors should be aware of the bidding process.

Equipment acquisition should be reviewed in terms of buying or leasing. With some products, such as copiers and computer equipment, leasing agreements offer options periodically to update the equipment. Leasing should also take into consideration the bidding process stated above.

Office Space

Office rental can be a big chunk of the monthly bills. So, before signing a lease, it's worthwhile to see if any free or especially inexpensive space exists. Consider creative space—room in a local church, school, or community center, for example. Or look for space that can be shared with an affiliated or nonaffiliated organization. This can be advantageous to both parties and can include the sharing of such features as meeting rooms, bathrooms, receptionists, copiers, other equipment, and security systems. Or office space can be tucked into a corner of a nonprofit's operational headquarters—say, a soup kitchen, shelter for abused women, or educationally oriented program.

Other factors to consider as you look for office space are:

- *Terms of contract.* Lease rather than purchase space, a factor dictated by the size and the financial status of the organization.
- *Location.* A determining factor if the nonprofit has close ties to a specific neighborhood. If a particular location is not necessary, modest rates may dictate your choice.
- *Size.* Ideally, an office should provide approximately 200 square feet of space per person including common space. At the start, the office space may be tight, so try to anticipate growth. Also take into consideration needed space for volunteers or board members.
- *Anticipated growth.* The potential growth of the organization needs to be anticipated as much as possible, since leases are mostly offered on a multiple-year basis. It is often difficult and expensive to break a lease and move to a new location.

- *Utilities in lease.* If the cost of utilities—heat, air conditioning, and electricity—is included in your lease payment, the building owner will handle monthly payments, but be aware that those rates may automatically increase each year. Utility rates are based on the consumer price index. If your hours are irregular, check to make sure the building will be heated, cooled, and lit when you need to be there.

- *Utilities separate from lease.* If you are in a nontraditional building, control of utilities—and the bills—is separate from the lease agreement. Landlords should be able to give estimates of monthly utility payments.

- *Cleaning service.* How the office gets cleaned can also be tied to the lease. In some larger office buildings, the landlord often adds janitorial services to all the leasees. In other places, the office manager may need to hire a janitorial service in a separate contract.

- *Security and life safety.* Some security and life safety measures are the responsibility of the leasee, regardless of the type of office building. If a security system is required, it must be installed by the leasee, although in some locations some security may be offered but only at the main entrance—such as a key pass or a security guard.

- *Space configuration.* It is essential to meet local codes, such as providing accessible fire extinguishers and fire exits. Offices with more than 15 employees must adhere to the Americans with Disabilities Act, which sets strict rules concerning accessibility in offices for disabled persons.

- *Furniture and equipment.* The most obvious way to furnish an office is to buy, lease, or rent new furniture. Look into buying used furniture. Clearinghouses link donators of used furniture with nonprofits looking for used, but decent, office furniture. Buying used equipment is tricky. For example, the repair of an used typewriter might cost as much as a new typewriter. When purchasing more sophisticated used equipment, it is advisable to get an expert opinion.

Before signing an office lease, consult your lawyer.

Communications

The phone system is one of the more expensive items acquired and is usually leased. The system selected should be based on the number of staff and lines required. Single-line phones can easily service a start-up organization with one to two people. The next step is a multiple line "key" systems that can support 20 to 30 people. There are two types of key systems: (1) *Squared-systems*, in which every line appears on each phone set and (2) *non-squared systems*, in which the lines are shared and not every line appears on each phone set. In the second system, a receptionist is required to transfer calls. When the staff reaches 100 persons or more, a PBX (Private Branch Exchange) system becomes a requirement.

Consider back-up for your telephones, either with a basic answering machine or answering service. The most sophisticated system called "voice" or "voice mail," adds a considerable amount to the cost of phone service, and may not be especially helpful for a small group.

Fax machines have become a mainstay of offices large and small. As the popularity of the fax has risen, prices of the machines have dropped, and this is an investment worth paying for. An extra telephone line (or a special split line) will be needed. Try sharing a fax with the organization down the hall.

Copying

It's unrealistic to think that even the smallest office can do without a copier for its routine needs. Access to copying equipment is a modern-day must. For start-up, estimate daily copying needs for a month-long period. Then actually track a few months' volume. A leasing agreement can provide periodic trade-ins for new equipment and for equipment of different sizes and features.

It may be more economical to send out large projects such as form letters, annual reports, and newsletters to a copy/printing company. Printers most often provide mail service.

Mail and Delivery Service

An organization's daily postage flow should determine what postage equipment is necessary. The most basic mailing system consists of stamps and a scale. When the volume increases, special metering equipment will be more cost-effective and can be leased from a mail equipment vendor. Sophisticated, computer-driven equipment is generally not cost-effective until the average number of daily pieces reaches 2,000.

To reduce mailing costs, nonprofits use reduced bulk third-class postage for mail that is not time-sensitive, like membership solicitations. Contact your local post office for Form 3624, *Application to Mail at Special Bulk Third-Class Rates.*

Mail houses provide stuffing, labeling, and mailing, and are up-to-date on technical specifications pertaining to factors that can affect one's postage charge, such as weight, size, folding, and placement of labeling. The mailing houses are also more capable of using ZIP+4 and presorting mail. Remember, however, that as a nonprofit organization with third-class bulk mail privileges, you must register independently with the appropriate post office.

Office Supplies

Buying supplies in bulk saves money. How do you determine your needs when you first start up? The answer: keep track of your needs of six months to a year. Those records can be a guide to the future purchase of supplies, including stationery. When buying in bulk, negotiation is the key; seek out three vendors and inform them that you are seeking competitive bids. Be careful not to overstock supplies that may not be in demand at a later time (such as typewriter correction tape, a product rendered nearly obsolete by the computer).

Insurance

Three types of insurance are needed for an office environment: liability, theft and fire, and vehicle (if used by the organization). Insurance companies' provisions will vary widely, and it is wisest to consult an insurance agent. Recommendations leading to the selection of an agent in a particular area can be obtained from other nonprofit organizations, lawyers, or accountants.

SUMMARY

In a broad sense, the people and the place make an organization. And if an organization hires and employs smart and equips well, it will enhance its own image in the world at large. That doesn't necessarily mean that money equals success. Nonprofits walk a much leaner line than for-profit organizations, but they also can offer more fulfilling work. For nonprofits, great things will come through choosing the best and the brightest, allowing them to grow in their job, and rewarding them for their efforts.

CHAPTER TWELVE

Knowing Important Legal Requirements

Like the foundations of a building, legal underpinnings are an essential part of your nonprofit's structure. As a manager, it is your duty to ensure that the essential legal documents — such as tax-exempt forms, bylaws, and articles of incorporation — are handled properly. This chapter outlines the rights, privileges, and obligations that your nonprofit has under the law.

Managing the affairs of a nonprofit organization within the laws of the United States and the various state and local jurisdictions is not tricky or difficult. The law actually provides some help to the executive in the everyday conduct of the organization's activities. A competent executive should, however, make himself or herself familiar with a few basic principles and provisions of the law to take advantage of the help they can provide and to avoid making any missteps which might result in trouble.

FORMING AND OPERATING A NONPROFIT ORGANIZATION

"In the beginning was the Word," and in the beginning of any nonprofit organization there should also be *the words*. There are three fundamental or "organic" documents which serve as the basis for establishing and operating a nonprofit organization:

- Articles of Incorporation.
- Bylaws.

- IRS Tax Exemption Letter.

These documents should be kept securely on file at the headquarters of the organization. They prescribe the scope and limits within which the organization operates, and they also can be the instruments which keep a nonprofit executive out of trouble.

Articles of Incorporation[1]

Strictly speaking, a nonprofit organization does not *have* to be incorporated. But failure to incorporate exposes the organization and the individuals involved to a variety of unhappy consequences, not the least of which could be personal liability for the organization's debts.

Corporations are created under the statutory authority of a state, and all states have specific statutory provisions relating to the formation of nonprofit corporations. Typical of the items required to be included in articles of incorporation for a nonprofit organization are:

- Name of the corporation;
- Duration of the corporation (usually perpetual);
- Purposes for which the corporation is formed;
- Provisions for conducting the internal affairs of the organization;
- Names and addresses of the incorporators;
- Names and addresses of the initial board of directors;
- Address of the initial registered office and name of the initial registered agent of the corporation;
- Provisions for distribution of the assets of the corporation on dissolution.

The statutes of each state are different, however, and legal counsel familiar with the requirements of the state chosen as the state of incorporation should be consulted to assure conformance with the particular requirements of that jurisdiction.

---

[1] "Certificate of Incorporation" or "Charter" are alternative terms used in some jurisdictions.

It is important that the articles qualify the organization as a nonprofit corporation by stating the nonprofit purpose of the organization. The stated purposes in the incorporating document should be broad enough to enable the organization to evolve as necessary to serve its constituency. Satisfying state law requirements for amending the articles of incorporation of the organization can be a nuisance if later circumstances warrant a significant departure from purposes that were too narrowly drawn originally.

Bylaws[2]

Articles of Incorporation provide only a broad outline of the organization's form, and the initial board of directors should quickly approve a set of bylaws which will supplement the articles by prescribing more detailed rules for governing the organization. Bylaws provide the discipline required for orderly operation of the organization, and they should be written with an emphasis on fair treatment.

Bylaws often begin with a restatement of the name and purposes of the organization consistent with the articles of incorporation, but they add basic rules for operating the organization:

- The frequency, notice, and quorum requirements for organizational meetings;
- Voting qualifications, proxies, and procedures;
- The number and term of the board of directors, scope of authority, method of nomination and election to the board, and provisions for filling vacancies;
- List of officers, method of nomination and election, terms of office, powers, duties, and succession;
- Title and scope of authority of the chief staff executive;
- Recordkeeping and financial reporting responsibilities; and
- Bylaw amendment procedures and provisions for dissolution of the organization.

---

[2] "Constitution" is a term sometimes used in place of Bylaws or Articles of Incorporation. However, because of the potential for confusion between "Constitution" and the term "Charter" which sometimes refers to the incorporating document, use of the term "Constitution" is not recommended.

Other provisions also may be included. For example, membership organizations may include a dues or participation fee structure (but never the rate); a definition of categories of membership; and qualifications for membership.

It is wise, however, to stop short of having too much detail contained in the bylaws so that the organization can retain some flexibility to change its operations without bylaw amendments. Bylaw amendments, although simpler than amendments to the articles of incorporation since the laws of the state are not involved, nevertheless often require a vote of the full membership of the organization, which can hamstring an executive and the officers and board in creating new operating structures to meet changing needs.

An illustration of the type of operating flexibility which should be preserved for board action is committee structure. The bylaws should prescribe the membership and authority of only one standing committee: an executive committee which is made up of officers who need to make policy decisions between board meetings. Beyond that, the bylaws should only provide that the board has authority to establish any other committees with whatever jurisdiction it prescribes. By preserving such organizational flexibility, the board is able to form new committees, or perhaps more importantly, eliminate obsolete committees without amending the bylaws.

Healthy organizations change over time. Let's say, for example, a nonprofit organization is formed for the protection of local wildlife. The organizers decide that a banquet to raise funds for wildlife food would be a good activity and establish a committee responsible for the event. Initially, the event is successful, but after a few years, attendance at the dinner declines, and the organizers decide to abandon the banquet and raise funds by commissioning and selling wildlife replicas. If the bylaws specifically mandate the existence of the banquet committee, the organization would have to labor through an amendment to make the operational change needed for the evolution to the new activity. It is better for the board to have the authority to abolish the old committee and establish a new one so that it may proceed with the new project.

With the articles and bylaws in place, most for-profit organizations have what they need for their basic organizational documents. Not so with a nonprofit organization. By their very nature, nonprofit organizations must take one more step in establishing their operations.

IRS Tax Exemption Letter

Nonprofit organizations must establish their tax-exempt status with the Internal Revenue Service. Section 1.501(a) of the Internal Revenue Regulations provides that there shall be an exemption from income taxation for qualified organizations. Section 1.501(c) of the regulations defines the organizations which qualify for the exemption and classifies them according to type. The 25 categories listed in section 1.501(c) include religious, charitable, scientific or educational organizations (c)(3); social welfare organizations (c)(4); labor organizations (c)(5); business leagues (c)(6); fraternal societies (c)(8); and credit unions (c)(14).

Application for exempt status should be filed with the IRS using either form 1023 (for 501(c)(3) organizations) or Form 1024 (for most other section 501(c) category organizations). Copies of the organization's articles of incorporation and bylaws must be included with the application, and a full description of the purposes and activities of the organization must be provided. IRS Publication 557 provides detailed information on the filing of applications for exempt status.

The business league category of exempt organization is commonly known as a trade organization, although it includes chambers of commerce and boards of trade as well. The purpose of such an organization is to promote the common business interests of its members, and not to engage in a regular business of a kind that is ordinarily carried on for profit. Its activities are typically directed to the improvement of business conditions in one or more lines of businesses, and not the performance of services for individuals.

Nonprofit organizations formed for purely charitable or public interest purposes qualify for tax exemption under the provisions of 501(c)(3) of the IRS code. Such organizations must meet the particular organizational and operational tests to be eligible for that designation. In general, an organization will qualify for status as a 501(c)(3) organization if it is organized and operated for one or more of the following purposes:

(a) Religious;
(b) Charitable;
(c) Scientific;
(d) Testing for public safety;
(e) Literary;

(f) Educational;

(g) Prevention of cruelty to children or animals.

These general purposes have been defined in much greater detail through IRS rulings and regulations. For example, "educational" purposes may be evidenced by the granting of scholarships or offering of lectures or other typical educational activities. "Charitable" organizations must provide that upon dissolution all of the donated funds will be used for charitable purposes and will not revert to the founding organization. "Scientific" organizations qualify only if the results of their activities are available to the public.

In some cases, a nonprofit organization which is qualified as tax-exempt under section 501(c)(6) of the tax code may decide to form a second nonprofit organization under the 501(c)(3) provisions of the code. There are many reasons for deciding to undertake such action, including eligibility for receiving tax-deductible gifts, objectivity and independence from the sponsoring organization's interests, and availability of favorable postal rates.

A sponsored foundation is formed in the same manner in which the sponsoring group was formed: through the creation and filing of articles of incorporation and bylaws. A separate application for tax-exempt status must be filed with the IRS for the sponsored organization. Because of these details, nonprofit executives would be wise to contact competent counsel to assist in the formation of any sponsored foundation.

If the IRS determines that an organization has met the test for exemption, it will issue a "determination letter," which should be kept safely on file with the other fundamental organizational documents. Issuance by the IRS of tax-exempt status does not eliminate the need for the organization to file annual information returns with the IRS. Tax-exempt organizations other than private foundations must file Form 990, or Form 990EZ, which is a shortened form designed for use by small organizations.

The nonprofit executive also should watch out for the potential need to obtain tax-exempt status from the state in which the organization is operating or is incorporated. Many states simply replicate the Federal tax exemption regulations, and qualification under the Federal regulations automatically qualifies the organization in the state. The District of Columbia is an example of a jurisdiction which requires an additional application for tax-exempt status and the filing of annual tax returns, and the executive should determine the requirements for the particular state in which the organization is located.

Selecting Officers and Directors

The minimum number of directors required for the board of a nonprofit organization is commonly prescribed by the statutes of the jurisdiction under which the organization is formed. The Model Non-Profit Corporation Act specifies a minimum of three directors. Beyond the statutory minimum, nonprofit organizations are at liberty to specify in their bylaws any number of directors, and the bylaws may be amended from time to time to increase or decrease that number.

Membership type organizations typically provide for election of directors on a rotating basis, and in some cases directors elected to represent specific categories of members may only be elected by the members in that category. In other types of nonprofit organization the incumbent directors may appoint their successors. In such cases, if new directors are not appointed, the incumbent directors may continue to hold office indefinitely unless they are removed "for cause" pursuant to "due process" by a majority of the other members of the board. This method of choosing new directors can create problems if a group of incumbent directors uses it to perpetuate their authority or policies to the detriment of the organization. Consequently, some mechanism for selecting new directors with fresh outlooks and energy is desirable.

In addition to specifying the number of directors on the organization's board, the bylaws of the organization should also provide for the mechanics of selection. Nomination of directors is often undertaken by a nominating committee appointed by the board chairman or president with the approval of the other members of the board. Local law may specify the duration of the terms of office for board members, but the organization's bylaws must specify the terms of office and the terms should be staggered to provide for continuity. The bylaws also should provide a method for filling vacancies in any director position. It is common to provide that the chairman or president should appoint a new director to fill the unexpired term of office of the vacant seat, with the approval of the remaining directors.

Officers of the organization may be elected directly by the members in the case of a membership organization, or they may be elected or appointed by the board members. In either case, it is wise to provide for a nominating process to assure the selection of qualified individuals who have adequate background and experience with the organization and its activities.

Membership Structure

If the organization is a *membership* type organization, the basis for membership is usually a commonality of interest. Such organizations often are more concerned with persuading members to join than with keeping them out, but qualifications for membership need to be sufficiently specific so that they include only those who are truly interested in the purposes of the organization. If membership qualifications are too broad in scope, the group may not be able to establish specific goals or interests. On the other hand, if the qualifications are too narrow, the group risks failure because of insufficient support for its programs and activities. An organization may, of course, have separate *classes* of membership with distinct qualifications and prescribed rights and privileges. The organization may, for example, establish a non-voting "associate" class of membership, which consists of individual or company members who have an interest in the overall purposes of the organization, but whose interest is somewhat different from that of the primary class of voting members. Suppliers of goods or services to the primary members for whom the organization was formed are an example of an associate class of membership.

Other common classes of membership in addition to "regular" or "active" members, include honorary, affiliate, inactive, or student members. It also is not uncommon for an organization to bestow "life" membership on individuals who have made a particular contribution to the organization. The life member designation does not mean that the organization cannot subsequently change the terms or conditions of such membership or even abolish the membership category in which the life member held membership.

A nonprofit organization also may define a specific geographic area which it serves and from which it will accept members. For example, a nonprofit organization may be formed to serve an international, national, state, or local constituency.

Any organization which wishes to limit membership must approach the issue of membership exclusivity carefully. While association membership is not a right explicitly guaranteed by the Constitution, organizations may not violate the civil or property rights of potential members by arbitrarily excluding them from participation. The more important an association is to its potential members, the more careful it must be to ensure that membership is not denied to anyone except upon strictly objective criteria related specifically to the purposes and goals of the organization. If the organization serves business or professional members, the basic principle of membership eligibility is that the organization may not exclude potential members for the purpose of reducing competition.

Minutes, Recordkeeping, and Reporting Requirements

Proper operation of a nonprofit organization entails sound practices for keeping records of the organization's official acts and filing the required reports with the appropriate authorities.

Who should keep the formal minutes of an organization's meetings? Recording and issuing the minutes of meetings is a burdensome task, and it may be difficult to motivate an elected volunteer secretary to generate them on a timely basis. It is often wise for the nonprofit executive to undertake the burden or to see to it that the responsibility for producing the minutes lies within his or her domain. While the minutes are subject to subsequent amendment and approval, the nonprofit executive will have significant influence over the outcome of the meetings if he or she is willing to accept the responsibility for producing them. This way, at least, you are sure the minutes will get done.

By accepting the responsibility for the minutes, the executive can assure that all of the relevant discussions and decisions are accurately reported, and that any off-hand, thoughtless, or potentially harmful comments are appropriately expunged. Handwritten notes from a meeting should be destroyed after the formal minutes of the meeting are typed and distributed. If a remark or observation at the meeting is worth preserving, it should be contained in the formal typed minutes. A complete record of everything that everyone said at the meeting is burdensome and unnecessary. Meeting minutes should accurately record the decisions made at the meeting with only as much of the discussion as is necessary to provide a record of the basis for the decisions. You should think of meeting minutes as a public document because they can be obtained by the plaintiff in any lawsuit against the organization or its members, and you should have no reason to want to prevent them from being examined.

Finally, there is the matter of filing required reports with governmental authorities. The jurisdiction in which the organization is incorporated will typically require the filing of an annual report. Normally, such reports simply require information regarding the identities of the officers and board of directors and confirmation of the name and address of the resident agent who is available to receive any service of legal process. In addition, an organization doing a substantial amount of work in a state which is not the state of its incorporation may be required to "qualify" to do business in that state. Additional reporting requirements may be imposed upon the organization by any jurisdictions in which the organization is "qualified" to conduct business.

Officer, Director, and Executive Liability

The officers and directors of a nonprofit organization have a position of trust *vis-a-vis* the organization. The fundamental power and authority of the organization reside in the organization itself and, in the case of a membership organization, in the collective members. The officers and directors are the custodians of that authority and have a responsibility to be faithful stewards of the organization's interests.

The nonprofit executive should be alert that the test of good faith is met by any of the actions or decisions of the officers and directors. Conflicts of interest are a hazard, which may increase as the organization becomes more successful. The executive should be careful that decisions or actions are not made for the benefit of one or more of the officers or directors. Contracting for services with the firm of one of the officers at a higher price than might be obtained through a competitive bidding process is a good example of the type of activity which could fail the good faith test and render the decision makers liable for restitution to the organization. Excessive compensation to executives, or compensation disguised as benefits, is a trap into which some major nonprofit organizations have recently fallen.

Because of the litigious nature of the society in which we live, it is wise to obtain some protection for the executive and the volunteer leaders through the purchase of Directors and Officers (D & O) Liability Insurance. This is particularly important for (c)(6) business league–type organizations. Such insurance will offer coverage for the payment of legal fees and expenses in defending against legal actions, but careful attention should be paid by the executive to the terms of the policy to assure that it covers all types of claims (such as administrative proceedings under the Equal Employment Opportunity Act or an investigation by the Internal Revenue Service or the Federal Trade Commission) and to be sure that the requirements for claiming indemnification are not overlooked in case of trouble.

AVOIDING POTENTIAL LEGAL PITFALLS

Executives in any organization must be careful to comply with local, state, and Federal laws relating to the employment of workers and other aspects of conducting a business. These issues are discussed in Chapter 11. Nonprofit organizations, of course, must be watchful to avoid legal problems which relate to their particular status.

Unrelated Business Income Tax (UBIT)

Having gone to the trouble of establishing tax-exempt status for a nonprofit organization, the nonprofit executive cannot presume that all revenues which are generated by activities which the organization undertakes are exempt from taxation. Revenues from a trade or business which a nonprofit organization *regularly carries on* and which is *unrelated to the exempt purposes* for which the organization exists may be taxed under section 1.511 of the IRS Regulation. The public policy objective of this provision of the tax code is to prevent unfair competition by nonprofit organizations with for-profit organizations.

With that rationale in mind, the nonprofit executive should remember the three touchstones which determine when revenues are subject to taxation: (1) they result from a "trade or business"; (2) they are "regularly" carried on; and (3) they are "unrelated" to the exempt purposes of the organization.

What kinds of activities have been found by the IRS to generate taxable revenues? Depending upon the specific circumstances involved, such activities might include: renting mailing lists; selling goods or services to the general public; operating a broadcast radio or TV station; performing laboratory test services.

Here is one example provided by the IRS of unrelated business income which is taxable:

> *"W is an exempt business league with a large membership. Under an arrangement with an advertising agency, W regularly mails brochures, pamphlets, and other advertising materials to its members, charging the agency an agreed amount per enclosure. The distribution of the advertising material does not contribute importantly to the accomplishment of the purpose for which W is granted exemption. Accordingly, the payments made to W by the advertising agency constitute gross income from an unrelated trade or business activity."* (Section 1.512(a)-1(e))

Publication of a periodical or magazine is a common activity among nonprofit organizations, and the nonprofit executive should remember that revenues from advertising in such publications are subject to the UBI tax. While such publications typically serve the exempt purposes for which the organization was founded, the revenues from advertising are firmly held to be unrelated business income. To determine the taxable income, from such advertising it is important to remember that the direct costs involved in producing the advertising may be deducted from the gross revenues.

There are a number of important exceptions in the UBI tax provisions which the nonprofit executive should remember:

1. If all the work in carrying on a trade or business is performed for the organization without compensation, it is *not* an unrelated trade or business.

2. Selling merchandise, substantially all of which has been received by the organization as gifts or contributions, is *not* an unrelated trade or business.

3. Conducting activities over a period of only a few weeks does not constitute the regular carrying on of a trade or business.

4. Income from dividends, interest, and annuities, as well as capital gains, are generally excluded in computing unrelated business taxable income.

Additional discussion of this and other aspects of nonprofit law may be found in *A Legal Guide to Starting and Managing a Nonprofit Organization* by Bruce R. Hopkins (John Wiley & Sons).

Postal Rates. Nonprofit organizations often are eligible for favorable postage rates which might not be available to for-profit organizations. And since many nonprofit organizations rely heavily upon the distribution of publications, solicitations, and other forms of communication through the mails, you should pay pecial attention to the opportunities for favorable rates.

Postal service regulations provide that a nonprofit organization may qualify for subsidized postal rates if its purpose is religious, educational, scientific, philanthropic, or agricultural, or if the organization is a labor, fraternal, veterans, or political organization. To qualify for such subsidy, none of the net income of such an organization can benefit any private person. If an organization has received an IRS designation as tax-exempt under sections 501(c)(3); 501(c)(5); 501(c)(8); or 501(c)(9) of the IRS Code, it is presumed by the postal service to qualify for the subsidized rates. Trade organizations qualified as tax-exempt under section 501(c)(6) of the IRS Code do not qualify for the subsidized rates.

Sales Taxes. Certain nonprofit organizations also may enjoy special privileges with regard to local and state sales taxes. State laws often contain sales tax exemptions for charitable and educational organizations, and the state laws typically follow the definitions contained in the Federal statutes and regulations. Consult with the state and local tax authorities to determine whether your organization qualifies for the sales tax exemption, which can be a very substantial benefit.

The Antitrust Laws. A major area of law which is of particular importance to nonprofit organizations of competitors within an industry or profession are the U.S. antitrust laws. The penalties for violation of these laws can be very severe, and nonprofit executives of business or professional organizations should be thoroughly familiar with the basic tenets of those laws to assure compliance.

America's antitrust laws were established to preserve free economic competition in response to the development of industrial monopolies. The Sherman Act established that "combinations . . . in restraint of trade" are illegal. Since nonprofit organizations are frequently organized as "combinations" of competing members, the first criterion for establishing illegal activity under the Sherman Act is inherent in the nature of the organization. The Supreme Court has adopted a "rule of reason" to determine if a combination or agreement violates the law.

Although the Supreme Court has determined that not *every* "combination" or agreement among competitors is a violation of the law, nevertheless it has held that there are some agreements among competitors which may be illegal regardless of their reasonableness. Such agreements are known as *per se* violations of the antitrust laws, and they include **price-fixing agreements, group boycotts, joint refusals to deal, market allocations,** and **tying arrangements** (requirements by a seller who has dominant market power that a buyer must purchase a second distinct product as a condition for being allowed to purchase the first). Nonprofit executives should put an immediate stop to any conversations among competing members of the organization which relate, even if in jest, to matters which might be a *per se* violation of the antitrust laws.

The Clayton and Federal Trade Commission Acts added to the list of activities which may be deemed to be an illegal restraint of trade. The Clayton Act covers tying arrangements, exclusive dealing contracts, price discrimination, mergers and acquisitions, and joint ventures. An important Federal Trade Commission (FTC) activity which should be kept in mind by the nonprofit executive is the availability from the FTC of advisory opinions regarding the legality of a proposed activity.

To protect themselves and their organizations from becoming entangled in an expensive and time-consuming antitrust litigation, executives of nonprofit organizations representing businesses or professionals should frequently remind their members about prohibited subjects and activities. Formal adoption of a set of "antitrust guidelines" for the organization is a worthwhile exercise, providing evidence of the organization's explicit intention to operate within the law. The minutes of meetings should reflect that the group was reminded of their responsibilities under the law, and a formal agenda for every meeting will help establish that there were no prohibited subjects on the agenda for discussion at the meeting.

Expulsion of Members.   Earlier in this chapter we reviewed the basic principles for defining allowable restrictions on membership when a nonprofit organization has such members. But what about the awkward and uncomfortable situation in which some members want to toss another member or group of members out of the organization for some real or imagined misconduct? This is a circumstance that is fraught with legal danger for the organization and for the executive, and should be handled with the utmost care.

Denying renewal of membership to a member who fails to pay the required dues is not a problem and may be done summarily as a matter of course. Other members pay their fair share of the burden of operating the organization, and a member who refuses to pay has no right to be carried by the others. The bylaws of a nonprofit organization typically provide for automatic expulsion of members for non-payment of dues.

Standards and Codes of Ethics.　A common and useful area of activity for a nonprofit organization is the development and promulgation of standards or codes of ethics. Standards can take many forms, including product standards and standards of conduct. Nonprofit organizations are natural vehicles for the development of standards because within them may reside the greatest concentrations of expertise in the subject areas involved.

Codes and standards can be a source of substantial legal trouble for a nonprofit organization and its executive, and they must be carefully and thoughtfully prepared. The general public may place great reliance upon such standards to protect their safety and well-being. The sponsor of a standard upon which the public relies has a duty to be reasonably sure that the standard is thorough, appropriate, and trustworthy.

Statistical Reporting.　Another area of activity which is a natural for nonprofit organizations is the gathering and reporting of statistical data. Sound judgments can only be made upon the basis of accurate facts, and nonprofit organizations involved in advocating public policies and providing social benefits must provide factual justification for their views and activities. Moreover, any business or profession must have accurate information about conditions in its field in order to compete effectively. Nonprofit organizations often have access to the individuals or companies which possess needed data, and they are best able to collect and aggregate the data to develop a basis for decisions.

If the data are gathered by a nonprofit organization representing competing members or companies, legal difficulties can arise in connection with statistical reporting activities when they cross the line to become an agreement among the participants regarding future prices, production, or conditions of sale. The key to propriety in statistical programs is to restrict the data collection to *past* prices and transactions, and to stay strictly away from reporting future intentions. Even if there is no express agreement among competitors regarding future prices, the mere reporting of future intentions provides the necessary basis for competitors to adjust their behavior in a subtle and unspoken conspiracy.

These are just some of the areas in which a nonprofit executive might find himself on the wrong side of the law in connection with management activities. Other areas which must be handled with care include responsibility for the activities and liabilities of affiliate groups; lobbying activities and the deductibility of membership dues for lobbying expenses (see Chapter 8); and a host of other activities such as buying organizational headquarters. As always, it is wise for the nonprofit executive to find good legal counsel upon whom he can rely for regular oversight of the organization's activities. It is much less expensive to have counsel keep you out of trouble than to get you out of trouble once you are in it.

SPECIAL CIRCUMSTANCES REQUIRING THE HELP OF COUNSEL

By becoming familiar with the basic principles related above, the nonprofit executive will be able to use the law as a tool to help manage the affairs of the organization and will largely be able to keep out of trouble. Sometimes, however, the activities of a nonprofit organization involve direct interaction with government, and in such cases the executive should be careful to obtain the help of counsel with particular expertise in the subjects involved.

Lobbying, Advocacy, and Regulatory Negotiation

As the government has become increasingly active in the business affairs and everyday lives of our citizens, it has developed mountains of laws, policies, and regulations which touch virtually every aspect of our lives. Americans have the right and the responsibility to "petition" their government in connection with these laws, but the government may prescribe rules and regulations for such activities and can also limit the tax-deductibility of expenses incurred in the activities.

Recall that President Grant coined the term "lobbying" to describe job-seekers who would linger in the lobby of a hotel he visited, waiting for an audience. Since then, the term has acquired a very specific definition. The Federal Regulation of Lobbying Act says that lobbying is the solicitation or collection of funds principally to aid or influence Federal legislation. In the Omnibus Budget Reconciliation Act of 1993, the term "lobbying" is defined as attempts to influence Federal or state legislation or to influence official action by "covered" executive branch officials at the Federal level. Under the 1993 Act, taxpayers are not allowed to take deductions for lobbying or political expenses, including any deduction for the portion of membership dues paid to a nonprofit organization which is used for lobbying expenses. A nonprofit executive of an organization with due-paying membership which attempts to influence state or Federal legislation should determine the effect of the law upon his or her organization. (This issue is also discussed in Chapter 8.)

Filing Lawsuits and "Amicus" Briefs

Occasionally, the members of a nonprofit organization will want the organization to pursue legal redress for some wrong which the members have suffered. The first step which must be taken in deciding on such an action is to determine whether the organization has a sufficient interest in the nature of the injury to give it the necessary "standing" to sue. Early cases held that only the party which has directly suffered the alleged injury has the necessary standing, but more recent cases have greatly liberalized that standard, and many nonprofit organizations have been found to have the necessary standing to file lawsuits on behalf of their members' interests. In addition, nonprofit organizations may undertake to file "amicus" briefs in support of a legal action involving one or more of its members. The filing of such briefs can be a substantial benefit for the parties and interests served by the organization, and can address issues of law which might not otherwise be fully explored.

Clearly, the initiation of such activities by a nonprofit organization requires the participation of legal counsel, and should be undertaken only after exhaustive review of the wisdom of the action by the organization's officers and board of directors.

IN CONCLUSION

There are other areas in which the nonprofit executive will want to seek out the particular expertise of specialized legal counsel who know the "prescribed formula" for achieving some legal end, such as trademark registration, copyright protection, the formation of for-profit subsidiaries, or the operation of political action committees. Such counsel is readily available and need not be expensive. Executives should keep current on legal developments affecting nonprofit organizations and keep repeating, "The law is my friend."

CHAPTER THIRTEEN

Selecting and Using Consultants

"Outsourcing" is a buzzword for the 1990s, and many non-profits turn to outside experts for help. This chapter provides insight and guidance on knowing when to seek outside assistance and then finding and hiring the right consultant.

HOW TO SELECT AND USE CONSULTANTS

The responsibilities of nonprofit organizations are wide, but their staff resources are usually limited. To carry out its strategic plan, almost every nonprofit organization will use outside services at some time. Of course, for-profit organizations also use consultants. But a nonprofit organization is even more likely to find that the expertise and resources it needs to get its job done fall outside the experience and the time available of its professional staff and of those board members and volunteers willing to commit enough time to get everything done.

The earlier chapters of this book outline how nonprofit executives and their in-house staff can carry out a range of complex activities. These ideas and case studies should make it possible for you to take on activities you might not have thought you could handle. But there's always a limit to time and staff, and it's a mistake to spread your staff too thin. The director of marketing who takes on additional responsibilities for community education programs may do that very well, but may self-destruct if asked to handle public relations or fund-raising.

The nonprofit executive frequently faces the question: Do I do it myself or do I need a consultant? An analogy from the private sector is the "make or buy" decision: Do I make my own gear shifts (pistons, axles, headlights, batteries) or am I better off buying them from a supplier? The same question comes up in a different form for a nonprofit.

When Should I Use a Consultant?

The first necessity, of course, is having a clear idea of your organization's goals and objectives. The long-range and strategic plans, at least if they're kept up-to-date, should lead the executive to a plan of action. The first consideration of whether or not to use a consultant begins as you face serious obstacles or opportunities to meet important goals of your organization.

This decision should not be made precipitously. It's usually a mistake to decide it's time to upgrade your information systems or start an ambitious new service program just because you were influenced by someone you met at a conference or who came to see you on the recommendation of a member of your board. Similarly, it's too easy to "set up a foundation" or agree with the board member who says "what we need is a public relations campaign" just because the idea sounds good at a meeting. While it's fine to get ideas this way, you should not base decisions about whether or when to take on a new project on the basis of personal contact. Improvisation—reacting to circumstances as they change—is sometimes needed when carrying out a project but not at the point of planning. Choosing to use a consultant should be a need-driven decision that fits within the outlines of your strategic plan.

Let's assume you have a project—maybe a membership campaign—that's been planned in advance and is carefully integrated with educational programs or other membership services. There are likely to be a number of pieces to this campaign. There will be letters to write, brochures to design. There's probably an outreach activity, involving staff or members calling prospects. There's research to be done on membership prospects, and analysis on why present members are (or are not) renewing. There may be brochures to design, prospective member receptions to plan and hold. There might even be a kick-off with a leading figure from the community or profession and media possibilities that go along with one or more of these functions.

Who is going to do all this? Your overworked secretary or administrative assistant? The vice president of personnel? Your bookkeeper, who took an art course in college and has always wanted to try graphic arts? Even if you think that you or others on your staff could do this, do they really have the skill or time or energy to do it, on time, in addition to their regular jobs?

At this point it may be helpful to make a checklist, such as the example in Exhibit 13-1, of the different tasks that go into this project. Put the different tasks involved on the left margin. On top of the page, write "Present Staff Can Do?" (don't leave out the question mark). Under that, set up four columns with these headings: "Well," "Satisfactorily," "With Luck," and "Not Possible."

Go through this twice, with your present staff in mind. The first time, just think of their ability and preparation. If they fall into either of the first three categories, put their initials in the box.

Put the worksheet aside for a day. (It's best to do this at home so you don't give in to the temptation to discuss it with your staff quite yet.) Then, the next day, review it with a different set of questions in mind: Does this person have the time? Would he or she enjoy doing this? Would I want to give them this assignment? And, if you've got those initials in the two "maybe" categories ("satisfactorily" or "with luck") is that good enough?

Now, you're getting close to your decision points. If you've got a staff person in the first category (that is, you're confident she or he could do the task just fine), you only have to face the question of whether or not it's the best use of the person's time. Maybe you

Exhibit 13–1   Checklist of Staff Responsibilities

PRESENT STAFF CAN DO?				
	Well	Satisfactorily	With Luck	Never
Plan Meeting?				
Solicit Corporate Sponsors?				
Obtain Speakers?				
Select Hotel and Negotiate Contract?				
Prepare Publicity Brochure and Press Releases?				
Develop Mailing List?				
Handle Registration and Accounting?				
Obtain Press Coverage?				

have to take her off something she's doing now to free up enough time, and you may not want to do that. On the other hand, if it's really an opportunity for job enrichment and learning, she may be glad to take on the assignment even if it is a stretch.

But if those initials are in one of the "maybe" categories, you don't want to do it with present staff if you can help it. Here, of course, budget realities have their impact. Often, in a nonprofit organization (it can happen in a for-profit too) the resources just aren't there to get additional help, even if you'd want to. You may have to settle for "satisfactorily" or gamble on "with luck." Just bear in mind that this staff person is going to need extra help and coaching along the way, either from you or from a talented board member or volunteer.

New Staff or Outside Consultants?

If you've concluded that some parts of the assignment are beyond your present staff, you can think about whether it is time to hire someone. If you've got the resources and the assignment is likely to be continuing, that may be the right thing. But not always.

The decision on whether to use a consulting firm or consultant is highly specific to the individual case. The right decision changes depending on the nature of the assignment, the nature and resources of your organization, and the relative strengths of both your own organization (which we've tried to assess above) and the services available to you locally that are within your budget.

Look back again to your organization's mission statement, the strategic plan, and the one-year plan. You've got a job to do and a budget to do it in. For a complex project, a consulting firm or agency might cost as much or more as bringing a new manager or an experienced professional on board. Why use an outside firm if you could hire your own?

If the budget is enough for a first-class professional, and if the job is going to keep him or her really occupied, not just for the first six months but into the future, a new hire may well be called for. But a few cautions.

Most managers have an in-built bias towards building up their own organization staff. A nonprofit organization may not have to measure success by increased sales or profits, like a for-profit organization. The "bottom line" (size of profit) does not constrain growth, as long as revenues cover expenses. As a result, we've heard nonprofit managers boast that they've doubled staff since they became CEO, as if the size of the staff is the measure of the organization's success.

First, you want to be sure you've looked at real costs, not just salary and fringes. Estimating overhead accurately can be complicated; we've tried to give some guidelines in Chapter 9, "Managing Your Finances." Those fringe benefit costs—social security, unemployment compensation, and, most likely, health insurance—add up fast. The new staff person is going to need an office, a desk, and probably a word processor. There will be increased time from your human relations director. Is this new staffer going to require an assistant? At the least, someone to answer the telephone when he or she is not at the desk?

A second question to ask yourself: Can I (or other members of your staff) give this person the guidance that will be needed? Of course, you'd look for a "self-starter," someone who knows what he or she is doing and doesn't need much supervision. But chances are the budget you've established is not going to attract a top-flight professional at the peak of experience. You will probably find that executive guidance is needed, and may find that this guidance is hard to come by. After all, if you really knew how to do this task yourself, you might not be looking to hire.

And third: Will this person really be busy—fully occupied—by the assignment you're giving? For how long? Suppose you put on four educational conferences in the course of a year, two board of directors meetings, and one or two major dinners or other events. That's clearly more than you or your administrative assistant can handle. Why not hire a full-time meeting manager? Because, most likely, that meeting manager is going to be extremely busy about half the year, and overloaded for two or three weeks of those six months. The rest of the time that person is going to sit there bored, or pretend that what he or she is doing will make the next meeting better. Travel costs to scout meeting sites will be a bigger item in next year's budget.

Is there a better way to do this?

Assignments for Consultants

Let's review assignments for which nonprofit organizations are most likely to call on outside consultants for help. These include:

- Accounting.
- Audiovisual production.
- Audit.
- Computer services.
- Curriculum development.
- Fund-raising.
- Government relations.
- Graphic arts.
- Legal.
- Meetings management.
- Public relations.
- Publications.
- Strategic planning.

Obviously, there is a different decision in each category in making that "make or buy" decision. Unless the organization is so small that you don't need (or want) an audited annual financial statement, you're going to have an outside auditor. And only very large nonprofits will have an attorney on staff; if you have a clear legal issue, you're going to contract out.

On the other end of the scale is accounting; most organizations do this themselves. But even here the choice may not be so obvious. Even fairly large organizations can find that the checks and balances needed for good financial controls are hard to build internally.

A membership organization with a $750,000 operating budget had employed a full-time bookkeeper to manage its financial affairs. The bookkeeper had several years of experience but could not implement financial controls and could not provide the executive director with meaningful information. Additionally, the association's software was inflexible so it could not meet the particular needs of this organization.

The bookkeeper became increasingly frustrated and left. Instead of replacing the bookkeeper and purchasing new accounting software, the organization retained the services of a management firm to handle the day-to-day *accounting responsibilities including cash receipts, cash disbursements, maintenance of the general ledger, and generation of the monthly financial statements. This organization then had the services of an entire accounting department at its disposal. The net savings to this group totaled $12,000 a year.*

Finding the Right Consultant

Once you've made the decision to go outside, the question is how to locate candidates and how to make your decision. We stress again: the make-or-buy decision should precede the decision on whom to buy from. Far too many nonprofits do this the other way around: they decide to undertake a project because a consultant sells them on that project. Even if one outside firm brings you an idea for a project that you then adopt, you should still get competitive bids and proposals. (Of course, you then keep the specific operational ideas of the original firm confidential, asking for proposals on a project outlined in general terms. Often, the original bidder wins out in a case like this; but if they object to your asking for competitive bids, it's probably not the right firm for you.)

The bidding process will be quite different depending on the nature of the project. Major consulting or public relations projects usually warrant a full-blown request-for-proposal (RFP). Selecting an attorney or auditor is usually a matter of interviewing recommended firms or individuals and carefully checking resumes. One important factor in deciding on your approach is whether you expect this to be a long-term or a single-project relationship. Another is the importance or financial size of the project—that is, what are the consequences of a mistake? The answers to these questions will affect the amount of time you will spend making your selection. Designing a brochure for your major fund-raising event of the year is important, but you aren't necessarily committing to using the same graphic design firm next year. If the design is less than great or if you get a better bid next year, it's easy to change. Choosing an attorney or auditor, on the other hand, builds a relationship that will be harder to change. That person will develop an understanding of the organization and a base of experience that you lose if you start over. More care is required in the initial selection.

The time-honored way of selecting a number of consultants to interview or from whom to request proposals is to gain recommendations from fellow professionals. The experience of people you trust and respect can be invaluable. Sometimes, however, what you get from them are the safe, predictable recommendations, the established firms. The firms recommended may be excellent, but they are unlikely (if cost matters) to be the low-cost suppliers.

By all means, get recommendations from your peers or the local grapevine. You may already know the names of the dominant firms in the area in which you're looking for help. Include one or two of those best-known or highly recommended firms in your list, but search out at least one small or less-known firm for comparison. At the very least, that will keep the established firms on their toes.

Some nonprofits, at this point, will simply put an RFP in the mail. That's usually not best. A better course is to ask some of your likely bidders to come by to discuss the project. Describe it to them orally. You'll find some that don't understand what you're after, some that offer sharp ideas right on the spot. You may even find that your RFP is off the mark, that what you're asking for is unrealistic or too ill-defined. If so, the sooner you learn that the better; revise your RFP now (even if this means going back to your executive committee) rather than facing reality later.

There's no one universally applicable model for a good RFP. You need to spell out what you want the consultant to accomplish and ask for specific recommendations as to how the consultant or consulting firm will execute the project. Ask for specifics on staff to be assigned and billing rates; as well as for information on the consultant's past projects and clients, including two or three you can call for references. While you need to include all details that will be important to you in making your decision, beware of making the RFP too long or too prescriptive. An overly detailed RFP may signal to potential bidders that you don't really want their advice and ideas and even discourage the best from responding. (See Exhibit 13-2 for a model RFP.)

After reviewing responses to the RFP, you should be able to pick out three finalists. The qualifications you look for will differ, of course, by the type of project. Thoroughness, creativity, and ability to work within budget are basic factors. It may be helpful to use an appraisal form in reviewing the RFP's with these qualifications, plus others specific to your project. If more than one person is reviewing the RFP's (a good idea on any major project), ask them to rate the respondents on a scale of one through five in each category. If there

Exhibit 13–2   Model RFP

Request for Proposals

Public Relations and Membership Campaign: Council for a Better Community

Background: The Council for a Better Community was founded in 1984 by Crescent City leaders concerned that the social fabric of our city was deteriorating, undermining public safety, schools, and our local economy. Initial support came from five local corporations. Program emphasis has been, and will continue to be, on citizen involvement in community affairs, especially local schools and those government agencies, such as public health, housing, and public safety, that work directly with our citizens.

Although community support has broadened, with over 100 local businesses and several foundations now funding the Council's activities, the Council has never before solicited membership or support from the general public. The board of directors has decided that a broad-based membership would not only widen the Council's base of financial support but would also improve public awareness and encourage greater citizen participation in the organization's activities. (Annual Reports summarizing the Council's recent activities are attached.)

Assistance desired: The Council is soliciting proposals from a public relations agency or other capable provider for a two-year program. Elements should include:

- Materials, including a membership brochure, to be used in direct mail and other membership promotion activities;
- Press releases and an action plan for developing media coverage that increases public awareness of the Council's activities and supports the membership campaign;
- Public relations materials and a plan for promoting the Council's annual award dinner, to be held later this year, and for incorporating this event into the new membership campaign;
- Plan of action for a direct mail membership campaign, including development of target lists and a plan of implementation.

The agency selected will report to the executive director and work closely with the Council's executive committee as well as Council staff responsible for communications and member recruitment.

Details for submission: The Council requests written proposals from qualified firms, to be submitted in triplicate to the Council's office by (date).

Submissions should include:

- An outline of how the firm would develop the plans and materials cited above;
- Any other suggestions for broadening the Council's membership base and increasing its public visibility and support;

Exhibit 13–2   *(Continued)*

- Examples of similar materials and summaries of campaigns that the firm created and carried out previously, for either nonprofit or for-profit organizations;
- Budget for the program, detailing the basis for the firm's charges; in particular, state whether the firm proposes to charge a fixed-fee retainer or on an hourly basis;
- List of references.

Additional information: please feel free to call (name), executive director of the Council, with any questions about the assistance desired.

The Council's executive committee intends to invite finalists to make a personal presentation of their proposal (next month, etc.). Finalists will be notified by (date).

are significant differences, meet to talk through the different reactions. At the end of this process, you should be able to identify your three best candidates. Invite them for the final presentations before your selection committee. Now that they know they are finalists, they may be able to refine their own ideas. You should expect discussions precisely focused on your organization and your specific project; consultants who talk too much about themselves or who give you the same "canned" presentation they make to all prospective clients probably won't give you individualized service in the future either.

Final interviews are usually conducted, for major projects, in groups of three or four interviewers. We all have different questions to ask and group dynamics are important. Also, for a large project, you want key board members to "buy in" to the decision.

The agreement should be summarized in a letter of understanding or, for larger projects, in a contract. Usually, this need not be elaborate. It should summarize what the organization expects from the consultant, when the work will be completed (often in stages), and the agreement on compensation. Where applicable, the agreement should spell out terms concerning how either party can terminate the agreement. Very large or complex projects sometimes require detailed contracts and legal review, but this should be avoided wherever possible. If a consultant's work turns out to be unsatisfactory, the only practical course is to terminate the arrangement as soon as this becomes evident. The purpose of the contract or letter of agreement is just to assure that both parties understand the expectations of each other, not to create a legally binding document. (See Exhibit 13–3 for a sample contract.)

Exhibit 13–3 Sample Consultant Contract

This letter is to confirm and constitute the understanding between WORTHY AGENCY and SUPERIOR CONSULTANTS, a _[name of state]_ partnership conducting the business of fund-raising consultation for not-for-profit organizations.

SUPERIOR CONSULTANTS will design and implement a fund-raising plan to increase contributions from individual donors.

[Person's Name] will coordinate the delivery of service under this contract, with the support of SUPERIOR CONSULTANTS.

It will be SUPERIOR CONSULTANTS' responsibility to:

1. Direct the development of a contributions data base containing information about past and present giving. Train volunteers in basic research techniques.

2. Identify potential contributors to the "challenge fund." Prepare and assist the president and board members in soliciting selected individuals for this purpose.

3. Develop and implement both short-term and ongoing fund-raising strategies involving board members, parents, and friends of WORTHY AGENCY.

4. Review suggestions for fund-raising for WORTHY AGENCY. Help set priorities and advise on the implementation of the best ideas.

5. Outline the basic functions of a development office for WORTHY AGENCY and prepare a model job description for a Director of Development.

6. Develop a proposal for a feasibility study for an Endowment Campaign and advise on sources of underwriting for such a study.

It will be WORTHY AGENCY'S responsibility to:

1. Provide SUPERIOR CONSULTANTS with information on prior and ongoing fund-raising efforts and outreach.

2. Identify key volunteers, donors, and community leaders for fund-raising leadership, and help with involving them in the annual giving program.

3. Enable the Executive Director to work closely with the consultants to ensure full and timely communication.

Exhibit 13–3 *(Continued)*

4. Furnish whatever secretarial and other office services the contributions program requires.

5. Pay or reimburse any out-of-pocket expenses, such as printed materials, special-event costs, and recognition items. All expenditures will be subject to prior approval.

6. Receive all monies; log and collect gifts and pledges; and provide periodic reports on income and expenses.

7. Implement public relations aspects of the campaign, if any.

WORTHY AGENCY will not be billed for telephone, postage, photocopying, clerical, and similar expenses incurred by SUPERIOR CONSULTANTS in WORTHY AGENCY's offices, or for travel within Home County.

WORTHY AGENCY has the right to cancel this contract upon 30 days' written notice. WORTHY AGENCY is responsible for all authorized expenditures committed up to the date of notification and for the final 30 days' fee owed to SUPERIOR CONSULTANTS.

The period covered by this contract is [Date] through [Date] . The fee for these services is [$X,000] , payable monthly at the beginning of each service period. Should WORTHY AGENCY wish to continue to receive these services after [Date] , SUPERIOR CONSULTANTS will provide them at no increase in fee.

If this letter correctly expresses our mutual understanding, please signify approval by signing the original and the attached copy and returning the original to me at SUPERIOR CONSULTANTS.

AGREED

_____   _____
              [Signature]   [Signature]
PRESIDENT   Partner
WORTHY AGENCY   SUPERIOR CONSULTANTS

Dated _____

Source: Nan D. Doty and Barbara M. Cox, "Annual Giving Programs" in *The Nonprofit Management Handbook*, edited by Tracy D. Connors (New York: John Wiley & Sons, 1993), p. 506. Reprinted by permission of Doty & Cox.

WORKING WITH YOUR CONSULTANT

Experienced nonprofit executives have different views of how best to work with consultants. Some executives simply sign the contract and turn their backs on the project until it's complete. Others will call the consultants every other day and expect them to be present at frequent staff meetings or consultations.

A middle course is usually best and should not be hard to follow. The nonprofit CEO or department head in charge of the project should be involved enough to know how it is progressing and be able to summarize where it stands. Is the project on schedule? Do preliminary findings confirm or call into question premises on which the project is based? What changes have been necessary in the plan of action? Are costs under control? The person on staff who is responsible for the project should be able to answer these basic questions at any time.

Over-management may seem harmless, but has problems. For one thing, it takes time—both your own time (to reduce your own or your staff's time is probably one reason you contracted out in the first place) and that of the consultant. If you're paying by the hour—typical of contracts with law firms or public relations agencies—every hour they spend in consultations with you or your staff is added to your bill. They should not be spending their time in unnecessary meetings and neither should you.

And over-management can call into question the basic reason you hired the consultant in the first place: they know more than you do in their field of expertise. At the worst, this may invalidate the results of a worthwhile project.

Research projects require realistic goals and the willingness to accept results, which at times can be different from what the organization anticipates at the outset. An organization that expects a contractor's report to buttress a case that it's already committed to can be disappointed.

Here are two examples to illustrate the importance of being open to research project results.

The Federated Council of Internal Medicine, representing four major organizations of internal medicine physicians, was skeptical of established projections showing a surplus of general physicians due to increased enrollments in medical school. The Council contracted with a recognized health care research firm to study trends in the practice patterns of internal medicine physicians. The consultants interviewed leaders of the sponsoring organizations and physicians at teaching hospitals and in the field. While different physicians had various pieces of information, none of them tried to force his own view on the consultants.

The consulting firm, able to "step out of the frame and look at the picture," found several factors that had been overlooked in deriving the projection of a physician surplus. First, they found that physicians working in managed care organizations typically put in somewhat shorter workweeks than those in private practice. They also found that women physicians, perhaps because of family demands but also because of different styles, not only worked slightly fewer hours but tended to spend more time with each patient. With enrollment of women in medical schools rising rapidly, this one factor changed trends sharply. The consultants also pointed out that any change in disease patterns could quickly create greater needs for medical generalists.

The study, when released and presented to a special governmental committee recommending changes in graduate medical education, prompted a shift in Federal policy to encourage teaching hospitals to emphasize general medical practice and was one factor in changing policies on payments of physicians to increase payments made to general practitioners.

At about the same time, another health care organization, whose members provided services to convalescent patients, faced cuts in payment under Federal policies and wanted to demonstrate that cost-cutters had overlooked essential costs of providing these services. A major consulting firm, which had done credible work for the association previously, set out to interview association members in the field about their own expenses and cost structures. First, it derived medians of costs in different companies and came up with a model cost structure. Unfortunately, the preliminary conclusion seemed to reinforce the view the association had set out to disprove: that prices were high in relation to costs.

The study was extended and the consultant returned to the field. But the only solution was to construct a new composite from the higher range of costs reported by the higher-cost firms in the industry. This supported the point desired, but at a heavy price; the study screamed "tilt." Although the board of directors seemed satisfied—the study now supported their preconception—the association's government relations staff knew the study would hurt, rather than enhance, the group's reputation and credibility. The study was buried in files.

Both organizations expected, at the outset, that the study would validate opinions they held and that the consultants' study would sway major decisions on health care policy. The first organization was correct; the second made the mistake of thinking the world could be remade to fit its preconceptions and compounded the error by pressuring the consultant into its own bias.

Controlling Costs

It's not always possible to price every project to the dollar. Research, for example, can justifiably take longer than predicted. But beware: whatever adjustments in estimates are permitted in the contract will always be up. If a supplier comes in under bid, be sure to use that firm next time.

Many projects, such as printing or convention management, are usually fixed-cost contracts. Accounting, audits, and legal services are usually based on hourly charges. Public relations can be either hourly or based on a monthly retainer, often with add-ons for any part of the project not specifically called for in the contract.

Major corporations, alarmed at rising legal bills, have begun in recent years to require that their law firms live with fixed contracts for all but complex litigation. Nonprofits, working with smaller budgets but without the same cost discipline, have been slow to follow their example.

At the very least, insist on timely billings and keep a running tally. (Law firms are notoriously late in billing; this makes it harder to control costs.) Some projects, for which the consultant is managing outside costs, might include a bonus if the overall project comes in under budget.

Monitoring Performance

For major projects, the contract should have appropriate reporting times built in. For a research project, this should usually be quarterly, if the project will take a year or more, and monthly if it is a short-term project. Public relations or government relations projects usually have a short monthly summary and a longer quarterly report. Other projects—such as an audit—are oriented to one task; timeframes for completion of preliminary tasks should be agreed upon, but there usually won't be any report until the project is over. Management of projects such as conventions or public events should be keyed to time lines, either as specified in the contract or worked out in detail between you and your consultant. For example, there should be dates by which hotel contracts will be pinned down, promotional pieces printed and mailed, speakers confirmed, etc. (see Chapter 6). The consultant should keep his or her own checklist of actions completed to make sure nothing is missed; it doesn't add to the consultant's cost to share this with you on a frequent basis.

If the contractor is off schedule, or over budget, or if performance is clearly differing from what you've expected, it's best to face this early. If you let it worry you or sit too long brooding, delay will sap your own energy and increase the risk that you'll end up in a confrontation with your consultant at the most critical time for the project. Work out any problems early, when they are most easily corrected. A good consultant will appreciate your honesty; after all, the consultant can't respond without knowing where you are coming from.

Occasionally, you'll have to take radical action to redirect or even terminate a project. This is hard to do, because it is a recognition either that the project was misconceived in the first place or that you made a mistake in hiring the consultant. If the consultant is tied in with influential members of your board of directors, you're in a worse bind. In that case, if possible, discuss it with that board member or with your executive committee. Ask for their advice on whether or not to proceed with the project. A smart consultant will be the first to say so if a project isn't working out as expected.

Soon after new regulations appeared, a nonprofit organization with expertise in helping service industries hire and promote workers with physical or emotional disabilities contracted with an industry organization to develop and put on an educational seminar in Washington to review what restaurants needed to do to comply with the Americans with Disabilities Act. While the seminar was valuable to the industry group as part of its overall educational program, the nonprofit organization had major responsibility and would get most of the profit of the meeting after expenses. The first seminar was over-subscribed, and in their enthusiasm the two organizations scheduled another in Chicago four months later. Contracts with some of the speakers had cancellation clauses that would require partial payment; other speakers were consultants also well known to members of the nonprofit organization. The director of the industry organization, who had been ecstatic at the success of the first meeting, was looking forward to press coverage of the second. Worse yet, the hotel contract had a cancellation penalty.

But registrations just didn't come in. As the deadline for hotel registrations approached, the executive director checked with the hotel and was able to negotiate a revised cancellation clause, at a reasonable but not disastrous penalty, but only if the cancellation was done immediately. He called a half dozen expected attendees who had not yet registered and found that it was not just delay; they had all attended other seminars on the subject or realized that compliance would not be nearly as difficult as early headlines had told them it would be. They could deal with the new law without having to send staff to Chicago for two days.

Reluctantly, the executive director of the nonprofit called the president of the industry association. A long silence followed as he explained the situation and recommended that the meeting be cancelled, accepting a small financial loss but avoiding the risk of a meeting that would flop. After that silence, the president finally said, "Well, I'm disappointed, but it looks like our timing is off on this one. We'll cover your costs, and let's think about another seminar next year. Thanks for realizing we needed to pull out of this one before it was too late."

ASSISTING THE CONSULTANTS

It stands to reason that nonprofit executives will be able to help the consultants do their work only if they understand what the consultants are doing. Most projects should be a partnership between the nonprofit staff and the consultant. Communication has to be good. Usually, this means frequent. But, as we've stressed above, that does not mean time-consuming. Two five-minute telephone calls are usually better than one one-hour meeting.

No consultant is going to know your own business as well as you do. Even if the consultant is a national expert on the subject to which your organization is devoted, he or she probably doesn't understand your local situation as well as you do.

The issue of how you can best work with the consultant, helping that person or firm to produce a report or put on a workshop or prepare a press conference that will serve your purpose, should be addressed in the selection process. How much help do they want from you? How do they want to communicate? Rapport is intangible, but if it's not there from the outset, it may be hard to develop later on.

FINAL REPORTS

For some projects—research projects most obviously—the final report is the purpose of the exercise. For other projects like fund-raising or organizing a meeting, the results will be in the numbers. But a summary of activities carried out under the contract and of results achieved is always useful. You'll usually circulate this to at least part of your board of directors. And it will be very useful next time you take on a similar project.

CHECKLIST/POINTS FOR REVIEW

Deciding on a Consultant:

- Make a cost/benefit analysis of doing the project in-house versus using a consultant. Be sure this includes the real costs, direct and indirect, of doing it yourself.
- Cast a wide net in targeting potential consultants; don't just use the first one suggested (long-established relationships are an exception).
- Discuss the project informally with one or two potential consultants even while developing the RFP. Be available to meet with all bidders at their request.
- Develop an RFP. This makes you think through the project, as well as giving potential consultants a guide to which to respond.
- Interview finalists in a small group of your staff or members.
- Delineate expectations and responsibilities clearly and summarize in a letter of agreement or contract.
- Make sure all costs are clearly spelled out and that fixed costs or caps on hourly charges are included.

Working with the Consultant:

- Maintain an open line of communication without wasting time in long meetings.
- Make sure you or someone on your staff knows where things stand at all times; don't just write a contract and then walk away from the project.

- Be honest with yourself and the consultant. If things aren't going well, have a meeting and discuss problems openly.
- If it's necessary to terminate a project—no matter what the cause—it's usually better to do this early than to struggle through to an unsatisfactory conclusion.

Index

A

Academic institutions:
  fund-raising example, 86–88
  marketing example, 109
Accounting function:
  accrual vs. cash basis, 228–229
  assets and liabilities, 232–233, 234, 235
  cash disbursements, 230–231
  cash receipts, 229–230
  closing procedures, 232–233
  defined, 220
  elements of, 221
  establishing system for, 225–227
  financial statement preparation, 234–236
  outsourcing, 225
  policies and procedures for, 244–245
  staffing for, 224–225, 302
  use of outside service, 302–303
Accrual basis accounting, 228–229, 231
ADA. See Americans with Disabilities Act (ADA)
Adverse publicity, 193–194
Advertising:
  crisis hotline example, 113
  for educational programs, 130–131
  as form of promotion, 111
  for hiring, 263–264
Affirmative action, 78
American Association of Blood Banks, 14, 20–21, 22–23

American Red Cross, 77
American Society for Psychoprophylaxis in Obstetrics, 16, 19
Americans with Disabilities Act (ADA), 127, 312–313
"Amicus" briefs, 295
Annual assessments, 66
Annual campaigns, 66–67
Annual meetings, 125–126
Annual reports, 185
Antitrust laws, 291–292
Articles of incorporation, 280–281
Asset accounting, 232, 234–235
Assets, analyzing, 11–12
Attorneys, 294–296, 303
Audiences. See also Consumers
  identifying, 97–98
  for public relations, 171–173
Auditors:
  hiring, 302, 303
  reports by, 242–243
  and tax returns, 244
Awards programs, 78, 79, 80

B

Bad publicity, 193–194
Baker, Gwendolyn Calvert, 52
Banking services, 221–224
Beer Baron Bill, 191–192
Beliefs, listing, 18–20
Benefits. See Job benefits

Board of directors:
  advocacy role, 39–40
  checklists for, 41, 58–59
  and committees, 42, 45–46
  and confidentiality, 36
  and conflicts of interest, 36
  and day-to-day administration, 37–39
  director's responsibilities, 45
  ethical considerations, 35–36
  examples, 34, 38–39, 40–41, 52, 53
  executive committee of, 32, 45–46, 47
  fiduciary responsibility, 34–35
  and fund-raising, 34–35
  liability of, 288–289
  meeting minutes, 287–288
  number of directors, 285
  and organizational mission, 33–34
  orientation for new members, 53–55
  position descriptions for, 42, 43–45
  president's responsibilities, 43
  and professionalism, 35–36
  recordkeeping, 287–288
  recruitment by, 40–41
  relationships among members, 35
  relationship with staff, 36–39, 51–55
  responsibilities of, 33–42
  roles of, 33, 37–40
  secretary's responsibilities, 44
  sizes of, 32–33
  and strategic planning, 5, 6, 7
  treasurer's responsibilities, 44, 46
  types of, 32–33
  vice president's responsibilities,
    43–44
Bookkeeping. *See also* Accounting
    function
  defined, 220, 221
  staffing needs, 224, 225, 302
Brady, Jim and Sarah, 213
Break-even analysis, 136
Broadcast media:
  for educational programs, 126–127
  interviews with, 188–190
Budgeting:
  capital, 234
  for educational programs, 135–137
  for marketing, 113–115
  for meetings, 150–152, 153
  overview, 233–234

Bulletin boards, 174–175
Burnout, 269
Businesses, soliciting funds from, 70–71
Business income, and UBI tax, 66,
    289–291
Business organizations:
  and antitrust laws, 291–292
  soliciting funds from, 74–75
  statistical reporting by, 293–294
Business plan. *See* Operational plan
Bylaws:
  committees in, 42, 45, 282
  writing, 281–282

C

Capital campaigns, 67
Cash basis accounting, 229
Cash disbursements, 230–231
Cash flows, 236, 241
Cash receipts, 229–230
CEUs (continuing education units),
    129–130
Chart of accounts, 226, 227–228
Chief executive officer. *See* Executive
    director
Chinese-Americans for Affirmative
    Action, 78
City Lights, 73
Classroom instruction, 124–125
Closing procedures, 232–233
Coalitions, 210
Codes of ethics, 35–36, 293
Committees:
  ad hoc, 45, 48
  and bylaws, 42, 45, 282
  criteria for success, 48, 49
  executive committee, 32, 45–46, 47
  finance committee, 46, 47
  for fund-raising project, 68
  for governance, 42, 45–46, 47
  nominations committee, 46, 47
  types of, 45, 46–47
Communications:
  between board and staff, 36–37,
    51–53
  choosing phone system, 275
  with constituents, 6, 52, 194–198
  in crises, 182, 192–193

and public relations, 173–185
Community relations, 190–191
Community service organizations,
    educational program examples,
    120, 127
Compensation, 267–268
Computer technology. *See also*
    Information systems
    in the office, 247–252
    as public relations tool, 174–175
Conferences, 125–126. *See also* Meetings
Constituents:
    communicating with, 52, 194–198
    involving in strategic planning, 6
Constitution. *See* Articles of
    incorporation; Bylaws
Consultants:
    ADA example, 312–313
    assisting, 313
    checklist for hiring, 314–315
    contracts with, 306–307
    and cost control, 311
    finding, 303–306
    health care study examples, 309–310
    likely assignments, 302–303
    for lobbying, 211–212
    monitoring, 311–313
    overview, 297–298
    as resource, 262, 298–300
    sample contract, 307, 308–309
    in strategic planning, 6–8
    vs. hiring new staff, 300–301
    when to use, 298–300
    working with, 307–313
Consumers, 93, 94. *See also* Audiences
    assessing needs, 99–102
    benefits to, 95–96
    educating, 184–185
    identifying, 97–98
Continuing education units (CEUs),
    129–130
Contracts:
    consultant, 306–307
    and cost control, 311
    meeting, 152–155
    monitoring, 311–313
    sample, 307, 308–309
Contributors. *See* Donors

Core constituency:
    communicating with, 52, 194–198
    involving in strategic planning, 6
Corporate recognition plan, 71, 72–73
Corporations, soliciting funds from,
    70–71
Council for Court Excellence, 203
Crisis communication, 182, 192–193
Crisis hotline, marketing by, 112
Critical dates list, 152, 154
Cross-training, for information
    systems, 253
Custom software, 251–252

D

Databases, 249
Decision-making, 2
Delphos, William, 74
Development officer, 69
Direct expenses, 135
Direct mail:
    crisis hotline example, 113
    for educational programs, 131
    as form of promotion, 111–112, 116
    for fund-raising, 76–77
Directors. *See also* Board of directors
    duties of, 42, 43–45
    election of, 285
    number of, 285
Direct sales, as form of promotion, 112,
    113
Disaster planning, 256
Donor prospect form, 68, 69
Donors, prospective:
    benefits for, 83–84
    categories of, 83, 85
    G.U. example, 87–88
    individual vs. corporate, 85
    research on, 70, 87
    sample pledge form, 83, 84
    sample prospect card, 68, 69
    solicitation packages for, 79–84
Drucker, Peter, 97
Dues revenue, 66

E

Educational programs:
    advertising, 130–131

Educational programs: *(Continued)*
  budgeting for, 135–137
  CEUs for, 129–130
  checklist for, 139–141
  choosing medium, 124–128
  competition in, 122
  credibility of, 128–130
  ease of access, 132–135
  evaluating, 137–139
  examples, 120, 124–125, 127, 129–130, 131
  expenses, 135–137
  and mission statement, 120–121
  needs assessment, 121–123
  planning, 123–124
  pricing, 132–133
  promoting, 130–132
  registration, 133–135
  speakers for, 128–129
Electronic mail, 250, 255
Electronic media:
  for educational programs, 126–127
  for public relations, 188–190
Emergencies, communicating about, 182, 192–193
Employees. *See* Staff
Employment laws, 270–272
Endowments, 67
Environmental analysis:
  alert matrix for, 12–13
  identifying priorities, 12–13
  in strategic planning, 8–10
  testing outcomes, 11–12
Equipment, office, 273
Ethics codes, 35–36, 293
Executive committee, 32, 45–46, 47
Executive director. *See also* Staff
  and budgeting, 233–234
  checklist for, 58–59
  and communications, 36–37, 51–53
  examples, 34, 38–39, 52, 53, 57
  fiscal responsibility, 55
  and meeting minutes, 287–288
  need for flexibility, 57–58
  position description, 48, 50
  relationship with board, 36–39, 51–55
  relationship with staff, 56–57, 268–269
  relationship with volunteers, 56, 262

roles and responsibilities, 48–58
  and strategic management, 56–57
Executive secretary. *See* Executive director
Expenses. *See also* Budgeting
  for educational programs, 135–137
  for meetings, 150–152, 153
External environment, 8, 9, 102–103

F

Facilitators, in strategic planning, 6–8
Federal Regulation of Lobbying Act, 295
Federal Trade Commission (FTC), 292
Federated Council of Internal Medicine, 309–310
Finance committee, 46, 47
Financial development. *See* Fund-raising
Financial management:
  accounting system for, 225–241
  bank account options, 221–224
  board responsibilities, 34–35
  defining accounting process, 220–221
  need for audit, 242–243
  staffing for, 224–225
  and taxes, 243–244
  writing policies and procedures, 244–245
Financial statements:
  preparing, 234–236
  review by treasurer, 236–241
Financial Stationers Association, 75
Firmware, defined, 249
Fish Middleton Jazz Scholarship Fund:
  goals, 21
  mission statement, 21
  strategic objectives, 23
Fixed vs. variable costs, 136, 137
Food Marketing Institute, 191–192
Foundations, soliciting funds from, 71, 73
Fund-raising:
  applying for grants, 71, 73–74
  awards programs, 78, 79, 80
  bibliography on, 90–91
  campaign worksheet, 85, 86
  checklist for, 88–89

cost estimating, 64–65
follow-up strategies, 79
Georgetown University example,
   86–88
in-house resources for, 65
letters, 77, 81, 82
need for, 63–66
organizational structure for, 68
planning for, 67–75, 87
program options, 66–67
resources for, 89–90
responsibilities in, 68–69
for smaller organizations, 85–86
solicitation packages, 79–84
special events, 78–79
strategies for, 76–79, 85–86
Furniture, office, 273

G

Georgetown University, 86–88
Goals:
   defined, 20
   examples, 20, 21
   for fund-raising, 63–66
   organizational, 20–21
   for public relations, 169–170
   testing, 21
Governing boards. *See* Board of
   directors
Government grants, 73–74
Government relations. *See also*
   Lobbying
   checklist for programs, 216–217
   coalitions for, 210
   effectiveness, 209, 212–214
   establishing local program, 202
   example, 203
   hiring for, 211–212
   importance of program, 203, 206–207
   letter-writing, 207–209
   presenting case, 207–209
   starting campaign, 204–205
Grant, Pres. Ulysses S., 201–202
Grants, applying for, 71, 73–74
Greenfield, Jim, 67
Guinier, Lani, 78

H

Hardware, computer:
   defined, 249
   maintenance, 256
Health organizations:
   educational program examples,
      124–125, 129–130
   marketing examples, 101–102, 103,
      108–109
   PSA example, 126–127
   public relations example, 191
   research example, 309–310
Hiring:
   advertising for, 263–264
   of consultants, 300–301, 314–315
   of employees, 263–268
Hopkins, Bruce R., 68, 290
Hospitals, marketing by, 94, 112
Human resources:
   hiring staff, 263–268
   overview, 260–261
   performance appraisal, 268–269
   personnel checklist, 266–267
   policies and procedures, 270–272
   sources of labor, 261–262

I

Income, and UBI tax, 66, 289–291
Income taxes. *See also* Tax-exempt
   status
   deductible expenses, 294–295
   paying, 243–244
   and unrelated business income,
      289–291
Incorporation, articles of, 280–281
Indirect expenses, 135
Individuals, soliciting funds from, 75
Information systems:
   basic services, 248–249
   centralized, 250–251
   and change, 253–255
   disaster planning, 256
   examples, 251, 252
   maintenance, 255–256
   selecting, 247–252
   staffing for, 252–253
   training for, 252–253

In-kind contributions, 114
Insurance, 276
Internal environment, 9, 103–104
Internal Revenue Service:
   determination letter, 284
   and tax-exempt status, 214, 244,
      283–285
   and tax returns, 243–244, 295
International trade, 74
Interviews:
   with broadcast media, 188–190
   with job applicants, 265–266

J

Job benefits, 267–268
Job descriptions:
   for board members, 42, 43–45
   for executive director, 48, 50
   for staff, 48, 50, 263, 264, 268
Jobs. *See* Staff

K

Keynote speakers, 78, 147–149
Kotler, Philip, 94

L

LANs, 249, 250
Laws. *See* Legal requirements
Lawsuits, 295
Lawton, Robert Brooks, 86–88
Lawyers, 294–296, 303
Legal counsel, 294–296, 303
Legal requirements:
   and antitrust, 291–292
   and employment, 270–272
   in forming organizations, 279–289
   and lobbying, 214–215, 295
   and unrelated business income,
      289–291
Legislative process, 191–192
Letters:
   checklist for writing, 208
   fund-raising, 77, 81, 82
   and government relations campaign,
      207–209
Liability accounting, 232, 235

Liability insurance, 276
Library, as marketing example, 115–116
Lobbying. *See also* Government
   relations
   effectiveness, 212–214
   grass roots, 210–211
   hiring professional, 211–212
   legal limitations, 214–215, 295
   at local level, 202
   origin of term, 201–202
   · tax-deductible expenses, 294–295
   and tax-exempt status, 214–216
Local area networks, 249, 250

M

Mail service, 275–276
Manager. *See* Executive director
March of Dimes, 103
Marketing:
   benefits of, 95–97
   budgeting for, 113–115
   checklists for, 105, 118
   defined, 93
   environmental analysis, 102–104
   evaluation of, 115–116
   examples, 94, 95, 101–102, 103, 106,
      108–109, 112, 115–116, 117
   identifying needs, 97–102
   for meetings, 155–156
   pervasiveness of, 96–97
   plan objectives, 106–107
   responsibility for, 117–118
   role in nonprofit organizations, 94–95
   targeting segments of, 97–98
   vs. selling, 93
   written plan for, 104–113
Marketing mix, 105–106, 107
Market niche, 108–109, 110
Market research, 99–102
Market segmentation, 97–98
Market share analysis, 116
Media. *See* News media
Meetings:
   budgeting for, 150–152, 153
   checklist for, 163–165
   content vs. administration, 144
   contracts for, 148–149, 152–155
   critical dates list, 152, 154

designing, 144–156
evaluation of, 162
examples, 129–130, 160
marketing for, 155–156
minutes of, 287–288
on-site logistics, 159–160
overview, 143–144
planning, 143–165
public relations for, 155–156
registration, 156–158
schedule planning, 145–146
scripts for, 159
site selection, 149–150, 163–165
speakers for, 147–149
special events at, 146–147
specification sheets for, 158–159
staff needs, 159–160
transportation for, 160
troubleshooting, 161
wrapping up, 162–165
Membership organizations. *See also*
    Core constituency
expulsion of members, 292–293
officers, 285–286
structure of, 286–287
Metropolitan area networks, 249
Mission statements:
changing, 17–18
defined, 15
examples, 17, 21
and fund-raising, 63–66
and strategic planning, 2, 15–17
testing, 18
Mothers Against Drunk Driving, 75
Museums:
educational program example, 131
fund-raising example, 83
marketing examples, 106, 117
Museum Trustees Association, 83

N

National Society for Fund-Raising
    Executives, 85
Networks, computer:
for public relations, 175
types of, 249
vs. stand-alone PCs, 249–250
News conferences, 182–184

Newsletters, 196–198
News media:
and adverse publicity, 193–194
crisis communication, 182, 192–193
for educational messages, 126–127
interviews, 188–190
outlets, 173–175
relations with, 187–188
News releases:
broadcast, 181
elements of, 178–181
style, 177–178
when to use, 175–177
Nickelsburg, Barry, 76
Nominations committee, 46, 47, 285,
    286
Non-dues revenue. *See* Fund-raising
Nonprofit organizations, forming,
    279–289

O

Objectives, strategic:
basing multi-year plan on, 23
defined, 22
developing, 22–23
Office management, 272–276
Office space, 273–274
Office supplies, 276
Off-the-shelf software, 251–252
Operational plans:
developing, 2, 4, 25–26
implementing, 26–28
and information systems, 248, 254,
    257
Operation Smile, 74
Opportunities, analyzing, 11–12
Organization charts, 261
Outside facilitators, in strategic
    planning, 6–8

P

Payroll, 226
Performance appraisal, 268–269
Personal computers:
software for, 248–249
vs. networks, 249–250
Personal fund solicitation, 76

Personal sales, as form of promotion, 112, 113
Personnel. *See* Human resources
Pet Food Institute, 75
Philosophical statements:
　examples, 18, 19
　testing, 20
Phone systems, 275
Photocopying, 275
Place (marketing mix), 105–106, 107
Plan documents, strategic. *See also* Strategic planning
　implementing, 25–26
　implications for organizations, 24–25
　writing, 24
Planned giving, 67
Planning. *See also* Strategic planning
　for disasters, 256
　educational programs, 123–124
　for fund-raising, 67–75, 87
　marketing, 104–113
　meetings, 143–165
　special events, 78–79
Plans, operational, 25–28
Policies and procedures:
　for accounting function, 244–245
　for human resource management, 270–272
　what to include, 58–59
Political action, 191–192. *See also* Lobbying
Position descriptions:
　for board members, 42, 43–45
　for executive director, 48, 50
　for staff, 48, 50, 263, 264, 268
Postal rates, 291
Price (marketing mix), 105, 106, 108, 110
Pricing educational programs, 132–133
Principles, listing, 18–20
Printed materials. *See* Publications
Priorities, identifying, 12–13
Private foundations, soliciting funds from, 71, 73
Professional organizations:
　and antitrust laws, 291–292
　soliciting funds from, 74–75
　statistical reporting by, 293–294

Program (marketing mix), 105, 106
Promotion:
　of educational programs, 130–132
　in marketing mix, 105–106, 110–113
Prospectus, 81–82
PTA, 212–213
Public. *See* Constituents; Consumers
Publications:
　annual reports, 185
　as background material, 181–182
　consumer brochures, 184
　for education, 127–128
　news releases, 175–181
　and unrelated business income (UBI) tax, 290
Public foundations, soliciting funds from, 71, 73
Publicity, as form of promotion, 112, 113
Public relations:
　and adverse publicity, 193–194
　to affect legislation, 191–192
　and annual reports, 185
　background material formats, 181–182
　channels for, 173–175
　and community involvement, 190–191
　consumer information, 184–185
　and crisis communication, 182, 192–193
　defined, 168
　goal setting for, 169–170
　and media relationships, 187–190
　for meetings, 155–156
　and news conferences, 182–184
　and newsletters, 196–198
　and news releases, 175–181
　and public service announcements, 126–127, 184
　researching audience for, 171–173
　resources available for, 170–171
　and shared vision, 168–169
　and speechmaking, 186
　tactics for, 186–198
Public service announcements (PSAs), 126–127, 184
Purposes. *See* Goals

Q

Questionnaires:
  for environmental analysis, 9, 10, 11
  for market analysis, 95, 99–102
  as program followup, 137–138
  for public relations, 172

R

Recordkeeping, 287–288
Registration:
  for educational programs, 133–135
  for meetings, 156–158
Requests-for-proposal (RFPs), 303, 304,
    305–306
Research:
  for marketing, 99–102
  for public relations, 171–173
Resumes, 264–265

S

Salaries, 267–268
Sales, as form of promotion, 112, 113
Sales analysis, 116
Sales tax, 291
Scenarios, 14
School programs, 184–185
Scripts, event, 159
Section 501(c)(3) organizations:
  applying for tax-exempt status,
    283–284
  determination letter, 284
  limitations on, 214–215
  and postal rates, 291
Selling. *See also* Marketing
  defined, 93
  as form of promotion, 112, 113
Seminars, 124–125
Sgt. Peppers Society, 16–17, 19, 20
Sister Cities International, 74
Site selection, for meetings, 149–150,
    163–165
Social service agencies:
  board example, 40–41
  marketing example, 95
Software:
  custom, 251–252
  defined, 249

  maintenance, 256
  off-the-shelf, 251–252
  upgrades of, 254
Solicitation packages, 79–84
Space, office, 273–274
Speakers:
  contracts for, 148–149
  for educational programs, 128–129
  for fund-raising events, 78
  for meetings, 147–149
Special events:
  as form of promotion, 131
  at meetings, 146–147
  planning for, 78–79
Speeches, 186
Spreadsheets, 249
St. Jude's Children's Hospital, 112
Staff. *See also* Executive director
  for accounting function, 224–225, 302
  checklist of responsibilities, 299
  firing, 269
  hiring, 263–268
  for information systems, 252–253
  management of, 56–57, 268–269
  performance appraisals, 268–269
  position descriptions, 48, 50, 263,
    264, 268
  relationship with board, 36–39, 51–55
  relationship with volunteers, 56, 262
  at start-up, 38, 261–262
  use of consultants, 300–301
Standards:
  for board and staff, 35–36
  producing, 293
Standing committees, 42, 45–46
Statement of activities, 234, 235–236,
    237–240
Statement of financial position, 234,
    235
Statistical reporting, 293–294
Strategic management, 1, 2–4, 56–57
Strategic objectives, developing, 22–23
Strategic planning:
  approaches to, 4–5
  and board members, 5, 6, 7
  checklist for, 28–29
  consultants for, 6–8
  defined, 2
  elements in, 5–25

Strategic planning: *(Continued)*
  environmental analysis for, 8–10
  and goals, 20–21
  implementing of plan, 25–26
  implications of plan, 24–25
  involving constituents in, 6
  leadership retreat for, 10–25
  listing principles in, 18–20
  and mission statements, 15–18
  pitfalls in, 4–5
  questions for, 2–3
  testing, 18, 20, 21
  use of outside facilitator, 6–8
  vs. traditional planning, 2, 3
  writing of plan, 24
Strategic thinking, 1, 2, 7, 23
Strengths, analyzing, 11–12
Stress, 269
Surveys:
  for environmental analysis, 9, 10, 11
  for market analysis, 95, 99–102
  of program participants, 137–138
  for public relations, 172
SWOT analysis, 11–12

T

Tax-exempt status:
  applying for, 283–284
  determination letter, 284
  and income taxes, 244, 295
  and lobbying, 214–216, 295
  and postal rates, 291
  and state taxes, 284–285
  and unrelated business income (UBI)
    tax, 289–291
Tax returns, 243–244, 295
Taylor, William, 14
Telemarketing, 77, 116
Telephone system, 275
Thinking strategically, 1, 2, 7, 23. *See
  also* Strategic planning
Threats, analyzing, 11–12
Trade issues, 74
Trade organizations:
  and antitrust laws, 291–292

  soliciting funds from, 74–75
  statistical reporting by, 293–294
Training, for information systems,
  252–253
Treasurer:
  and finance committee, 46, 47
  and financial statement review,
    236–241
  position description for, 44
Troubleshooting meetings, 161

U

Universities:
  fund-raising example, 86–88
  marketing example, 109
Unrelated business income (UBI) tax,
  66, 289–291

V

Values, listing, 18–20
Video cassettes, 126, 127
Visions:
  identifying, 13–14
  translating into strategic objectives,
    22–23
Visiting Nurses Association, 191
Volunteers:
  coordinating activities of, 262
  and fund-raising projects, 69
  recognizing, 160–161
  recruiting, 40–41
  relationship with staff, 56, 262

W

Weaknesses, analyzing, 11–12
Wide area networks, 249
Word processing, 248
Workshops, 124–125

Y

YWCA, 52